Helping Babies Learn

Developmental Profiles and Activities for Infants and Toddlers

Setsu Furuno, Ph.D.

Katherine A. O'Reilly, PT, MPH

Takayo T. Inatsuka, OTR

Carol M. Hosaka, M.A.

Barbara Zeisloft Falbey, M.S., CCC-SP

Illustrations drawn under contract by Cathie Lowmiller

Communication Skill Builders

3830 E. Bellevue/P.O. Box 42050
Tucson, Arizona 85733
(602) 323-7500

Reproducing Pages from This Book

Many of the pages in this book can be reproduced for instructional or administrative use (not for resale). To protect your book, make a photocopy of each reproducible page. Then use that copy as a master for photocopying or other types of reproduction.

Published by
Communication
Skill Builders, Inc.
3830 E. Bellevue/P.O. Box 42050
Tucson, Arizona 85733
(602) 323-7500

ISBN 0-88450-660-6   Catalog No. 7898

10 9 8 7 6 5 4 3 2 1
Printed in the United States of America

For information about our audio and/or video products, write us at:
Communication Skill Builders, P.O. Box 42050, Tucson, AZ 85733.

Acknowledgments

The authors are grateful to the staffs and families of Healthy Start and the Kamehameha Schools Pre-Kindergarten Educational Program for field testing the contents of this book. We are also grateful to our families for their patience and support while we met on weekends and evenings, and to Josie Woll for her unwavering persistence in presenting the parents' point of view.

We owe a lot to our publishers also, for their encouragement, for keeping us on course with their questions, and for their insistence on our meeting essentially generous deadlines.

Dedication

To the graduates of our Enrichment Project for Handicapped Infants, 1971-1975, some of whom are now in college, or working full time or half time, who have kept in touch with the authors by serving as volunteers in present special needs programs, and some of whom are in sheltered workshops, in group homes, and at home. May they and their families serve as an inspiration to us all and affirm the importance of early intervention programs.

About the Authors

Helping Babies Learn was developed by an interdisciplinary group of professionals experienced in working directly with environmentally at-risk infants and toddlers and their families. This book was originally developed for the Kamehameha Schools Parent-Infant Educational Services and for Healthy Start. The Kamehameha Schools Parent-Infant Educational Services focuses on families of Hawaiian descent. Healthy Start is a home visiting program for overburdened families with infants and children throughout the islands of Hawaii.

Setsu Furuno, Ph.D., is a professor emeritus with the University of Hawaii. She is a clinical psychologist who continues to work with children in private practice. She is a member of the Governor's Early Intervention Council in Hawaii and an advisory board member for Healthy Start. **Katherine A. O'Reilly, PT, MPH,** is director of Rehabilitation Services Department at Kapiolani Medical Center for Women and Children in Honolulu. **Takayo T. Inatsuka, OTR,** is coordinator of Occupational Therapy Service at Kapiolani Medical Center for Women and Children. **Carol M. Hosaka, M.A.,** is a curriculum developer with the Kamehameha Schools Parent-Infant Educational Services. **Barbara Zeisloft Falbey, M.S., CCC-SLP,** is an early intervention specialist in Newberg, Oregon.

Contents

Activities and Developmental Skills for 3-6 Months

Activities and Developmental Skills for 6-9 Months

Activities and Developmental Skills for 9-12 Months

Activities and Developmental Skills for 12-15 Months

Activities and Developmental Skills for 21-24 Months

Activities and Developmental Skills for 24-27 Months

Activities and Developmental Skills for 27-30 Months

Activities and Developmental Skills for 30-33 Months

Activities and Developmental Skills for 33-36 Months

Introduction

Helping Babies Learn is a series of developmental activities and concerns that caregivers and babies are involved in every day. By "babies," we mean from newborns through 36 months of age; by "caregivers," we mean parents, other family members, and others who provide care for the child. The purpose is to provide ideas and suggestions about parent-infant interactions and child development activities that caregivers and babies can enjoy together as they learn with and about each other.

The book is designed for easy use, organized by three-month intervals (for example, for babies 0-3 months, 3-6 months, and so forth) and by activities that reflect daily family life. The activities are grouped by:

- Home routines
- Indoor activities
- Excursions
- Social development
- Health and safety

To track a child's development, we recommend using the Hawaii Developmental Charts that accompany this book. The charts can be useful in creating a visual picture of a child's development.

The charts are designed to reflect the book's organization and approach. *Helping Babies Learn* focuses on activities in which families are involved daily and relates to multiple developmental skills within each three-month sequence. Overall, the charts list six developmental areas by year, up to three years of age. The developmental skills associated with each activity are also listed in the text. Each developmental domain is referred to by its first letter (for example, social and emotional skills are referred to in the text lists by "S"). Definitions of the skills listed in the charts are provided in an appendix to this book.

Background

The authors who developed the *Hawaii Early Learning Profile and HELP Activity Guide* in 1979 have continued to work with infants in various settings and with an expanded target population. The original population for the *HELP Activity Guide* was primarily infants with disabilities or significant developmental delays. With the passage of PL 102-119, Hawaii became one of the first states to incorporate the environmentally "at-risk" population as part of the target population to be served. Healthy Start, a home visiting program for overburdened families with infants and children, was already in place on all of the islands of Hawaii. Program directors asked the authors to assist in developing an intervention curriculum for the program's home visitors.

A second project, the Kamehameha Schools Parent-Infant Educational Services, had similar needs for materials to be used by Parent-Infant Educators working specifically with families of Hawaiian descent. This program supports families in their efforts to promote their child's development with an emphasis on cognitive, language, and social skills.

Goals

The goals of this book are to:

- Be a resource for parents, paraprofessionals, or professional staff who are helping parents develop appropriate interactions with their infants
- Provide enjoyable activities that can be incorporated naturally into the daily lives of families
- Serve home- and center-based programs

The intent is to make parents aware of how they may enrich their child's development by taking advantage of opportunities in their daily experiences. As noted earlier, each activity in the book is followed by a list of the specific developmental skills incorporated into that activity.

To program personnel using this book, we suggest that the ultimate goal is to have parents become good observers of their child and be able to independently plan appropriate activities for their child that integrate developmental, physical health, and safety aspects of care.

Target Population

The target population for this book are families with children considered environmentally at risk for delays in development. Children and their families may be seen in their home or in center-based programs. The presumption is made that there are no obvious delays in any developmental domain; therefore, the activities described assume that the child is functioning at about the same developmental age in all domains (cognitive, language, social, motor, and self-help). As a result, the activities presented here have incorporated, as much as possible, examples of how an interaction with a child could integrate all aspects of development into one activity.

The activities reflect integrated age-appropriate activities, and thus this book can easily be used by any parent with a normally developing child. However, the activities might have to be adapted for a child with one or more significant developmental delays. For example, an activity for a 24-month-old child presumes the child can stand and walk. If a child has a condition that has interfered with gross motor development, the activity may need to be adapted to reflect a sitting position or use of a wheelchair.

Important Features of *Helping Babies Learn*

- One unusual and important feature of *Helping Babies Learn* is that the baby does the talking throughout. "Babyspeak" helps adults look at the world through baby's eyes and realize that babies may view themselves and their environment differently than do parents. By listening to baby, parents and other adults may be less likely to think in terms of "do this" and "do that" as the way to help babies learn. Having babies do the talking emphasizes the parent-child partnership. It also teaches us that, for baby, learning occurs mostly through play, that it can occur in many different environments, and that every interaction provides an opportunity for learning. Baby doing the talking (and frequently with a sense of humor) also emphasizes that learning can be fun.

- The activities encompass the range of skills from the domains of social, cognitive, language, motor, and self-help development. The intent was to describe play interactions that encompass as many skills as possible in an integrated way.

- A major emphasis of this book is demonstration of the value of watching for and responding to baby's cues, thus increasing parenting skills and the child's communication skills.

- The activities are designed for use by people without special training in educational or health fields.

- The focus is on normal child development, as opposed to curricula designed for babies with disabilities.

- The fundamental concept of this book, which is demonstrated throughout, is that *every* interaction between caregiver and child is an opportunity for promoting cognition, communication, socialization, movement, self-care, and health and safety.

- The authors are aware that babies are not all alike. This understanding is well stated by Dr. T. Berry Brazelton in his book *Infants and Mothers*, which describes the behaviors of average, active, and quiet babies. We also understand and appreciate that each culture has certain prescribed patterns of child behavior and child-rearing practices. For these reasons, we expect that users will be selective and creative about their use of the material in this book.

Suggestions for Using the Hawaii Developmental Charts

1. Record personal identifying information in the blanks on the charts.

2. With a read-through marker (one that doesn't obscure the print beneath it), draw a vertical line indicating the child's age. Use the same color to mark all skills the child can accomplish, based on your observations and on the parent's report. You should arrive at a fairly clear picture of the child's development.

   (Note: Definitions of the skills on the charts are provided in an appendix to this book.)

3. After this informal assessment, the staff person and parent can decide which skills to work on with the child. Remember that each activity in *Helping Babies Learn* relates to a number of skills from which you can choose. Most children's developmental skills should fall within their age range.

4. Select activities oriented to parent and infant to enhance confidence in caring for the child.

   For example, assume the staff member is working with the mother of a five-month-old infant. The mother talks about how the baby seems to want to put things in her mouth. The staff person could reaffirm the mother's observations by turning to a cognitive activity such as "Exploring Objects" (page 33) and talking with the mother about why mouthing is an important and appropriate way for the baby to learn at this point in her life.

   In another example, a father is talking about his baby's reaction to strangers. After asking the father to describe the baby's behavior and then reinforcing his observations, the staff person could share the suggestions provided by "Reducing Stranger Anxiety" (page 41).

5. At the next assessment, use a marker of a different color to show the child's progress.

The Individual Family Service Plan (IFSP)

Under PL 102-119 regulations, all programs must develop an IFSP for each family they serve. The purpose is to develop goals and objectives for the baby and family that are agreed to both by parents and staff persons. These goals and objectives are for a set time, followed by evaluation by both parents and staff.

For the baby, goals are related to health and development. For the parents, goals may relate to caretaking skills, family attitudes, job skills, education, economic independence, and self-enhancement. All goals and objectives are choices introduced by the parents with collaboration of the staff member in relation to what might realistically be accomplished. Our discussion of developing the IFSP will be confined to the baby's development.

It is important from the outset that the staff person become well acquainted with the parents and the child. This knowledge can come partly from family history, but should come mostly from initial visits with the family, with the parents discussing their feelings and concerns about the baby and themselves.

The eventual goal is that the parents will take the initiative in planning for the child. First, we want to reinforce the parents' capacity to make accurate and caring observations about the child and to discuss these observations with the staff person. Activities should be based as much as possible on these observations and on parents' questions about the child's development.

Suggestions for Developing the IFSP

1. Determine the level of the child's functioning informally by using the Hawaii Developmental Charts, or by formal testing. (Formal testing should not be necessary unless a specific problem is reported or the staff member is working with a developmentally delayed child for whom testing was requested.)

2. The parent and staff member would then decide on what skills the child needs to develop. Both the staff member and parents may want to look at the skills listed in the Hawaii Developmental Charts and select skills slightly beyond what the child is presently able to accomplish.

3. The selected skills may then be converted into behavioral objectives to be accomplished at a specific stated time.

4. *Helping Babies Learn* could then be scanned and activities selected to meet the objectives. Since the activities relate to multiple skills, it may well be that a given activity will help develop additional skills beyond the ones selected.

5. The parents and staff member then meet as scheduled after the stated date of goal completion to determine the child's accomplishment and discuss new goals.

6. Parent objectives within this context may be related to increasing caretaking skills, observations, self-confidence, literacy, sharing information, counting to ten before "flying off the handle," and enhancing self-image.

References

Brazelton, T. B. 1969. *Infants and mothers.* New York: Dell.

Breakey, C., and B. Pratt. April 1991. Healthy growth for Hawaii's Healthy Start: Toward a systemic statewide approach to the prevention of child abuse and neglect. *Zero-to-Three* XI (No. 4).

Furuno, S., K. A. O'Reilly, C. M. Hosaka, T. T. Inatsuka, T. L. Allman, and B. Zeisloft. 1979. *Hawaii early learning profile (HELP) and activity guide.* Palo Alto, CA: Vort Corp.

Peet, C. Y., and C. M. Hosaka. 1990. Home visiting. In *The Kamehameha Journal of Education,* edited by G. E. Speidel and K. Inn. Vol. I, No. 2.

Activities and Developmental Skills for 0-3 Months

Getting Ready for Sleep

Activities

A quiet, safe place is what I need most. I'm likely to fall asleep almost anywhere I'm comfortable. Sometimes I'll seem to do it to "get away" from too much activity or attention. Some of the ways I might let you know I'm ready for sleep are fussing and crying when I'm not hungry or wet, avoiding eye contact, closing eyes, squirming, yawning, and grimacing. Sometimes I'll fall asleep as you feed me.

If you rock me, sing to me, or pat my back it will probably help me relax, but don't do all three at once—it might be more stimulation than I can stand. If I am very irritable, difficult to console, move too much, or thrash about, I may quiet and become calmer if swaddled in a blanket.

I will go through changes in my sleep pattern. Different babies need different amounts of sleep, so let me sleep as much as I need to.

A snug-fitting mattress in the crib makes it safe, so that part of me cannot be wedged between the mattress and crib. I don't need a pillow; it's best to keep my sleep area clear for safety. If I'm not sleeping in a crib, be sure I can't fall if I should happen to roll over.

Developmental Skills

Social and Emotional
S.01	Enjoys and needs a great deal of physical contact and tactile stimulation (0-3 months)
S.02	Regards face (0-1 month)
S.03	Smiles reflexively (0-1½ months)
S.04	Establishes eye contact (0-2 months)
S.05	Molds and relaxes body when held; cuddles (0-3 months)
S.06	Draws attention to self when in distress (0-3 months)

Cognitive
C.01	Quiets when picked up (0-1 month)
C.02	Shows pleasure when touched and handled (0-6 months)
C.04	Responds to voice (0-2½ months)

Language
L.01	Cry is monotonous, nasal, one breath long (0-1½ months)
L.02	Cries when hungry or uncomfortable (0-1 month)
L.03	Makes comfort sounds—reflexive vocally (0-2½ months)
L.04	Makes sucking sounds (½-3 months)
L.05	Cry varies in pitch, length, and volume to indicate needs such as hunger, pain (1-5 months)

Self-Help
SH.03	Sleeps nights for 4- to 10-hour intervals (1-3 months)
SH.04	Stays awake for longer periods without crying, usually in p.m. (1-3 months)
SH.05	Naps frequently (1-3 months)

Enjoying Mealtime

Activities

One of the best times of day for me is when you feed me. Hold me safely and securely while you sit comfortably in a chair. If you are nursing me, you can even lie down with my body cuddled next to you. You may hear me making sucking or lip-smacking sounds.

I may become excited and wiggly or reach as I anticipate being fed. I'll watch you move about the room as you bring my bottle or prepare to nurse me. Let me know you are going to feed me.

If I'm quiet, you can stroke my cheek gently as you say my name. I'll turn toward you to show you I'm ready to be fed. If I'm crying, I'll stop after a taste or two.

While you are feeding me, look at me, smile, and touch me gently as you admire what a beautiful baby I am. Say my name so I will begin to recognize it. Watch me stare back at you with devotion. As I begin to get full, I may stop sucking to smile or coo at you, but don't interrupt me by removing the nipple from my mouth. When I pause on my own, I may reach for your face or your clothing. My first smile is likely to come at a time like this, when you are feeding and smiling at me.

When you hold me at your shoulder to burp me, I'll lift my head briefly and turn it to one side or the other. I'll like hearing you say my name and telling me what a great burper I am.

Caution: If I drink my milk while lying on my back with the bottle propped up, I might inhale some milk into my lungs and choke. If I drink prepared formula that you pour ahead of time and keep in the refrigerator, I should drink it within 24 hours. Don't let me drink milk that has been at room temperature for more than one hour (it might be spoiled).

© 1993 by Hawaii Early Learning Partners
Published by Communication Skill Builders, Inc./(602) 323-7500. This page may be reproduced for instructional use. (Catalog No. 7898)

Developmental Skills

Social and Emotional
S.01	Enjoys and needs a great deal of physical contact and tactile stimulation (0-3 months)
S.02	Regards face (0-1 month)
S.03	Smiles reflexively (0-1½ months)
S.04	Establishes eye contact (0-2 months)
S.05	Molds and relaxes body when held; cuddles (0-3 months)
S.06	Draws attention to self when in distress (0-3 months)
S.07	Responds with smile when socially approached (1½-4 months)

Cognitive
C.01	Quiets when picked up (0-1 month)
C.02	Shows pleasure when touched and handled (0-6 months)
C.04	Responds to voice (0-2½ months)
C.06	Shows active interest in person or object for at least 1 minute (1-6 months)
C.07	Listens to voice for 30 seconds (1-3 months)
C.08	Shows anticipatory excitement (1½-4 months)

Language
L.01	Cry is monotonous, nasal, one breath long (0-1½ months)
L.02	Cries when hungry or uncomfortable (0-1 month)
L.03	Makes comfort sounds—reflexive vocally (0-2½ months)
L.04	Makes sucking sounds (½-3 months)
L.05	Cry varies in pitch, length, and volume to indicate needs such as hunger, pain (1-5 months)
L.07	Coos open vowels (ahh), closed vowels (ee), diphthongs (oy as in boy) (2-7 months)
L.08	Disassociates vocalizations from bodily movement (2-3 months)

Gross Motor
GM.01	Neck-righting reactions (0-2 months)
GM.02	Turns head to both sides in supine (0-2 months)
GM.03	Lifts head in prone (0-2 months)
GM.04	Holds head up 45° in prone (0-2½ months)
GM.05	Holds head to one side in prone (0-2 months)
GM.06	Lifts head when held at shoulder (0-1 month)

Fine Motor
FM.04	Follows with eyes moving person while in supine (½-1½ months)
FM.05	Stares and gazes (1-2 months)
FM.06	Follows with eyes to midline (1-3 months)
FM.07	Brings hands to midline in supine (1-3½ months)

Self-Help
SH.01	Opens and closes mouth in response to food stimulus (0-1 month)
SH.02	Coordinates sucking, swallowing, and breathing (1-5 months)
SH.06	Suck and swallow reflex inhibited (2-5 months)
SH.07	Brings hand to mouth (2-4 months)

© 1993 by Hawaii Early Learning Partners
Published by Communication Skill Builders, Inc./(602) 323-7500. This page may be reproduced for instructional use. (Catalog No. 7898)

Taking a Bath

Activities

Does bathing me sound scary to you? It can be to me, too. If we work together, though, it can be fun for both of us.

Remember to test the water temperature yourself before you actually put me into the tub. Make sure the water is warm—not too hot or too cold. Since burns can happen from very hot water, it would help if the water heater can be adjusted at no more than 120° F. Prepare me for getting wet by getting just my hand or foot wet before the big plunge. If I cry when I'm undressed, you can cover my body with a washcloth or your hand to make me feel more secure.

Look at my face and talk to me as you wash me. Tell me what you're doing. Teach me how to splash with my hands and feet. At first I'll extend both legs together; I might even surprise myself with a kick and a splash. Admire me and my splashes!

I enjoy watching you and can follow your face as you wash and talk to me. When you dry me off, watch me kick my legs out again. Help me roll to the side and even over to my tummy.

Bath time will be easier if all the bath items are laid out ahead of time. If I feel slippery during the bath, you might want to use a light cotton diaper or towel around me so that I won't slip through your hands.

A portable tub would be the right size for me. It may help to put the bathtub on a counter at a comfortable level so you don't need to stoop over and strain your back.

Developmental Skills

Social and Emotional

S.01	Enjoys and needs a great deal of physical contact and tactile stimulation (0-3 months)
S.02	Regards face (0-1 month)
S.04	Establishes eye contact (0-2 months)
S.06	Draws attention to self when in distress (0-3 months)
S.07	Responds with smile when socially approached (1½-4 months)

Cognitive

C.02	Shows pleasure when touched and handled (0-6 months)
C.03	Responds to sounds (0-1 month)
C.04	Responds to voice (0-2½ months)
C.05	Inspects surroundings (1-2 months)
C.06	Shows active interest in person or object for at least 1 minute (1-6 months)
C.07	Listens to voice for 30 seconds (1-3 months)
C.08	Shows anticipatory excitement (1½-4 months)
C.10	Searches with eyes for sound (2-3½ months)
C.11	Inspects own hands (2-3 months)
C.12	Watches speaker's eyes and mouth (2-3 months)

Language

L.02	Cries when hungry or uncomfortable (0-1 month)
L.03	Makes comfort sounds—reflexive vocal (0-2½ months)
L.05	Cry varies in pitch, length, and volume to indicate needs such as hunger, pain (1-5 months)
L.06	Laughs (1½-4 months)
L.07	Coos open vowels (aah), closed vowels (ee), diphthongs (oy as in boy) (2-7 months)
L.08	Disassociates vocalizations from bodily movement (2-3 months)
L.10	Squeals (2½-5½ months)
L.11	Responds to sound stimulation or speech by vocalizing (3-6 months)

Gross Motor

GM.02	Turns head to both sides in supine (0-2 months)
GM.03	Lifts head in prone (0-2 months)
GM.07	Holds head up 90° in prone (1-3 months)
GM.09	Extends both legs (1½-2½ months)
GM.10	Rolls side to supine (1½-2 months)
GM.11	Kicks reciprocally (1½-2½ months)
GM.15	Holds chest up in prone—weight on forearms (2-4 months)

Fine Motor

FM.01	Regards colorful object momentarily (0-1 month)
FM.02	Moves arms symmetrically (0-2 months)
FM.03	Regards colorful object for few seconds (½-2½ months)
FM.04	Follows with eyes moving person while in supine (½-1½ months)
FM.05	Stares and gazes (1-2 months)
FM.06	Follows with eyes to midline (1-3 months)
FM.07	Brings hands to midline in supine (1-3½ months)
FM.08	Activates arms on sight of toy (1-3 months)
FM.10	Follows with eyes past midline (2-3 months)
FM.11	Follows with eyes downward (2-3 months)
FM.12	Indwelling thumb no longer present (2-3 months)

Self-Help

SH.07	Brings hand to mouth (2-4 months)

Watching People

Activities

Your face is the most interesting part of my environment. I'll work hard to be able to watch your face as you talk to me.

When I am on my stomach, call my name and come talk to me. Make sure I can see you and follow you as you place your face in front of me. I'll learn to lift my head to see your wonderful face!

As my neck gets stronger, I'll be able to do more lifting to see what's going on around me. Be sure to give me lots of opportunities to follow and watch family members and people by putting me where I can do this (for example, placed securely in an infant seat in the kitchen). I also just like to be near people and the sound of their voices.

Developmental Skills

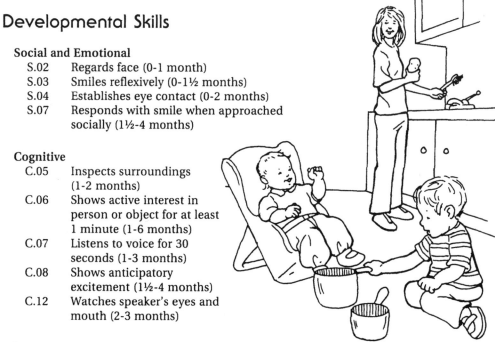

Social and Emotional
S.02	Regards face (0-1 month)
S.03	Smiles reflexively (0-1½ months)
S.04	Establishes eye contact (0-2 months)
S.07	Responds with smile when approached socially (1½-4 months)

Cognitive
C.05	Inspects surroundings (1-2 months)
C.06	Shows active interest in person or object for at least 1 minute (1-6 months)
C.07	Listens to voice for 30 seconds (1-3 months)
C.08	Shows anticipatory excitement (1½-4 months)
C.12	Watches speaker's eyes and mouth (2-3 months)

Language
L.03	Makes comfort sounds—reflexive vocally (0-2½ months)

Gross Motor
GM.03	Lifts head in prone (0-2 months)
GM.04	Holds head up 45° in prone (0-2½ months)
GM.05	Holds head to one side in prone (0-2 months)
GM.07	Holds head up 90° in prone (1-3 months)
GM.15	Holds chest up in prone—weight on forearms (2-4 months)

Playing with Rattles

Activities

Here are some games to play with me when I am sitting comfortably in an infant seat.

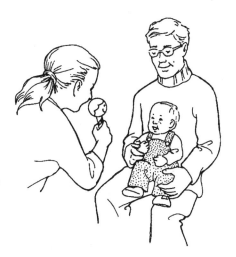

Watch the Rattle
Hold a bright rattle in midline 8 to 10 inches from my face so I can see it clearly. When I'm watching it, move it to the left slowly. Next time, see if I can follow it to the right. How about down?

When I'm older, move the rattle from one side to the other and see if I can keep my eyes on it.

Listening to Sounds
Watch to see my response when you shake a rattle about 6 inches from my ear. When I react, move the shaking rattle to the front so I can see it. Show me the rattle, then put it in my hands so I can hold it. Describe to me what wonderful things I am doing and seeing. Talk about the expressions on my face.

Developmental Skills

Cognitive
C.03	Responds to sounds (0-1 month)
C.09	Reacts to disappearance of slowly moving object (2-3 months)
C.10	Searches with eyes for sound (2-3½ months)
C.13	Begins play with rattle (2½-4 months)

Fine Motor
FM.01	Regards colorful object momentarily (0-1 month)
FM.03	Regards colorful object for few seconds (½-2½ months)
FM.06	Follows with eyes to midline (1-3 months)
FM.08	Activates arms on sight of toy (1-3 months)
FM.09	Blinks at sudden visual stimulus (2-3 months)
FM.10	Follows with eyes past midline (2-3 months)
FM.11	Follows with eyes downward (2-3 months)
FM.12	Indwelling thumb no longer present (2-3 months)
FM.13	Grasps toy actively (2-4 months)
FM.16	Reaches toward toy without grasping (2½-4½ months)

Going for a Ride

Activities

I love to be held, but when we go for a ride in the car I should be in a car seat. The infant seat in which you carry me is not safe enough to be used as a car seat. Until I weigh 20 pounds or am 26 inches tall, I am safer in an infant car seat that faces the back of the car. The safest car seats are the ones that have passed the dynamic or crash test. (Check the label on the box.) The car seat should fit my size and weight and fit our car and seat belt.

I may show you that I know we're going for a ride by becoming excited when I see the car seat. I like riding because of the soothing motion. You also put up interesting pictures for me to look at, taped just at my eye level in the car. Sometimes you sing songs to me, which also makes the ride fun. I may try to make some sounds to copy you.

If the ride is long, I may take a nap along the way. Some days I may not be as happy about riding in my seat; just be patient and try to soothe me. You will need to be sure I stay in my seat for safety, even if I cry.

Do not leave me alone in the car even if you think you will be gone only for a short time; anything can happen while you are away.

Developmental Skills

Cognitive
C.04   Responds to voice (0-2½ months)
C.08   Shows anticipatory excitement (1½-4 months)

Language
L.07   Coos open vowels (aah), closed vowels (ee), diphthongs (oy as in boy) (2-7 months)

Fine Motor
FM.03   Regards colorful object for few seconds (½-2½ months)

Self-Help
SH.05   Naps frequently (1-3 months)

© 1993 by Hawaii Early Learning Partners
Published by Communication Skill Builders, Inc./(602) 323-7500. This page may be reproduced for instructional use. (Catalog No. 7898)

Going for a Walk

Activities

I love to go outside for walks in the early morning or late in the afternoon when the sun is not too bright. When you take me outdoors, it's nice to be protected from the direct sunlight. The stroller roof, an umbrella, or a hat would protect me from overexposure to the sun.

When you carry me cradled in your arm, I like to look at your face. It's also fun to face forward so I can see the sights. Part of the time carry me in your right arm, and part of the time in your left arm. If you do this, I won't get too heavy for you and I'll have a chance to turn my head in different directions.

Tell me the names of what we see and make the sounds of animals we see, like birds or cats. Hold me at your shoulder so I can look behind you. Sometimes I will lift my head to see something interesting. I especially like it if someone will come up and talk to me in this position. If they move around where I can see them, I'll be able to follow them with my eyes.

Developmental Skills

Cognitive
C.05   Inspects surroundings (1-2 months)
C.10   Searches with eyes for sound (2-3½ months)

Gross Motor
GM.02   Turns head to both sides in supine (0-2 months)
GM.06   Lifts head when held at shoulder (0-1 month)

Fine Motor
FM.05   Stares and gazes (1-2 months)
FM.06   Follows with eyes to midline (1-3 months)
FM.10   Follows with eyes past midline (2-3 months)
FM.11   Follows with eyes downward (2-3 months)

Enjoying Your Company

Activities

You are the most important people in my world and I learn a lot by watching, listening, and playing with you. When you come to pick me up, change my diaper, or visit with me, call my name and let me know you are coming.

Let me follow you with my eyes as you come closer. Watch my face and body movements to see me welcome you. I may smile, sigh, make sucking sounds, or open my eyes wide. My body may become more active or very quiet in response to your approach and face.

When you hear me make a sound or smile, tell me you like my *talking* to you by imitating what I do and say. I also like to listen to your voice as you talk or sing to me. Bringing your face close to me and looking into my eyes helps me to pay attention to you.

I enjoy it when you hold and gently move my hands or play with my legs. You might try pressing on the bottoms of my feet or moving them in a bicycle motion.

Developmental Skills

Social and Emotional

S.01   Enjoys and needs a great deal of physical contact and tactile stimulation (0-3 months)
S.02   Regards face (0-1½ months)
S.03   Smiles reflexively (0-1 month)
S.04   Establishes eye contact (0-2 months)
S.05   Molds and relaxes body when held; cuddles (0-3 months)
S.07   Responds with smile when socially approached (1½-4 months)

Cognitive

C.02   Shows pleasure when touched or handled (0-6 months)
C.06   Shows active interest in person or object for at least one minute (1-6 months)
C.07   Listens to voice for 30 seconds (1-3 months)
C.08   Shows anticipatory excitement (1½-4 months)
C.12   Watches speaker's eyes and mouth (2-3 months)

Language

L.03   Makes comfort sounds—reflexive vocally (0-2½ months)
L.04   Makes sucking sounds (½-3 months)
L.06   Laughs (1½-4 months)
L.07   Coos open vowels (aah), closed vowels (ee), diphthongs (oy as in boy) (2-7 months)
L.08   Disassociates vocalization from bodily movement (2-3 months)
L.10   Squeals (2½-5½ months)

Fine Motor

FM.04   Follows with eyes moving person while in supine (½-1½ months)
FM.05   Stares and gazes (1-2 months)
FM.08   Activates arms on sight of toy (1-3 months)

Holding Me Close

Activities

I like being close to you. I feel safe and secure if you hold me firmly but in a relaxed fashion. If you hold me over your shoulder, I get a chance to see what's happening behind you, and that's fun. Grandma, Grandpa, and Dad frequently come by to talk and sing to me, and that makes me feel good and important. You will feel my legs pushing as I respond to them, or I might feel so content that I'll mold my body to yours and snuggle.

I also like to be held so I can see you and have you sing and talk to me. I love your smile and touch as you stroke and pat me. Because you hold me so securely, I can move my arms and legs without worrying about falling and show you how much I enjoy being with you.

There are times when I need to take a break from close contact. I'll tell you this by pulling back or turning away. You will learn my signals easily—I'm not shy about communicating them. Please don't ever think I'm rejecting you. I still love you and need your love.

Sometimes you may need to take a break from me, too. Part of taking care of me is taking care of yourself. Just be sure that I am with someone who can take good care of me until I'm with you again.

Developmental Skills

Social and Emotional
S.01   Enjoys and needs a great deal of
         physical contact and tactile stimulation (0-3 months)
S.02   Regards face (0-1 month)
S.04   Establishes eye contact (0-2 months)
S.05   Molds and relaxes body when held; cuddles (0-3 months)

Cognitive
C.02   Shows pleasure when touched and handled (0-6 months)
C.05   Inspects surroundings (1-2 months)

Gross Motor
GM.06   Lifts head when held at shoulder (0-1 month)

Fine Motor
FM.05   Stares and gazes (1-2 months)

Crying to Communicate

Activities

When I cry, I'm trying to tell you that I'm hungry, wet, or uncomfortable or I don't like all that hard rock music noise. You shouldn't leave me alone to cry, but should try to learn what my crying means.

It'll take a while, a couple of weeks perhaps if you're with me a lot, but before you know it you'll surprise your friends by knowing exactly why I'm crying. You'll feed me if I'm hungry, you'll change me if I'm wet, you'll swaddle me in a blanket if I'm feeling upset and disorganized. You'll recognize my cry of anger or pain. Sometimes you will just hear me whimper because I need your company—I want to be held and hear your voice.

Remember, at this age, you won't spoil me if you pick me up and cuddle me. If you can't pick me up, you can do other things to console me:

- Talk to me softly.

- Help me bring my hand to my mouth so I can suck on my fingers.

- Put your hand on my chest or trunk.

- Hold my hands across my chest.

- Change my position: Put me on my stomach or my side.

- Put one hand on my feet and one on my head with my body slightly flexed.

- Sometimes eye contact at these times may be too much for me, so you might try being very quiet with your eyes and face turned away.

- Put your finger in my mouth so I can suck on it if I don't seem to want to suck on my own.

- When you pick me up, you can hold me on your shoulder in a cradled position; you can talk to me as you rock me gently; or you can try patting, juggling, and walking around with me.

Developmental Skills

Social and Emotional
S.06   Draws attention to self when in distress (0-3 months)
S.08   Stops unexplained crying (3-6 months)

Cognitive
C.01   Quiets when picked up (0-1 month)
C.02   Shows pleasure when touched and handled (0-6 months)
C.03   Responds to sounds (0-1 month)
C.04   Responds to voice (0-2½ months)

Language
L.01   Cry is monotonous, nasal, one breath long (0-1½ months)
L.02   Cries when hungry or uncomfortable (0-1 month)
L.05   Cry varies in pitch, length, and volume to indicate needs such as hunger, pain (1-5 months)

"Colicky" Crying

Activities

I am sure there is nothing that bothers you more than what doctors refer to as "infant colic," or excessive inconsolable crying. It usually starts after the evening feeding and goes on and on for several hours. Not all of us have it, but for some of us who do, the crying starts when we're about six weeks old (maybe even earlier). Such crying can make our parents and even our doctors feel helpless and inadequate. Well, *don't:* It's not your fault or anybody else's.

What to do about "colicky" crying?
First, check to make sure there's nothing wrong with me except for my crying. If your usual way of quieting me doesn't work, just be calm, pick me up for a while and try to talk and comfort me. I may quiet so you can put me down.

1. Don't be surprised if I start my loud crying again. Leave me be to continue for about 15 to 20 minutes; just be sure I'm safe as you take refuge somewhere. Don't forget to check me periodically.

2. Parents have tried a lot of ways of soothing babies like me, such as taking me for a ride in the car, turning on music, turning me over from my back to my stomach, holding my arms across my chest, and swaddling. These efforts may stop me for a short while.

Be forewarned that I might continue to cry for a good long period: two, three, or even four hours. But by the time I'm 12 weeks old or even sooner, it'll all be over and you'll find me communicating in a more civilized and delightful way.

Remember that it's not your fault (nor is it mine) that I cry so hard and long. I can't stop myself. We both need to hang in there until I'm about 12 weeks old.

Developmental Skills

Social and Emotional
S.06   Draws attention to self when in distress (0-3 months)
S.08   Stops unexplained crying (3-6 months)

Cognitive
C.01   Quiets when picked up (0-1 month)
C.02   Shows pleasure when touched or handled (0-6 months)
C.03   Responds to sounds (0-1 month)
C.04   Responds to voice (0-2½ months)

Language
L.01   Cry is monotonous, nasal, one breath long (0-1½ months)
L.02   Cries when hungry or uncomfortable (0-1 month)
L.05   Cry varies in pitch, length, and volume to indicate needs such as hunger, pain (1-5 months)

Knowing When to Call the Doctor

Activities

If I have a fever (rectal temperature of over 100.4° F under 2 months age and over 104° F over 2 months of age), look unusually pale, flushed, puffy, or blue, call the doctor for advice. You might also want to consult the doctor if I am unusually cranky or fussy and you can't figure out what's wrong with me.

If you have some concerns about me and your questions can wait until my next regular visit to the doctor, it would be helpful to write these concerns and questions down in a notebook. It would also be fun to write down the things I am starting to do. These notes will help us remember my developmental milestones.

Developmental Skills

Social and Emotional

S.06   Draws attention to self when in distress (0-3 months)

Language

L.05   Cry varies in pitch, length, and volume to indicate needs such as hunger, pain (1-5 months)

Visiting the Doctor

Activities

When I go to the doctor's office for my regular checkup, the doctor measures my weight, height, and head size to see how I am growing. We each grow at our own rate; some babies are bigger and some are smaller than others, depending on our parents' size and other special reasons. A caution: I might develop a fever, rash, or swelling where I was given an injection. Ask my doctor what should be done about this.

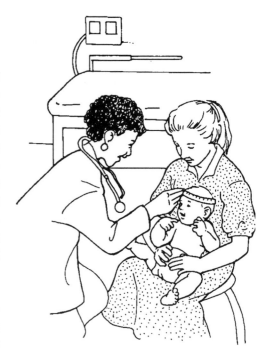

Remember to bring the list of concerns and questions you have been writing in your notebook about my care and development to each office visit. Ask the doctor about my hearing and vision if I consistently do not seem to startle to a sudden loud sound, or if my eyes do not seem to move together, to move smoothly together, or to follow a slow-moving object.

Developmental Skills

Cognitive
C.03	Responds to sounds (0-1 month)
C.04	Responds to voice (0-2½ months)
C.09	Reacts to disappearance of slowly moving object (2-3 months)
C.10	Searches with eyes for sound (2-3½ months)
C.12	Watches speaker's eyes and mouth (2-3 months)

Fine Motor
FM.04	Follows with eyes moving person while in supine (½-2½ months)
FM.06	Follows with eyes to midline (1-3 months)
FM.10	Follows with eyes past midline (2-3 months)
FM.11	Follows with eyes downward (2-3 months)
FM.14	Looks from one object to another (2½-3½ months)

© 1993 by Hawaii Early Learning Partners
Published by Communication Skill Builders, Inc./(602) 323-7500. This page may be reproduced for instructional use. (Catalog No. 7898)

Choosing My Furniture

Activities

Crib

A snug-fitting mattress in the crib makes it safe for me, keeping any part of me from being wedged between the mattress and the crib. A bumper pad placed around the crib would keep me from hurting or bumping myself.

Please make sure that the lock and latches on the drop side of the crib are secure. Keep only a blanket for me in my bed; I do not need a pillow. Also, please be sure that the mobile above me is securely attached to the crib so it won't fall on me.

Infant Seat

If you purchase an infant seat, please make sure that it is made of sturdy material with firm supports, has a wide base to keep it stable, and a safety strap. If there isn't a nonskid surface on the bottom, you can put on nonskid adhesive strips. Whenever you put me into the infant seat, don't forget to fasten my safety straps. Always stay nearby in case I accidentally topple over.

Developmental Skills

Social and Emotional

S.06   Draws attention to self when in distress (0-3 months)

Gross Motor

GM.10   Rolls side to supine (1½-2 months)
GM.11   Kicks reciprocally (1½-2½ months)
GM.17   Rolls prone to supine (2-5 months)

Self-Help

SH.03   Sleeps nights for 4- to 10-hour intervals (1-3 months)
SH.04   Stays awake for longer periods without crying, usually in p.m. (1-3 months)
SH.05   Naps frequently (1-3 months)

Activities and Developmental Skills for 3-6 Months

Changing Diapers

Activities

Changing my diaper gets a little trickier as I become more active. Never leave me where I can fall because I may roll over at any time. Even with you right by me, I may flip over from my back to tummy, then push up to look around.

Call my name and ask me if I need to be changed. You'll need to check, of course, because I can't really tell you. Use my name again and again as you point out my arms, legs, feet, toes, hands, and tummy. Say things like "Up you go!" as you raise my bottom and "There, is that better?" or "Let's get rid of that yucky diaper."

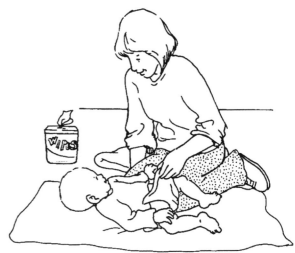

When you've finished, say "Want up?" When I raise my arms to you, gently pull me to sitting. Help me stay in my sitting position and see how I can hold my head up. Say my name and admire me some more, waiting to see if I answer with a cooing or babbling sound. Try a little "I'm gonna get you!" to see how I react (but don't let me fall in my excitement).

Once you've put me in a safe place, dispose of my diaper and then wash your hands. When you need to get back to something else, keep me near you and hand me a rattle or other toy to explore with my hands and mouth.

Developmental Skills

Social and Emotional

S.07   Responds with smile when socially approached (1½-4 months)
S.13   Vocalizes attitudes (pleasure and displeasure) (3-6 months)
S.15   Enjoys social play (3-6 months)
S.17   Recognizes mother visually (4-8 months)
S.18   Enjoys frolic play (4-8 months)
S.21   Lifts arms to mother (5-6 months)

Cognitive

C.06	Shows active interest in person or object for at least 1 minute (1-6 months)
C.08	Shows anticipatory excitement (1½-4 months)
C.10	Searches with eyes for sound (2-3½ months)
C.13	Begins play with rattle (2½-4 months)
C.15	Uses hands and mouth for sensory exploration of objects (3-6 months)
C.29	Brings feet to mouth (5-6 months)

Language

L.05	Cry varies in pitch, length, and volume to indicate needs such as hunger, pain (1-5 months)
L.06	Laughs (1½-4 months)
L.07	Coos open vowels (aah), closed vowels (ee), diphthongs (oy as in boy) (2-7 months)
L.09	Cries more rhythmically with mouth opening and closing (2½-4½ months)
L.10	Squeals (2½-5½ months)
L.14	Vocalizes attitudes other than crying (joy, displeasure) (5-6 months)
L.16	Looks and vocalizes to own name (5-7 months)
L.18	Babbles to people (5½-6½ months)

Gross Motor

GM.15	Holds chest up in prone—weight on forearms (2-4 months)
GM.21	Holds head steady in supported sitting (3-5 months)
GM.22	Sits with slight support (3-5 months)
GM.28	Rolls supine to side (4-5½ months)
GM.29	Sits momentarily leaning on hands (4½-5½ months)
GM.32	Moves head actively in supported sitting (5-6 months)

Fine Motor

FM.13	Grasps toy actively (2-4 months)
FM.26	Reaches for object bilaterally (4-5 months)
FM.27	Reaches for toy followed by momentary grasp (4-5 months)
FM.28	Uses palmar grasp (4-5 months)

Self-Help

SH.09	Brings hand to mouth with toy or object (3-5 months)

© 1993 by Hawaii Early Learning Partners
Published by Communication Skill Builders, Inc./(602) 323-7500. This page may be reproduced for instructional use. (Catalog No. 7898)

Discovering My Body

Activities

I'm becoming more of a "wiggle worm" now as I work to discover my body from head to toe. I love to be touched and handled by familiar persons. Play with me and admire me as I explore my body.

While you're fixing dinner or folding laundry or putting away the groceries, have me in a safe place near you, perhaps on a blanket on the floor. While you work, talk to me and tell me what I'm doing. I'll put my hands in my mouth for a taste. I'll also grab at my toes and even bring them to my mouth for a good look and maybe a taste. If you touch my tummy, I may look serious as I reach down to find the same spot on my body to touch.

As I wiggle around, you may see me roll from my tummy to my back. If I start sounding angry, that means I got stuck! Please help me roll back to my tummy. On my tummy, I'll push up on my hands, lift my head, and look all around. I may even manage to turn my body around so I'm looking in a new direction. If I can be near a mirror, I'll watch the "other baby."

Remember to talk to me and admire me. I'll reward you with smiles, happy sounds, and even try to talk with you by taking turns making sounds.

Developmental Skills

Social and Emotional

S.09	Vocalizes in response to adult talk and smile (3-5 months)
S.13	Vocalizes attitudes (pleasure and displeasure) (3-6 months)
S.15	Enjoys social play (3-6 months)
S.16	Makes approach movements to mirror (3-5½ months)
S.23	Smiles at mirror image (5½-8½ months)
S.27	Struggles against supine position (6-12 months)
S.28	Responds playfully to mirror (6-9 months)

Cognitive

C.15   Uses hands and mouth for sensory exploration
of objects (3-6 months)

C.16   Turns eyes and head to sound of hidden voice
(3-7 months)

C.17   Plays with own hands, feet, fingers, toes (3-5 months)

C.19   Localizes sound with eyes (3½-5 months)

C.22   Localizes tactile stimulation by touching the same spot
or searching for object that touched body (4-6 months)

C.29   Brings feet to mouth (5-6 months)

Language

L.11   Responds to sound stimulation or speech by vocalizing
(3-6 months)

L.14   Vocalizes attitudes other than crying (joy, displeasure)
(5-6 months)

L.18   Babbles to people (5½-6½ months)

Gross Motor

GM.15   Holds chest up in prone—weight on forearms (2-4 months)

GM.17   Rolls prone to supine (2-5 months)

GM.31   Circular pivoting in prone (5-6 months)

GM.38   Rolls supine to prone (5½-7½ months)

Fine Motor

FM.21   Clasps hands (3½-5 months)

FM.23   Looks with head in midline (4-5 months)

Self-Help

SH.07   Brings hand to mouth (2-4 months)

SH.09   Brings hand to mouth with toy or object (3-5 months)

Exploring Objects

Activities

I like to explore the many interesting objects you give me directly, or place where I can reach them. Don't worry if you see me putting them in my mouth: this is one of my favorite ways of touching things. Just make sure that the things within my reach are safe for me to put in my mouth. I'm most interested in finding out all I can from objects that are colorful, make a sound, and have different textures. I also pay more attention if I'm in a secure position and the objects fit into my hands.

If you place me on my stomach and place a roly-poly toy where I can hit it with my hands, I can watch it move and make sounds. I am learning that the movement of my hands and arms can cause interesting things to happen.

You can also show toys to me while I am on my back and encourage me to roll to my stomach to play with them. I'll be able to roll to my side, but may need your help getting all the way over to my stomach.

When you see that I am able to move my body while on my stomach, try placing the toy just out of reach to the side of me. Soon I'll be able to move my body in a complete circle to get toys that interest me.

When we play these games, please talk to me. I'm interested in what I am holding and doing, so tell me the words that describe my actions at the same time I do them. Also, listen to what I have to say about the toy or what I've managed to discover.

When I make a sound, repeat it back to me. When you imitate my sounds immediately after I make them, I begin to understand that vocalizing is important to you. This understanding will encourage me to make more sounds.

© 1993 by Hawaii Early Learning Partners
Published by Communication Skill Builders, Inc./(602) 323-7500. This page may be reproduced for instructional use. (Catalog No. 7898)

Developmental Skills

Social and Emotional

S.09   Vocalizes in response to adult talk and smile (3-5 months)
S.13   Vocalizes attitudes (pleasure and displeasure) (3-6 months)
S.19   Repeats enjoyable activities (4-8 months)

Cognitive

C.06   Shows active interest in person or object for at least 1 minute (1-6 months)
C.08   Shows anticipatory excitement (1½-4 months)
C.14   Enjoys repeating newly learned activity (3-4 months)
C.15   Uses hands and mouth for sensory exploration of objects (3-6 months)
C.19   Localizes sound with eyes (3½-5 months)
C.25   Reaches for second object purposefully (5-6½ months)

Language

L.11   Responds to sound stimulation or speech by vocalizing (3-6 months)
L.14   Vocalizes attitudes other than crying (joy, displeasure) (5-6 months)
L.18   Babbles to people (5½-6½ months)

Gross Motor

GM.15   Holds chest up in prone—weight on forearms (2-4 months)
GM.17   Rolls prone to supine (2-5 months)
GM.28   Rolls supine to side (4-5½ months)
GM.31   Circular pivoting in prone (5-6 months)

Fine Motor

FM.13   Grasps toy actively (2-4 months)
FM.14   Looks from one object to another (2½-3½ months)
FM.16   Reaches toward toy without grasping (2½-4½ months)
FM.26   Reaches for object bilaterally (4-5 months)
FM.27   Reaches for toy followed by momentary grasp (4-5 months)
FM.37   Reaches for object unilaterally (5½-7 months)

Self-Help

SH.09   Brings hand to mouth with toy or object (3-5 months)

Playing with Toys

Activities

When I am sitting comfortably in your lap or in my infant seat, call my name to get my attention. Then, place a rattle or a squeeze toy in my hands. I can bring it to my mouth and sometimes shake and bang it. When I drop it, let me look for it first and try to pick it up myself. Help me when it looks like I need your assistance. Later I will be able to reach for toys myself.

Sometimes hold a toy at eye level but to the side of me until I look at it. Then move it slowly from one side to the other to let me practice following it with my eyes. When I try to get the toy, help me be successful at reaching for and grasping the toy. At first, you may need to put it into my hands so that I can grasp it. Later, I'll be able to reach further and use one hand. Sometimes let me follow the toy with my eyes as you move it above my head. Then, smile and tell me how clever I am as you give me the toy to explore.

Let me explore small objects, such as toy people. Offer me one toy and then another so I can hold one in each hand. Watch the way I reach for the toy so you will be able to assist me. I may need you to bring it closer or hold it longer until I really have it, or to offer it to me again if I drop it.

Encourage all my attempts with smiles and nods. Describe to me what I'm doing by saying things like, "Now you have one in each hand!" and make suggestions, such as, "Try to put it in that hand."

When I am playing by myself, help me select toys that are safe for me. Do not let me play with toys with sharp corners or ones that can easily break off when I gum or chew on them. I shouldn't play with rattles small enough to fit into my mouth.

I love to grasp things and put things in my mouth, so you will need to keep dangerous things away from my reach. Toys with many small pieces and toys with long strings attached to them can be hazardous. Do not keep toys on a long string because the string can wrap around my neck, arm, or leg.

I love to look at balloons, but be careful! Don't let me suck on rubber balloons. If the balloon pops, be sure to throw all the pieces away so I can't put a piece in my mouth and choke on it.

Developmental Skills

Social and Emotional
S.09	Vocalizes in response to adult talk and smile (3-5 months)
S.13	Vocalizes attitudes (pleasure and displeasure) (3-6 months)

Cognitive
C.13	Begins play with rattle (2½-4 months)
C.15	Uses hands and mouth for sensory exploration of objects (3-6 months)
C.19	Localizes sound with eyes (3½-5 months)
C.25	Reaches for second object purposefully (5-6½ months)

Language
L.16	Looks and vocalizes to own name (5-7 months)

Gross Motor
GM.21	Holds head steady in supported sitting (3-5 months)
GM.32	Moves head actively in supported sitting (5-6 months)

Fine Motor
FM.08	Activates arms on sight of toy (1-3 months)
FM.13	Grasps toy actively (2-4 months)
FM.14	Looks from one object to another (2½-3½ months)
FM.16	Reaches toward toy without grasping (2½-4½ months)
FM.17	Follows with eyes 180° (3-5 months)
FM.19	Follows with eyes upward (3-4 months)
FM.22	Uses ulnar palmar grasp (3½-4½ months)
FM.24	Follows with eyes without head movement (4-6 months)
FM.26	Reaches for object bilaterally (4-5 months)
FM.27	Reaches for toy followed by momentary grasp (4-5 months)
FM.28	Uses palmar grasp (4-5 months)
FM.29	Reaches and grasps object (4½-5½ months)
FM.30	Uses radial palmar grasp (4½-6 months)
FM.33	Drops object (5-6 months)
FM.34	Recovers object (5-6 months)
FM.35	Retains small object in each hand (5-6 months)
FM.37	Reaches for object unilaterally (5½-7 months)
FM.38	Transfers object (5½-7 months)
FM.39	Bangs object on table (5½-7 months)
FM.40	Attempts to secure tiny object (5½-7 months)

Self-Help
SH.07	Brings hand to mouth (2-4 months)
SH.09	Brings hand to mouth with toy or object (3-5 months)

Going to the Park

Activities

I would feel most comfortable if you would dress me for the weather, to protect me from the sun, wind, rain or cold. Since I burn easily, I don't enjoy staying out in the sun for too long. A hat or stroller roof would help me from getting overheated or getting a sunburn. Let's take a mat or a blanket to sit on. Be sure to be aware of which plants may be poisonous or cause an allergic reaction.

Let's start by exploring the park and searching for natural objects to play with. I can sit on your lap or on the mat with your help and hold a seed pod. You may need to gently redirect my hand if I try to put it in my mouth. Help me to hit it on the mat or on something hard from your diaper bag that would make a noise. I may do it over and over again, especially if you imitate me or take turns with me.

I like to watch other children playing and listen to sounds of animals. Tell me the names of what I see and hear. Talk to me enthusiastically or ask questions so that I hear how your talking changes. The excitement in your voice will make me feel excitement, too!

Pick a leaf for me to touch and smell. Tickle my foot with the leaf and I will look where you touched me; maybe I'll touch my foot, too. Tell me "I tickled _____'s foot," using my name. Touch my leg and my arm and I will respond with a look, a touch, or a laugh. If you stop this game, I may touch your arm or kick my legs to get you to do it again.

Let me lie on my stomach on the mat. I'll enjoy moving around a little to explore the grass at the edge of the mat and the outdoor things we've collected. I like to look at tiny things, too, such as a beetle crawling across the mat.

If someone else says hello to me, I'll be friendly and smile, but I will know that this is not my family. If you get busy talking with this other person, I may make a loud noise to get your attention again.

Hold me around the chest and lift me high in the air over your head. Bring me down close to you, then lift me rapidly again in the air. I love a game like this and it may make me squeal with excitement. Remember: this movement should not be a vigorous shaking that could hurt me.

Developmental Skills

Social and Emotional

S.10   Discriminates strangers (3-6 months)

S.11   Socializes with strangers/anyone (3-5 months)

Cognitive

C.06   Shows active interest in person or object for at least 1 minute (1-6 months)

C.10   Searches with eyes for sound (2-3½ months)

C.14   Enjoys repeating newly learned activity (3-4 months)

C.17   Plays with own hands, feet, fingers, toes (3-5 months)

C.19   Localizes sound with eyes (3½-5 months)

C.21   Continues a familiar activity by initiating movements involved (4-5 months)

C.22   Localizes tactile stimulation by touching the same spot or searching for object that touched body (4-6 months)

Language

L.06   Laughs (1½-4 months)

L.10   Squeals (2½-5 ½ months)

Gross Motor

GM.21   Holds head steady in supported sitting (3-5 months)

GM.22   Sits with slight support (3-5 months)

GM.31   Circular pivoting in prone (5-6 months)

Fine Motor

FM.18   Follows moving object with eyes in supported sitting (3-4½ months)

FM.26   Reaches for object bilaterally (4-5 months)

FM.27   Reaches for toy followed by momentary grasp (4-5 months)

FM.28   Uses palmar grasp (4-5 months)

FM.29   Reaches and grasps object (4½-5½ months)

FM.31   Regards tiny object (4½-5½ months)

FM.32   Looks at distant objects (5-6 months)

FM.39   Bangs object on table (5½-7 months)

Self-Help

SH.09   Brings hand to mouth with toy or object (3-5 months)

Socializing

Activities

You saw me smile a little when I was younger, but now that I'm older, I'm *really* ready to party.

- It's fun to have you tickle, swing, and toss me gently. Remember, don't shake me too hard; I can be hurt easily from too vigorous a movement.

- You can play "This little piggy went to market" with me.

- I love to hear all the funny sounds you make and to try imitating them.

- Your different funny faces really make me laugh.

- It's fun too to have you clap my hands together or bounce me on your knee.

- I love to have you hold me as you dance to music.

One of my favorite ways to have a good time is for you to talk and sing to me, then wait for me to talk and sing back to you (or try to, anyway).

I sure have a lot more fun socializing with you than crying, but remember to watch for my cues that tell you I've had enough and need a rest. About 5 minutes of an activity usually is enough; after that, I need to rest and be on my own for a minute or two. Don't leave me alone too long, though; I'll get bored and may start to scream for attention.

It's also good to interchange active activities, gentle activities, and rest periods to help me organize myself.

Developmental Skills

Social and Emotional
S.07	Responds with smile when socially approached (1½-4 months)
S.09	Vocalizes in response to adult talk and smile (3-5 months)
S.12	Demands social attention (3-8 months)
S.15	Enjoys social play (3-6 months)
S.18	Enjoys frolic play (4-8 months)
S.19	Repeats enjoyable activities (4-8 months)

Cognitive
C.02	Shows pleasure when touched or handled (0-6 months)
C.06	Shows active interest in person or object for at least 1 minute (1-6 months)
C.08	Shows anticipatory excitement (1½-4 months)
C.16	Turns eyes and head to sound of hidden voice (3-7 months)
C.17	Plays with own hands, feet, fingers, toes (3-5 months)

Language
L.06	Laughs (1½-4 months)
L.11	Responds to sound stimulation or speech by vocalizing (3-6 months)
L.12	Laughs when head is covered with a cloth (3½-4½ months)
L.14	Vocalizes attitudes other than crying (joy, displeasure) (5-6 months)
L.15	Reacts to music by cooing (5-6 months)

Fine Motor
FM.16	Reaches toward toy without grasp (2½-4½ months)
FM.18	Follows with eyes moving object in supported sitting (3-4 months)
FM.19	Follows with eyes upward (3-4 months)
FM.21	Clasps hands (3½-5 months)

© 1993 by Hawaii Early Learning Partners
Published by Communication Skill Builders, Inc./(602) 323-7500. This page may be reproduced for instructional use. (Catalog No. 7898)

Reducing Stranger Anxiety

Activities

I like being with Mom most of the time, but I like being with Dad and Grandma too. Just recently I became acquainted with my babysitter, Mary. She's fun to be around, too. Knowing that there are other people as nice as Mom makes me better able to face new people, places, strange sounds, and animals when I'm taken to the park or to other people's homes. I really like seeing and experiencing new things, but not too much at a time.

I may sometimes act shy and frightened in this new and strange outside world, but if I'm with Mom or someone with whom I feel very secure, I'm going to profit from these new experiences.

I want to go with Mommy to the supermarket, and to Grandma and Grandpa's home. I want to go on picnics, too, so I can learn to eat and drink in a different place from home.

Developmental Skills

Social and Emotional
- S.10   Discriminates strangers (3-6 months)
- S.11   Socializes with strangers/anyone (3-5 months)
- S.14   Becomes aware of strange situations (3-6 months)

Cognitive
- C.27   Distinguishes between friendly and angry voices (5-6½ months)

Gross Motor
- GM.22   Sits with slight support (3-5 months)
- GM.23   Bears some weight on legs (3-5 months)

Taking Medications

Activities

Consult my doctor before giving me any medicine. If you measure the medicine accurately in the medicine dropper and place it at the corner of my mouth, it will be easier for me to swallow it. If you use a spoon, use a measuring spoon to accurately measure the medicine. (You can also use a small medicine cup with measurements on the cup.)

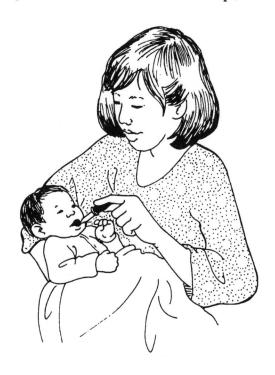

© 1993 by Hawaii Early Learning Partners
Published by Communication Skill Builders, Inc./(602) 323-7500. This page may be reproduced for instructional use. (Catalog No. 7898)

Activities and Developmental Skills for 6-9 Months

Beginning to Self-Feed

Activities

I'm ready to sit in a high chair now, but please make sure I'm secure with a seat belt. I'm learning so much, so quickly, you can't count on me to stay sitting without a safety belt and your close attention.

I'm a messy eater, so remember to either put old clothes on me (or at least a bib) and put a cloth or newspaper under where I'm sitting. If I try to grab the spoon when you are feeding me, see if you can help me guide it to my mouth. If I won't "share," get another spoon out so I can hold one by myself.

I'm probably beginning to get some teeth. Even if I don't have any teeth yet, I'll chew crackers with a munching pattern with my gums. If you offer me something, I'll take a bite, and I'll feed myself little bites of things like cereal. Be careful to give me just a few at a time. I'm still learning, and I might just stuff everything in my mouth without swallowing!

You can help me begin to drink from a cup. Let me watch you take a sip. Put just a little in a small cup, hold it for me, and let me taste. Eventually I'll want to put my hands on the cup, too.

Talk to me and encourage others to call my name and greet me. Even if I can't see who is talking, I'll turn to look.

Tell me about what I'm eating, how it tastes, feels, looks, and smells. Try to remember that I'm interested in my food and learning about it with all my senses. Messiness is normal for someone my age.

Developmental Skills

Social and Emotional
S.13   Vocalizes attitudes (pleasure and displeasure) (3-6 months)

Cognitive
C.16   Turns eyes and head to sound of hidden voice (3-7 months)
C.19   Localizes sound with eyes (3½-5 months)
C.25   Reaches for second object purposefully (5-6½ months)
C.34   Smells different things (6-12 months)
C.38   Looks for family members or pets when named (6-8 months)
C.41   Turns head and shoulders to find hidden sound (7-10 months)
C.43   Responds to simple request with gesture (7-9 months)

Language
L.26   Shows understanding of words by appropriate behavior
        or gesture (9-14 months)

Gross Motor
GM.34   Sits independently indefinitely but may use hands
        (5-8 months)

Fine Motor
FM.25   Keeps hands open most of the time (4-8 months)
FM.26   Reaches for object bilaterally (4-5 months)
FM.35   Retains small object in each hand (5-6 months)
FM.37   Reaches for object unilaterally (5½-7 months)
FM.38   Transfers object (5½-7 months)
FM.40   Attempts to secure tiny object (5½-7 months)
FM.44   Rakes tiny object (7-8 months)
FM.45   Uses inferior pincer grasp (7½-10 months)

Self-Help
SH.11   Uses tongue to move food in mouth (4-8½ months)
SH.17   Mouths and gums solid foods (5-8 months)
SH.19   Bites food voluntarily (6-8 months)
SH.20   Drinks from cup held by other (6-12 months)
SH.21   Feeds self a cracker (6½-8½ months)
SH.24   Chews food with munching pattern (8-13½ months)

© 1993 by Hawaii Early Learning Partners
Published by Communication Skill Builders, Inc./(602) 323-7500. This page may be reproduced for instructional use. (Catalog No. 7898)

Having Fun at Mealtime

Activities

There are a lot of learning activities to do in the high chair as I sit up more independently. I can hold my head steady while sitting now and even turn to watch you get my food ready. I like to watch you and smell the food, too. If I sound fussy, it's probably because I can't wait to eat. Bring me a little to smell and taste as you work.

I'm as curious as ever and will pick up small objects like cereal. I put them in my mouth, take them out, move them from one hand to another, and drop them on the floor.

"Fetch the Toy" is a favorite game to play with you or my brothers, sisters, or cousins. You put a toy on my high-chair tray and I drop it on the floor. You pick it up, put it back on my tray, and talk to me in a friendly voice, and I'll drop it again. I'll do this game until you get tired of it.

"Peek-a-boo" is fun to play with my bib or napkin over my face. You can play this with me by calling my name from behind me, then peeking out at me from one side of the high chair, then the other. Listen to me squeal and giggle with delight! If you try to stop it before I'm ready to stop, I'll call to you to try to start it again.

Developmental Skills

Social and Emotional
S.12 Demands social attention (3-8 months)
S.13 Vocalizes attitudes (pleasure and displeasure) (3-6 months)
S.15 Enjoys social play (3-6 months)
S.19 Repeats enjoyable activities (4-8 months)
S.26 Cooperates in games (6-10 months)
S.30 Shows like/dislike for certain people, objects, places (7-12 months)

Cognitive

C.33 Plays peek-a-boo (6-10 months)
C.34 Smells different things (6-12 months)
C.35 Plays 2-3 minutes with single toy (6-9 months)
C.36 Slides toy or object on surface (6-11 months)
C.38 Looks for family members or pets when named (6-8 months)
C.39 Responds to facial expressions (6-7 months)
C.41 Turns head and shoulders to find hidden sound (7-10 months)
C.43 Responds to simple request with gesture (7-9 months)
C.45 Retains two objects and reaches for third (8-10 months)
C.48 Listens selectively to familiar words (8-12 months)
C.50 Guides action on toy manually (9-12 months)
C.52 Drops objects systematically (9-12 months)

Language

L.14 Vocalizes attitudes other than crying (joy, displeasure)
      (5-6 months)
L.16 Looks and vocalizes to own name (5-7 months)
L.18 Babbles to people (5½-6½ months)
L.21 Shouts for attention (6½-8 months)
L.23 Vocalizes in interjectional manner (7½-9 months)
L.25 Babbles single consonant "ba" (8-12 months)
L.26 Shows understanding of words by appropriate behavior
      or gesture (9-14 months)

Gross Motor

GM.34 Sits independently indefinitely but may use hands
       (5-8 months)

Fine Motor

FM.25 Keeps hands open most of the time (4-8 months)
FM.32 Looks at distant objects (5-6 months)
FM.33 Drops objects (5-6 months)
FM.37 Reaches for object unilaterally (5½-7 months)
FM.38 Transfers object (5½-7 months)
FM.39 Bangs object on table (5½-7 months)
FM.40 Attempts to secure tiny object (5½-7 months)
FM.43 Uses radial digital grasp (7-9 months)
FM.44 Rakes tiny object (7-8 months)
FM.45 Uses inferior pincer grasp (7½-10 months)

Self-Help

SH.11 Uses tongue to move food in mouth (4-8½ months)
SH.17 Mouths and gums solid foods (5-8 months)
SH.19 Bites food voluntarily (6-8 months)
SH.20 Drinks from cup held by other (6-12 months)
SH.21 Feeds self a cracker (6½-8½ months)
SH.24 Chews food with munching pattern (8-13½ months)

Enjoying Bath Time I

Activities

Bath time has become an adventure for me! Now that I can sit up and hold objects, there's so much to do.

This is still an important time for me to learn about my body. Be sure to tell me, "Wash your tummy," "Let me wash your neck," "Dry your feet," and things like that so I begin to learn the names of my body parts. Offer me the washcloth and tell me to "wash Mommy's face." I love touching your face and will try to get your eyes, nose, and mouth.

Bath time games to play while you wash me or after the work is done might be "Kick Your Feet and Splash Mommy" or "Splash the Water with Your Hands." Help me do these the first few times. Remember that I still might be a little unsteady while sitting, so let me use my hands to help when I need it.

Now is a good time for me to hold a plastic cup to practice pouring. Try pouring water on my hands while I watch, then let me try doing it to you.

There are lots of plastic bath books that I will enjoy looking at while in the bathtub. Talk about the pictures with me. I'll enjoy holding the book, moving it from hand to hand, sinking it, and maybe even banging it on the tub.

When it's time to dry off, let me stand and bounce myself as I hold on to you. Tell me again how clever and wonderful I am!

Precaution: Stay right with me during my bath. Don't leave me even for a moment because accidents can easily happen in the tub.

Developmental Skills

Social and Emotional
S.12	Demands social attention	(3-8 months)
S.19	Repeats enjoyable activities	(4-8 months)
S.22	Explores adult features	(5-7 months)

Cognitive

C.24	Touches toy or adult's hand to restart an activity (5-9 months)
C.25	Reaches for second object purposefully (5-6½ months)
C.33	Plays peek-a-boo (6-10 months)
C.36	Slides toy or object on surface (6-11 months)
C.39	Responds to facial expressions (6-7 months)
C.43	Responds to simple request with gesture (7-9 months)

Language

L.18	Babbles to people (5½-6½ months)
L.24	Babbles with inflection similar to adult speech (7½-12 months)

Gross Motor

GM.34	Sits independently indefinitely but may use hands (5-8 months)
GM.41	Protective extension of arms to side and front (6-8 months)
GM.45	Bears large fraction of weight on legs and bounces (6-7 months)
GM.46	Stands, holding on (6-10½ months)

Fine Motor

FM.37	Reaches for object unilaterally (5½-7 months)
FM.38	Transfers object (5½-7 months)
FM.39	Bangs object on table (5½-7 months)
FM.42	Reaches and grasps object with extended elbow (7-8½ months)
FM.46	Bangs two cubes held in hands (8½-12 months)

Self-Help

SH.22	Bites and chews toys (7-8 months)

Getting to Know My Family

Activities

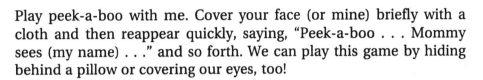

When you play with me, use my name. This helps me learn that not only am *I* special, but I have a special name, too! I'll learn that you also have your own name if you tell me what it is whenever you play with me.

Play peek-a-boo with me. Cover your face (or mine) briefly with a cloth and then reappear quickly, saying, "Peek-a-boo . . . Mommy sees (my name) . . ." and so forth. We can play this game by hiding behind a pillow or covering our eyes, too!

Encourage me to wave bye-bye to family and friends when they leave. Point to them and use their names often so I'll learn to look for them when I hear just their names.

Because you use my name when you call me or talk to me, I will learn to look and vocalize when I hear you use it. When I hear your voice or the voice of familiar people that I cannot see, I will try to find the person who is talking. Watch to see if I turn my eyes and head to find the person. If I can't, help me by having the person move closer and in front of my eyes until our eyes make contact.

As I get older and more experienced, I will be able to show you that I recognize the names of the special people in my life—you, my sisters and brothers, pets, or anyone who plays a lot with me. It is a great accomplishment when I begin to look for these people or for pets when I hear just their names mentioned.

Show me pictures of myself and our family from our family album. It will be fun for me to sit in your lap as you point out and name the members of my family and our friends.

Developmental Skills

Social and Emotional
    S.19   Repeats enjoyable activities (4-8 months)
    S.26   Cooperates in games (6-10 months)

Cognitive
    C.16   Turns eyes and head to sound of hidden voice (3-7 months)
    C.33   Plays peek-a-boo (6-10 months)
    C.38   Looks for family members or pets when named (6-8 months)
    C.43   Responds to simple request with gesture (7-9 months)
    C.48   Listens selectively to familiar words (8-12 months)

Language

L.07   Coos open vowels (aah), closed vowels (ee), diphthongs
(oy as in boy) (2-7 months)

L.13   Babbles consonant chains ("babababa") (4-6½ months)

L.16   Looks and vocalizes to own name (5-7 months)

L.17   Babbles double consonants ("baba") (5-8 months)

L.18   Babbles to people (5½-6½ months)

L.19   Waves or responds to bye-bye (6-9 months)

L.20   Says "dada" or "mama" nonspecifically (6½-11½ months)

L.23   Vocalizes in interjectional manner (7½-9 months)

L.24   Babbles with inflection similar to adult speech (7½-12 months)

L.25   Babbles single consonant "ba" (8-12 months)

Gross Motor

GM.34   Sits independently indefinitely but may use hands (5-8 months)

GM.51   Sits without hand support for 10 minutes (8-9 months)

© 1993 by Hawaii Early Learning Partners
Published by Communication Skill Builders, Inc./(602) 323-7500. This page may be reproduced for instructional use. (Catalog No. 7898)

Reaching for and Holding Small Toys

Activities

Around this time, I'm learning to reach for and hold on to small toys such as peg people, cars, and small blocks. Hold toys out to me so I need to stretch a little to the left, right, above, or below to get them. When you offer me a second object, see what I do with the one I am holding: do I drop it, or have I learned to transfer it to my other hand?

When I can easily hold two objects (one in each hand), offer me another more interesting toy and see what I do then. At first, one of the toys may drop out of my hand as I reach for the third object. Later, I will purposefully try to figure out how I can get the third object without letting go or losing what I already have. This may mean that I reach for the third with my mouth or with both hands full, or that I might deliberately place one of my objects down to get the third toy.

Sometimes when we play together see if I will imitate an action you have already seen me do in my own play. The important thing is for me to learn to copy the action in response to seeing you do it. (For example, pat a toy and see if I'll do the same.)

Remember that I can play these games while I am sitting up or on my stomach or on my back. Looking at and playing with toys in these positions present different challenges and ways of finding out about my world.

Precaution: I learn by exploring with my hands and mouth, but be sure that toys are large enough so that I can't hurt myself.

Developmental Skills

Cognitive

C.25	Reaches for second object purposefully	(5-6½ months)
C.30	Shows interest in sounds of objects	(5½-8 months)
C.35	Plays 2-3 minutes with single toy	(6-9 months)
C.36	Slides toy or object on surface	(6-11 months)
C.40	Retains two of three objects offered	(6½-7½ months)
C.42	Imitates familiar, then new gesture	(7-11 months)
C.45	Retains two objects and reaches for third	(8-10 months)

Language

L.17   Babbles double consonants "baba" (5-8 months)

L.23   Vocalizes in interjectional manner (7½-9 months)

Gross Motor

GM.34   Sits independently indefinitely but may use hands (5-8 months)

Fine Motor

FM.25   Keeps hands open most of the time (4-8 months)

FM.37   Reaches for object unilaterally (5½-7 months)

FM.38   Transfers object (5½-7 months)

FM.39   Bangs object on table (5½-7 months)

FM.41   Manipulates toy actively with wrist movements (6-8 months)

FM.42   Reaches and grasps object with extended elbow (7-8½ months)

FM.43   Uses radial digital grasp (7-9 months)

FM.46   Bangs two cubes held in hands (8½-10 months)

© 1993 by Hawaii Early Learning Partners
Published by Communication Skill Builders, Inc./(602) 323-7500. This page may be reproduced for instructional use. (Catalog No. 7898)

Finding and Playing with Toys

Activities

If you give me toys of different textures, shapes, and sizes to explore I will learn what happens when I shake, squeeze, bang, drop, slide, or mouth the toys. As I explore these toys, watch to see how I learn to hold them. Do I turn my wrists to move them? Can I use both hands independently?

I'll soon learn to bang two objects together and even to transfer objects from one hand to the other. If I accidentally drop a toy, let me look for and try to get it all by myself.

Sometimes a toy will bounce and roll away from me. Watch to see if my eyes follow the path the toy takes, especially if the toy rolls behind or under another object. When this happens, it is a challenge for me to follow the same path to get my toy. Encourage me to roll or crawl to get the toy. By watching my eyes and actions, you will be able to tell if I need help finding or reaching for the toy. Remember to let me do as much as I can before you give me hints.

I am also beginning to learn that objects in my environment do not disappear just because I do not see them. Help me learn how to find objects that are hidden. When I begin to reach for a toy, cover it quickly with a cloth and watch to see what I do. Do I look surprised? Do I turn to play with the cloth or something else as if I have forgotten all about the toy? If I do not look for the toy, lift the cloth and show it to me and let me play with it. Then try again.

Whenever we play together, it is important for me to hear the words that teach me what I am holding or doing. I will need to hear your words to learn that they are important and useful labels for things and actions that I will need as I grow. I may not use them right away, but I will remember, so talk with me.

Developmental Skills

Social and Emotional
S.26   Cooperates in games (6-10 months)

Cognitive

C.26	Works for desired out-of-reach object (5-9 months)
C.30	Shows interest in sounds of objects (5½-8 months)
C.31	Anticipates visually the trajectory of a slowly moving object (5½-7½ months)
C.32	Finds hidden object using 1 screen, 2 screens, then 3 screens (6-9 months)
C.35	Plays 2-3 minutes with single toy (6-9 months)
C.36	Slides toy or object on surface (6-11 months)
C.37	Follows trajectory of fast-moving object (6-8 months)
C.43	Responds to simple request with gesture (7-9 months)
C.46	Overcomes obstacle to obtain object (8-11 months)

Language

L.07	Coos open vowels (aah), closed vowels (ee), diphthongs (oy as in boy) (2-7 months)
L.13	Babbles consonant chains "babababa" (4-6½ months)
L.17	Babbles double consonants "baba" (5-8 months)
L.23	Vocalizes in interjectional manner (7½-9 months)
L.24	Babbles with inflection similar to adult speech (7½-12 months)
L.25	Babbles single consonant "ba" (8-12 months)

Gross Motor

GM.34	Sits independently indefinitely but may use hands (5-8 months)
GM.38	Rolls supine to prone (5½-7½ months)
GM.48	Brings one knee forward beside trunk in prone (6-8 months)
GM.49	Crawls backwards (7-8 months)
GM.52	Crawls forward (8-9½ months)

Fine Motor

FM.25	Keeps hands open most of the time (4-8 months)
FM.37	Reaches for object unilaterally (5½-7 months)
FM.38	Transfers object (5½-7 months)
FM.39	Bangs object on table (5½-7 months)
FM.41	Manipulates toy actively with wrist movements (6-8 months)
FM.42	Reaches and grasps object with extended elbow (7-8½ months)
FM.43	Uses radial digital grasp (7-9 months)
FM.46	Bangs two cubes held in hands (8½-12 months)

Self-Help

SH.22	Bites and chews toys (7-8 months)

Looking at Picture Books

Activities

I am not too little to enjoy looking at picture books with you. Cardboard books are easiest for us to share. The most important thing, though, is that we are doing this together. We can look at pictures with me in your lap, or you can join me on the floor on your stomach.

The kinds of picture books I pay attention to best are photographs of babies and animals. When you point to the pictures and tell me about them, I will look at what you are touching and listen to the sound of your voice. Your excitement and interest in what you are telling me teaches me that books are important to you, and so they will become important and fun for me, too.

You will find that I will listen and sometimes laugh at the sounds you make when you tell me how the animals talk. I will enjoy watching your face and will want you to make these sounds often. As we look at the animal pictures, I may even begin to "talk" to the pictures, too. Encourage any sounds I make. I may not be able to pay attention to all the pictures, so a few at a time would be just fine.

Books with colorful pictures of things in my environment are also fun for me. I like cars, airplanes, phones, and other things that make noise when I see them at home or outside. I will also learn to make these sounds as I imitate you.

I can play by myself with plastic books. I may bite and drool on them and occasionally look at some of the bright pictures.

Developmental Skills

Cognitive
C.23   Plays with paper (4½-7 months)
C.42   Imitates familiar, then new gesture (7-11 months)
C.43   Responds to simple request with gesture (7-9 months)
C.44   Looks at pictures 1 minute when named (8-9 months)
C.48   Listens selectively to familiar words (8-12 months)

Language

L.07 Coos open vowels (aah), closed vowels (ee), diphthongs (oy as in boy) (2-7 months)

L.13 Babbles consonant chains ("babababa") (4-6½ months)

L.23 Vocalizes in interjectional manner (7½-9 months)

L.25 Babbles single consonant "ba" (8-12 months)

Gross Motor

GM.34 Sits independently indefinitely but may use hands (5-8 months)

Playing in My Yard

Activities

Have a mat or blanket available to place on the grass or concrete in our yard. Let me crawl around to explore some of the different things we find on our walk around the yard: a flower, a seedpod, a stick, a leaf. When I am sitting, give me one of the items and let me hold it. Tell me its name and then offer another object to the same hand. Help me to transfer the first item to the other hand so I can take the new item.  I will probably try to put these interesting things in my mouth, so you will need to redirect my play by saying something like, "Let's put the flower in my hair, not in your mouth." I may also enjoy being held up in a standing position during some of our play.

We can use our outdoor time for frolic play. Hold me close to you, support my head, and spin in a circle. I may indicate to you by sounds and gestures to do it again. Respond by saying, "Oh, (baby's name) likes to spin" and then repeat the activity to show you understand.

When you call my name during different activities, be alert to my turning to my name, and sometimes I may respond with vocalizations. Respond to my sounds with something like, "Yes, I called your name, (baby's name)." When going back inside, help me wave good-bye to the trees, the cars, the cat, the fence. Say, "Bye-bye, we're going home now."

Developmental Skills

Language
L.16   Looks and vocalizes to own name (5-7 months)
L.19   Waves or responds to bye-bye (6-9 months)

Gross Motor
GM.46   Stands, holding on (6-10½ months)
GM.49   Crawls backwards (7-8 months)
GM.52   Crawls forward (8-9½ months)

Self-Help
SH.22   Bites and chews toys (7-8 months)

Discovering My Neighborhood

Activities

The outdoors right where we live provides wonderful opportunities for us to explore and learn. When we go exploring in our neighborhood, I could ride in a stroller, a baby carriage, or on your back.

If you decide to buy a back carrier, take me with you when you purchase it to be sure there is a good fit for my size and weight. The carrier should be deep enough to support my back and the leg openings the right size to prevent me from slipping out or scraping my legs. The materials of the back carrier should be strong and sturdy. When you are leaning or stooping over, remember to bend from your knees so that I won't fall out of the back carrier. Having a safety belt that goes around my waist within the carrier is a good idea.

Before we go on our walk, remember to dress me for the weather; I'll need sunscreen if it's a sunny day.

As we walk around our neighborhood, let's look together for moving things that I can follow with my eyes: a bird flying, a cat running, a car or bike moving on the street. Walk me around in our yard and find different things to smell. Some of these things may be pleasant (a flower, leaf, or fruit); some may be unpleasant (bagged garbage, animal odors). Use appropriate language and gestures: for pleasant smells, smile and say, "(Baby's name), smell the pretty flower"; for unpleasant smells, wrinkle your nose and say, "That smells yucky!" Let's collect some of the items we find to play with later when we get home.

Developmental Skills

Social and Emotional
S.18   Enjoys frolic play (4-8 months)

Cognitive
C.31   Anticipates visually the trajectory of a slowly moving object (5½-7½ months)
C.34   Smells different things (6-12 months)
C.37   Follows trajectory of fast-moving object (6-8 months)
C.39   Responds to facial expressions (6-7 months)

Learning Who I Am

Activities

I used to feel that I was part of mother, but I am suddenly aware that I'm separate from her and my own person. I'm on the road to becoming independent, and I feel good about that. But I'm also frightened, and feel I need her even more.

Earlier, I could be with others and feel okay, but nowadays I find that I don't want her out of sight. I want you, Mom, to keep reassuring me that you're around. Otherwise, I find myself whimpering and sometimes I feel like crying. I need to be held and cuddled during this important phase of my growing up.

To help me feel that it's okay to be a separate person, you might:

- Play games with me in front of the mirror; point out where you are and where I am.

- Talk to me and have me respond, smile and laugh with me, and play peek-a-boo.

- Allow me to play by myself while you do chores, but check with me frequently so I begin to learn that you aren't going to be gone forever.

- Have my brother or babysitter play with me while you are busy doing something else, but check in frequently and talk to me.

- Have the babysitter or my sister distract me (for example, by showing me a nice toy) when I am about to fuss.

What's important is that you be close and be aware of my anxiety about becoming independent, and that you help me to begin to enjoy becoming a separate person.

Developmental Skills

Social and Emotional

S.16	Makes approach movements to mirror	(3-5½ months)
S.17	Recognizes mother visually	(4-8 months)
S.22	Explores adult features	(5-7 months)
S.23	Smiles at mirror image	(5½-8½ months)
S.24	Distinguishes self as separate from mother	(6-9 months)
S.25	Shows anxiety over separation from mother	(6-9 months)
S.28	Responds playfully to mirror	(6-9 months)
S.29	May show fear and insecurity with previously accepted situation	(6-18 months)

Cognitive

C.32   Finds hidden object using 1 screen, 2 screens, then 3 screens
(6-9 months)

C.33   Plays peek-a-boo (6-10 months)

C.37   Follows trajectory of fast-moving object (6-8 months)

C.38   Looks for family members or pets when named (6-8 months)

Language

L.16   Looks and vocalizes to own name (5-7 months)

L.20   Says "dada" or "mama" nonspecifically (6½-11½ months)

L.26 S hows understanding of words by appropriate behavior or
gesture (9-14 months)

Coping with Separation

Activities

I've come to understand that I'm separate from Mom, but I still find myself depending on her a lot and missing her when she's away from me. I guess my missing her is pretty obvious to everybody because I make such a fuss and scream and wail when she's away. I understand that some children don't react the same way, perhaps because they have a lot more people taking care of them.

Strange as it may seem, I'm going to continue to demonstrate how much I miss her even as I grow older. Suddenly, when I'm a year old or even later, until I'm about three years old, I may act out my need for her. Thus, even as it appears that I'm able to do a lot more things and to be more responsive, I will also appear quite dependent on mother.

I know some mothers have to go to work. It would be wonderful if moms could be home for about a year. To make separating easier for both of us, let me suggest some of the steps that you might take:

- Prepare me for our separation by letting me get acquainted with a gentle, caring babysitter. Plan to stay with us for the first few times. You may leave the room for short periods, but be sure to return.

- The babysitter should initiate playing, talking, and laughing with me while we are all together.

- Stay with me for the first few times, whether the babysitter comes to our home or I'm cared for at the baby-sitter's home.

- Help in any way you can to focus my attention on the babysitter. You should try not to get so involved that I find myself wanting you to do everything for me.

- Before you actually start working, it would help if you left me with the babysitter for very brief periods, told me you were coming back, and did so after not too long a period. Then I can gradually get used to the babysitter or day-care setting without you being there, but before I begin to miss you.

- You should also remember that having my *lovey* (my favorite toy) will be consoling when I am missing you.

- It's important that you leave me without lingering. You and I may cry, but off you go after you've said good-bye and told me that you'll return.

Developmental Skills

Social and Emotional
S.17 Recognizes mother visually (4-8 months)
S.20 Displays stranger anxiety (5-8 months)
S.22 Explores adult features (5-7 months)
S.23 Smiles at mirror image (5½-8½ months)
S.24 Distinguishes self as separate from mother (6-9 months)
S.25 Shows anxiety over separation from mother (6-9 months)
S.29 May show fear and insecurity with previously accepted situations (6-18 months)

Cognitive
C.31 Anticipates visually the trajectory of a slowly moving object (5½-7½ months)
C.32 Finds hidden object using 1 screen, 2 screens, then 3 screens (6-9 months)
C.33 Plays peek-a-boo (6-10 months)
C.37 Follows trajectory of fast-moving object (6-8 months)
C.38 Looks for family members or pets when named (6-8 months)
C.49 Finds hidden object under three superimposed screens (9-10 months)

Language
L.16 Looks and vocalizes to own name (5-7 months)
L.20 Says "dada" or "mama" nonspecifically (6½-11½ months)
L.26 Shows understanding of words by appropriate behavior or gesture (9-14 months)

© 1993 by Hawaii Early Learning Partners
Published by Communication Skill Builders, Inc./(602) 323-7500. This page may be reproduced for instructional use. (Catalog No. 7898)

Keeping Mealtime Safe

Activities

When buying commercially prepared jars of food, check the expiration date on the label. When opening a jar or can of food, make sure the lid is not swollen. If the lid is swollen, do not use the food because it may be spoiled. When using a new jar of food, spoon out only the amount needed for one feeding and refrigerate the remainder, which should be used within three days.

If you warm up my food in the microwave oven, please stir the contents and check the temperature to be sure it is not too hot for me. As I start to gum and chew foods and learn to finger feed, it would help me to start with foods that soften, crumble, or melt in my mouth. The best way to know if the food is like this is to try it yourself. Stay with me while I attempt these new foods just in case I choke on them. Keep dangerous foods that I can choke on, like popcorn, peanuts, or grapes, away from me.

Developmental Skills

Self-Help
SH.08   Swallows strained or pureed foods (3-6 months)
SH.11   Uses tongue to move food in mouth (4-8½ months)
SH.17   Mouths and gums solid foods (5-8 months)
SH.21   Feeds self a cracker (6½-8½ months)

Dealing with Choking

Activities

When I am choking on something but am able to cough, let me try to cough up the object without interference. If I continue to cough, call the emergency telephone number (911).

Call 911 immediately when I am choking on something and cannot breathe, cough, or cry. My cough may sound very weak and my breathing may have a high-pitched or whistling sound. I will need immediate first aid to clear my airway.

The following first-aid steps are a guide. More detailed techniques should be learned and practiced by taking a course in cardiopulmonary resuscitation (CPR).

1. Turn me over face down on your forearm. Put me on your thigh with my head lower than my hips.

2. Give four back blows between my shoulder blades with the heel of your hand.

3. Turn me on my back, still keeping me on your thigh with my head lower than my hips.

4. Press down four times on my breastbone with your middle and index fingers.

5. Repeat steps 1-4 until the object is coughed up or until I start to cough, cry, or breathe.

If I become unconscious, let me lie on a firm and flat surface and:

1. Look for the object in my throat.

2. Try to sweep out the object with your finger.

3. Tilt my head back and lift my chin to open my airway.

4. Seal my nose and mouth with your mouth and give two slow breaths.

5. Give me four back blows between my shoulder blades with the heel of your hand.

6. Turn me over and place me on your thigh with my head lower than my hips.

7. Give me four chest thrusts by pressing my breastbone with your middle and index fingers.

Repeat steps 3-7 until my airway is cleared and I am breathing again, or until the ambulance arrives.

Even if I seem to be breathing without difficulty after a serious choking episode, please take me to the emergency room or the doctor for a thorough checkup.

Developmental Skills

Self-Help

SH.09	Brings hand to mouth with toy or object (3-5 months)
SH.17	Mouths and gums solid foods (5-8 months)
SH.21	Feeds self a cracker (6½-8½ months)
SH.24	Chews food with munching pattern (8-13½ months)
SH.25	Finger feeds self (9-12 months)

Swallowing Objects—Knowing What to Do

Activities

If I swallow something like a bead or button without discomfort or distress, watch my bowel movements for a few days to check whether I've passed the object. If I am in pain, swallow something sharp, or start to vomit, call the doctor immediately. If I swallow anything poisonous, call the doctor or Poison Center for advice.

Please be sure that I do not get hold of button batteries. Should I swallow any, the battery acid is very dangerous and can be fatal. If you even suspect that I swallowed a button battery, take me immediately to the emergency room.

If you know that I suck on my pacifier especially hard and vigorously, please check it periodically and give me a new one when it becomes soft. I might suck off a piece of a softened nipple and have it lodged in my throat. Pacifiers made from one piece of material so they will not break off are better for me to use.

Developmental Skills

Self-Help
SH.17   Mouths and gums solid foods (5-8 months)
SH.22   Bites and chews toys (7-8 months)

© 1993 by Hawaii Early Learning Partners
Published by Communication Skill Builders, Inc./(602) 323-7500. This page may be reproduced for instructional use. (Catalog No. 7898)

Keeping Equipment Safe

Activities

Stroller

Now that I am able to sit by myself (and am even beginning to pull to standing), help keep me safely in my stroller by fastening my belt or harness and keep me well supervised. Please check to see if the brakes can be locked securely.

Crib

You may need to drop my mattress lower in the crib because I'll be sitting up and pulling up to standing. Please be sure to keep the crib rail up and securely locked when I am in the crib.

Keep my bed free of objects, such as powder, lotion, and diapers. Also, do not keep toys that can harm me in the crib, such as toys with sharp edges, toys that can break off, toys small enough to go into my mouth, and toys with long strings that can entangle me. If my crib has posts that extend above the crib, it would be a good idea to saw them off to prevent me from getting my clothing caught on the posts.

High Chair

When you purchase my high chair, please buy one that has a wide base for stability so it won't easily tip over. I should have a seat belt to keep me securely in the chair in case I try to climb out or the tray slides off.

Please check to see that the tray is securely latched each time I sit in the chair. It would be best if my high chair is away from the doorway, refrigerator, stove, oven, and other kitchen equipment.

Playpen

The hinges on folding playpens should lock tightly and have no sharp edges on which I can hurt myself. The smaller the weave of the mesh netting, the better; this will keep me from getting anything caught in it.

The floor of the playpen should be firm so that it will not collapse. When hanging toys on the playpen, use short cord or string so the toy cannot accidentally wrap around my neck, leg, or arm.

Developmental Skills

Gross Motor

GM.45   Bears large fraction of weight on legs and bounces (6-7 months)
GM.46   Stands, holding on (6-10½ months)
GM.47   Pulls to standing at furniture (6-10 months)

Teething and Dental Care

Activities

I may be fussy when I am teething. You can help relieve my teething pain by gently rubbing my gums with your finger or by giving me a teething ring. When my first teeth erupt, they can be kept clean by wiping them with a wet cheesecloth or with a soft baby toothbrush and water.

Activities and Developmental Skills for 9-12 Months

Helping with Dressing

Activities

Time to get dressed! Tell me what we're getting dressed for (playtime, bedtime, shopping, visiting a friend) and what I'll be wearing. Describe my clothes by name (shirt, dress, pants), color, and other characteristics (big, warm, pretty).

Tell me how it goes on and what to do, and I'll help as best I can. Say, "Sit up," "Give me your foot," or "Over your head." You might also ask me to, "Come here," "Stand up," or "Can you get your shoes?"

When you talk to me, give me time to respond. I might look at what you named or I might make sounds like I'm talking. You might even hear something like "Mama" or "Dada."

Remember that some days I might want to just play. I'll crawl away and laugh when you call me. I'm not trying to make you angry; I want to play. If you play "Peek-a-boo, I see you" as you put my shirt on over my head, that might satisfy me. Then tell me we need to finish getting dressed.

Developmental Skills

Social and Emotional
S.30   Shows like/dislike for certain people, objects, places (7-12 months)
S.34   Tests parental reactions at bedtime (9-12 months)
S.35   Engages in simple imitative play (9-12 months)

Cognitive
C.33   Plays peek-a-boo (6-10 months)
C.43   Responds to simple request with gesture (7-9 months)
C.48   Listens selectively to familiar words (8-12 months)
C.54   Listens to speech without being distracted by other sources (9-11 months)
C.55   Knows what "No-No" means and reacts (9-12 months)
C.56   Responds to simple verbal requests (9-14 months)

Language
L.20   Says "dada" or "mama" nonspecifically (6½-11½ months)
L.24   Babbles with inflection similar to adult speech (7½-12 months)
L.25   Babbles single consonant "ba" (8-12 months)
L.26   Shows understanding of words by appropriate behavior or gesture (9-14 months)
L.27   Babbles in response to human voice (11-15 months)

Gross Motor
GM.44   Gets to sitting without assistance (6-10 months)
GM.46   Stands, holding on (6-10½ months)
GM.52   Crawls forward (8-9½ months)
GM.59   Creeps on hands and knees (9-11 months)
GM.60   Stands momentarily (9½-11 months)
GM.61   Walks holding on to furniture (9½-13 months)
GM.64   Creeps on hands and feet (10-12 months)
GM.68   Stands a few seconds (11-13 months)

Fine Motor
FM.50   Releases object voluntarily (9-11 months)

Self-Help
SH.29   Cooperates with dressing by extending arm or leg (10½-12 months)

Celebrating My First Birthday

Activities

My first birthday is a day to celebrate! You can see how much I've grown and changed.

I won't remember my first birthday; you keep that in mind when you plan a celebration. Big birthday parties at this age are really opportunities for the family to get together and enjoy each other's company. I may not like all the attention lavished on me by aunts, uncles, grandparents, and friends who have come to admire me, and I may even cry. I really prefer you and the safety of my routines.

If you plan a big party (lots of parents do; the memories and pictures can be great), here are some things you can do to help me be at my best.

- Be sure I am well rested and in good health. If I should become ill before the party, have the party without me. My health is more important than my presence at the party.

- If I get upset from too much activity and attention, be sure there is a quiet place and a familiar, loved person who can be with me for some rocking, cuddling, and even a nap.

- Don't expect me to go happily from one lap to another. I might, but it might also be too much for me. You hold me and let others come to you to see me. I'll smile and laugh more from the safety of your lap.

- Ask someone to help you act as host or hostess so you can attend to me.

- Take lots of pictures of everybody, my cake, my presents, you and me together, and—of course!—me exploring my birthday cake.

- Give me a cupcake without a candle or hard candies that could make me choke. I'll entertain myself and everyone around by poking my fingers in it, smearing it on my face and hair, and maybe even tasting it. Another big cake for the guests can have candles and candies. Ask the older children to help blow out my candles and serve the cake. They'll feel important and helpful.

- Be sure to have at least one change of clothes for me for my party.

- Enjoy all the wonderful things people say about me. You've done a great job with me this first year. When they praise me, they are praising you, too!

Developmental Skills

Social and Emotional

S.29   May show fear and insecurity with previously accepted situations (6-18 months)

S.30   Shows like/dislike for certain people, objects, places (7-12 months)

S.31   Lets only mother meet needs (8-12 months)

S.37   Likes to be in constant sight and hearing of adult (12-13 months)

S.49   Tends to be quite messy (12-18 months)

S.50   Enjoys being center of attention in family group (12-18 months)

Cognitive

C.56   Responds to simple verbal requests (9-14 months)

C.61   Unwraps a toy (10½-12 months)

C.77   Recognizes several people in addition to immediate family (12-18 months)

Language

L.26   Shows understanding of words by appropriate behavior or gesture (9-14 months)

Fine Motor

FM.51   Pokes with index finger (9-12 months)

FM.54   Uses both hands freely; may show preference for one (11-13 months)

Self-Help

SH.25   Finger feeds self (9-12 months)

SH.26   Holds spoon (9-12 months)

SH.27   Sleeps nights 12-14 hours (9-12 months)

SH.28   Naps once or twice each day 1 to 4 hours; may refuse morning nap (9-12 months)

Learning to Imitate

Activities

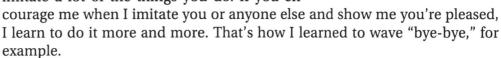

Imitation is one of the first ways I learn. Even as a newborn baby, I may imitate you sticking out your tongue. By five or six months, you will hear me make sounds I've been hearing since (or possibly even before) I was born.

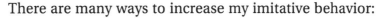

Watching and imitating what I do will help me imitate a lot of the things you do. If you encourage me when I imitate you or anyone else and show me you're pleased, I learn to do it more and more. That's how I learned to wave "bye-bye," for example.

There are many ways to increase my imitative behavior:

- When I feed myself a cracker, you could say, "Oh, great! (Baby's name) is feeding himself."

- Show your enthusiasm when you hear me say "Dada" or "Mama." (Won't that be a great day!)

- The more you talk to me, the more sounds I'll make. Eventually, these sounds will be words you can understand.

- Playing singing games with lots of motions will help me learn to imitate the singing and the motions.

- If I make a funny face or sound, you can imitate what I've done in a playful manner. See if I do it again. After you've imitated my behavior a few times, you might make a sound or gesture and see if I try it.

- Don't forget to talk about what I'm doing as you see me trying to comb my hair or use a washcloth in the bath. You can comb your hair and say, "Mom is now combing her hair."

- Remember, the more you applaud my imitations, the more I'll continue to imitate as one of the important ways I learn about the world.

Developmental Skills

Social and Emotional

    S.26   Cooperates in games (6-10 months)

    S.35   Engages in simple imitative play (9-12 months)

Cognitive

    C.42   Imitates familiar, then new gesture (7-11 months)

    C.48   Listens selectively to familiar words (8-12 months)

    C.66   Imitates several new gestures (9-12 months)

Language

    L.18   Babbles to people (5½-6½ months)

    L.19   Waves or responds to bye-bye (6-9 months)

    L.20   Says "dada" or "mama" nonspecifically (6½-11½ months)

    L.23   Vocalizes in interjectional manner (7½-9 months)

Putting Things In and Taking Them Out

Activities

As I explore the things in my environment, I am discovering that I can take things apart and put them together again. For example, I find containers with small toys inside and have lots of fun taking them all out. Sometimes I take them out one at a time, but they all fall out if I shake the container or turn it over.

When you let me play with containers made of different materials and sizes, I learn which ones I can see into from the top or sides, and which ones reflect my face! I also can make the most interesting sounds as I bang or push the container over. I can reach into some cans such as coffee cans easily, while plastic bottles need more experimentation to find out how to get things out.

As I learn to release objects, I can start to put things into the containers. Whether I drop them in by mistake or figure out how to put them in, it is still an accomplishment for me, so please tell me how well I'm doing.

Good containers are plastic bottles, large coffee cans, shoe boxes, or margarine tubs. Items to put into containers are spools, peg people, clothespins, cubes, small toys, and other things common to my environment. Please remember to make sure my playthings are safe. When using metal cans, hammer the edges down and put tape over the edges.

Join me sometimes as I play and ask me to give you a toy so you can drop it into my container, too. You can also pretend we are taking turns by dropping a toy after I do. We can take turns taking plastic rings off the ring stack. While we play, tell me about the toys I am using, what they are called, their color, size, or where I might have seen them before.

Developmental Skills

Social and Emotional
S.26   Cooperates in games (6-10 months)
S.32   Extends toy to show others, not for release (9-12 months)

Cognitive
C.48   Listens selectively to familiar words (8-12 months)
C.52   Drops objects systematically (9-12 months)
C.54   Listens to speech without being distracted by other sources (9-11 months)
C.56   Responds to simple verbal requests (9-14 months)
C.58   Takes ring stack apart (10-11 months)

Language
L.26   Shows understanding of words by appropriate behavior or gesture (9-14 months)
L.28   Babbles monologue when left alone (11-12 months)

Gross Motor
GM.51   Sits without hand support for 10 minutes (8-9 months)

Fine Motor
FM.45   Uses inferior pincer grasp (7½-10 months)
FM.48   Takes objects out of container (9-11 months)
FM.50   Releases object voluntarily (9-11 months)
FM.54   Uses both hands freely; may show preference for one (11-13 months)
FM.56   Puts objects into container (11-12 months)

© 1993 by Hawaii Early Learning Partners
Published by Communication Skill Builders, Inc./(602) 323-7500. This page may be reproduced for instructional use. (Catalog No. 7898)

Playing with Balls

Activities

Let's play "roll the ball." I will be better at holding and pushing a large rubber or plastic ball, but I like to play with small tennis or foam balls, too! Just remember that I still like to bite toys and might bite a piece off. Don't let me play with it by myself.

Encourage me to throw the ball to you. It will most likely slip out of my hands, get thrown by accident, or simply stick in my arms. It is playing ball with you that is most important.

Even if I have a hard time throwing the ball to you, I get excited watching you throw the ball to me. Let me try to hold onto the ball you roll to me. When I miss the ball, encourage me to creep or crawl to get it.

Another way to play with the ball is to roll the ball under or behind furniture. Let me try to figure out how to get it back. I may need to go over or around something that is in my way or to reach under something. If I need help, use gestures and make suggestions like, "Come this way . . . go around the chair."

Developmental Skills

Social and Emotional
S.26   Cooperates in games (6-10 months)

Cognitive
C.46   Overcomes obstacle to obtain object (8-11 months)
C.48   Listens selectively to familiar words (8-12 months)
C.51   Throws objects (9-12 months)
C.56   Responds to simple verbal requests (9-14 months)

Language
L.25   Babbles single consonant "ba" (8-12 months)
L.26   Shows understanding of words by appropriate behavior or gesture (9-14 months)

Gross Motor
GM.51   Sits without hand support for 10 minutes (8-9 months)
GM.52   Crawls forward (8-9½ months)
GM.59   Creeps on hands and knees (9-11 months)
GM.64   Creeps on hands and feet (10-12 months)

Fine Motor
FM.50   Releases object voluntarily (9-11 months)
FM.54   Uses both hands freely; may show preference for one (11-13 months)

Making Toys Move

Activities

I am very curious about toys and things that move and make sounds. It's especially exciting when I do something that makes the movement occur!

Since I like to watch and listen to real garbage trucks, cars, and buses, I like to play with toy ones too. I will try to make each toy go by sliding or pushing it. Make sounds such as "vroom" as I make the bus move. If I'm interested, we can put small peg people in or take them out.

Show me how to push the toy and let it go so that it continues by itself. Encourage me to creep on my hands and knees toward the bus and resume playing. I am not able to let go of the toy yet, but I love to watch you let it go.

Try driving the car under a pile of things like a cloth, box, and pillow. See if I can find it by removing first the pillow, then the box, and finally the cloth. This gives me practice looking for things I want even if they are not easy to find.

Other toys that help me discover how I can make things happen with my own actions are toys like pop-up boxes, push-and-go vehicles, and animals. I learn to push, turn, pull, flip, or press different parts of the toy to make something pop up, squeak, go somewhere, or turn on music. Sometimes put my busy pop-up box on the sofa or low table so I can practice standing while I play.

This is a wonderful time to show me how mechanical toys work and make suggestions to help me look for ways of making them move.

© 1993 by Hawaii Early Learning Partners
Published by Communication Skill Builders, Inc./(602) 323-7500. This page may be reproduced for instructional use. (Catalog No. 7898)

Developmental Skills

Social and Emotional
S.26   Cooperates in games (6-10 months)
S.35   Engages in simple imitative play (9-12 months)

Cognitive
C.36   Slides toy or object on surface (6-11 months)
C.48   Listens selectively to familiar words (8-12 months)
C.49   Finds hidden object under three superimposed screens (9-10 months)
C.50   Guides action on toy manually (9-12 months)
C.56   Responds to simple verbal requests (9-14 months)
C.61   Unwraps a toy (10½-12 months)

Language
L.24   Babbles with inflection similar to adult speech (7½-12 months)
L.26   Shows understanding of words by appropriate behavior or gesture (9-14 months)

Gross Motor
GM.46   Stands, holding on (6-10½ months)
GM.47   Pulls to standing at furniture (6-10 months)
GM.51   Sits without hand support for 10 minutes (8-9 months)
GM.59   Creeps on hands and knees (9-11 months)
GM.64   Creeps on hands and feet (10-12 months)

Fine Motor
FM.45   Uses inferior pincer grasp (7½-10 months)
FM.47   Removes pegs from pegboard (8½-10 months)
FM.49   Extends wrist (9-10 months)
FM.50   Releases object voluntarily (9-11 months)
FM.54   Uses both hands freely; may show preference for one (11-13 months)

Exploring Outdoors

Activities

Find or clear a small, enclosed, outdoor area where I can safely move around and explore without too many restrictions. Make the area safe for crawling. Include small sturdy objects for me to support myself on in standing and walking.

When it's time to go outside, tell me what you're planning to do and enlist my cooperation in putting on a hat or jacket (if one is needed). Have shoes and socks or sandals if foot protection is needed because of rough surfaces or hot or cold weather.

Please allow me to move around the area freely; I will probably try crawling, creeping, pulling to standing, and walking with support as I explore the objects available to me (such as a ball, sturdy cardboard box, tree stump, or fence). The box can be used for pulling up to standing and walking with support. If both ends are open and the box is tilted on its side, I can crawl through it.

You might join in the play by saying, "Roll the ball to me" or, "Come to Mommy." Expect more physical responses than verbal ones during this active playtime.

Developmental Skills

Social and Emotional
S.36   Explores environment enthusiastically; safety precautions important (9-12 months)

Cognitive
C.53   Uses locomotion to regain object and resumes play (9-12 months)
C.56   Responds to simple verbal requests (9-14 months)

Language
L.32   Unable to talk while walking (11½-15 months)

Gross Motor
GM.46   Stands, holding on (6-10½ months)
GM.47   Pulls to standing at furniture (6-10 months)
GM.52   Crawls forward (8-9½ months)
GM.58   Lowers to sitting from furniture (9-10 months)
GM.59   Creeps on hands and knees (9-11 months)
GM.61   Walks holding on to furniture (9½-13 months)
GM.65   Walks with both hands held (10-12 months)

Self-Help
SH.29   Cooperates with dressing by extending arm or leg (10½-12 months)

Taking a Trip to the Supermarket

Activities

Taking a trip to the supermarket can be fun for me and a wonderful new expe-rience. However, take me when we're both well rested and not hungry. Plan ahead what you need to buy. Try to keep the trip short so that we both enjoy it.

Be sure I am safely seated in the grocery cart's special seat and with seat belt on, if there is one. Don't leave me alone in the cart; I may try to stand up.

Keep me interested in the event by talking about what you are doing and naming the items you pick up. Show me pictures on packages of cereal; perhaps I could hold one to look at as you shop. Provide something easy for me to hold, such as a bread stick or a small toy from your purse. Let me touch items with my finger: the bread feels soft, for example, or the ice cream container is cold.

If I make babbling sounds as you go, repeat the sounds back to me and then turn them into the appropriate language, such as, "Ba-ba-ba, yes, we're buying bread." Are there some simple jingles from radio or TV ads that I may recognize? If you see the item for sale in the store, you might sing the song to me.

If I am having a bad day, it may be best to leave the store quickly. Don't become upset and yell at me; I'm still quite young.

Developmental Skills

Cognitive
C.48   Listens selectively to familiar words (8-12 months)
C.60   Enjoys looking at pictures in books (10-14 months)

Language
L.25   Babbles single consonant "ba" (8-12 months)

Gross Motor
GM.51   Sits without hand support for 10 minutes (8-9 months)

Fine Motor
FM.51   Pokes with index finger (9-12 months)

Self-Help
SH.26   Holds spoon (9-12 months)

Expressing Myself at Mealtime

Activities

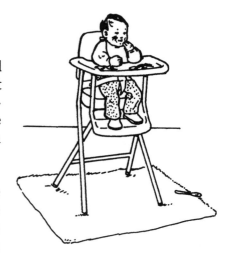

This is about the age when I begin to feel that I have to express myself. I know that Mom thinks it's important that I eat properly, but it's hard sometimes because there are so many interesting experiments I can do with food.

It's a learning experience for me to feel the texture of foods, to hear the sound of the spoon or a dish, and to get my fingers into the different kinds of food and splash them about. It's great fun to be messy.

I can tell from both Mom and Dad's facial expressions and their body language that I'm a handful, but I can't help myself.

Let me make some suggestions about managing this kind of behavior:

- Don't worry if I don't eat a lot or don't eat the kinds of food you think are good for me. I'll eat if I'm hungry. It's more important and fun for me to explore and learn about my world. Sometimes I'm discovering what your reactions are to my different actions.

  It's also fine for me to use my fingers. I'm just not ready to use a spoon or a cup, even if you want me to.

- If you don't like what I'm doing, give me as little attention as possible.

- If you have the floor under me covered, you won't have to worry about it if I throw food and spill things. If I keep playing with the food, you can always take the food away. If I look like I want it back, you may want to give me another chance. If I play around again, just take me away from the table.

- Don't let me control the situation; let me know that you're in charge.

Developmental Skills

Social and Emotional
S.33   Tests parental reactions during feeding (9-12 months)

Cognitive
C.51   Throws objects (9-12 months)
C.52   Drops objects systematically (9-12 months)

Managing Bedtime Dawdling

Activities

I like testing you at bedtime just as I did at mealtime. That's because I like having you with me as long as possible. Remember, however, that even if I like to make you get up and do things for me, I would rather have you in charge.

Let me suggest ways to make bedtime easy for you and me:

- Establish a routine and stick to it.

- You may choose to read me a story before you tuck me in with my teddy bear or my favorite safe toy. Don't allow me to ask you for this and that; it may become a habit.

- If I call after you've said goodnight, just call back from your bedroom so I know you're near.

- If I want a night light left on, don't hesitate to let me have it.

Developmental Skills

Social and Emotional
  S.34   Tests parental reactions at bedtime (9-12 months)

Cognitive
  C.44   Looks at pictures 1 minute when named (8-9 months)
  C.60   Enjoys looking at pictures in books (10-14 months)

Being Safe at Home

Activities

As I become more curious and begin to explore everything around me, it is time to child-proof the house for my safety. Here are some things to do:

- Put a protective gate at the stairway. Keep doors closed, locked, or latched.

- One of my favorite pastimes is to explore the kitchen and bathroom cupboards where the cleaning agents are kept. Keep cleaners where I cannot reach them or keep a safety lock on these doors.

- Safety caps on unused electrical sockets would keep me from poking an object into the socket and getting shocked.

- Keep electrical appliances and their cords (such as the iron, electric skillet, and toaster) out of my reach.

- Keep medicines out of my reach and in childproof containers, just in case I get hold of one.

If I should swallow any medicines, cleaning agents, poison, or any other dangerous nonedible material, contact the doctor, the Poison Control Center, or the hospital emergency room for advice. Look at the container for information about the contents. It would be helpful to keep on hand a bottle of syrup of ipecac designed to make me vomit (ask your doctor or druggist) just in case you are advised to give it to me.

Developmental Skills

Social and Emotional
S.36   Explores environment enthusiastically; safety precautions important (9-12 months)

Preventing Putting Objects in Nose and Ears

Activities

Watch me to make sure I don't put small objects in my nose or ears. Don't suggest that I not do this, as it might arouse my curiosity about doing it.

If I do put a small object (like a bead, pellet, or wad of cotton or paper) in my nose, try to have me sneeze it out by encouraging me to imitate you blowing your nose. If I should sniff inward rather than blow out through my nose and the object stays in my nose, take me to the doctor.

If the object in my ear is soft, you might try to take it out with tweezers while I lie very still. However, be cautious if the object is smooth and hard; you might push it in further by trying to pry it out. To be safe, have the doctor remove it.

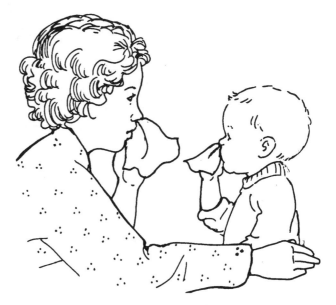

Developmental Skills

Fine Motor
FM.51   Pokes with index finger (9-12 months)
FM.52   Uses neat pincer grasp (10-12 months)

Caring for My Teeth

Activities

I have about six teeth by now (four front-upper teeth and two front-lower teeth). Don't let me get into the habit of taking my bottle to bed with me to help me to go to sleep. This habit will make it hard for me to give up the bottle, and the milk or juice on my teeth will cause tooth decay.

Encourage me to brush my teeth while you brush yours. I will need your help in brushing my teeth. Have me use only water and a soft brush if I don't like the toothpaste.

Developmental Skills

Self-Help
SH.18   Holds own bottle (5½-9 months)
SH.24   Chews food with munching pattern (8-13½ months)

© 1993 by Hawaii Early Learning Partners
Published by Communication Skill Builders, Inc./(602) 323-7500. This page may be reproduced for instructional use. (Catalog No. 7898)

Preventing Accidents

Activities

Crib and Playpen

When I start to stand and climb, lower the crib so the mattress is at the lowest position. Keep large toys and boxes out of the crib and playpen because I may use them to climb out. I may do the same if the holes of the mesh webbing are large enough for my toes. When I am able to climb out of the playpen, it is time for me to stop using it.

Toys

To prevent accidents, periodically check my toys. Repair the ones that can be fixed and discard the dangerous ones. Help me be careful of electronically operated toys so that I don't get electric shocks or burns. Be careful that I don't chew on the batteries.

Developmental Skills

Gross Motor
GM.44	Gets to sitting without assistance (6-10 months)
GM.46	Stands, holding on (6-10½ months)
GM.47	Pulls to standing at furniture (6-10 months)
GM.60	Stands momentarily (9½-11 months)
GM.61	Walks holding on to furniture (9½-13 months)
GM.67	Stands by lifting one foot (11-12 months)
GM.68	Stands a few seconds (11-13 months)

Fine Motor
FM.54	Uses both hands freely; may show preference for one (11-13 months)

Being Safe around Water

Activities

During my bath time I need you to stay with me, even if I can sit and play by myself in the tub. A nonslip rubber mat or strips would keep me from slipping and falling. If you need to leave for even just a few minutes to answer the telephone or the doorbell, take me with you. Accidents can happen so quickly, and drowning can happen in very shallow water.

When we're near a swimming pool or at the beach, keep me with you and watch me, because I might wander off into the water. When you take me into the pool or beach, I need you to stay with me even if I'm wearing floaters or inflatables.

Since I burn easily, don't keep me in the sun for too long; a shady place would be nice. The best time to be out in the sun is mid-morning or late afternoon when it is cooler, rather than right at noontime when the sun is hottest.

Developmental Skills

Gross Motor

GM.44	Gets to sitting without assistance	(6-10 months)
GM.46	Stands, holding on	(6-10½ months)
GM.47	Pulls to standing at furniture	(6-10 months)
GM.51	Sits without hand support for 10 minutes	(8-9 months)
GM.57	Goes from sitting to prone	(9-10 months)
GM.59	Creeps on hands and knees	(9-11 months)
GM.60	Stands momentarily	(9½-11 months)
GM.61	Walks holding on to furniture	(9½-13 months)
GM.67	Stands by lifting one foot	(11-12 months)
GM.68	Stands a few seconds	(11-13 months)
GM.69	Assumes and maintains kneeling	(11-13 months)
GM.70	Walks with one hand held	(11-13 months)
GM.71	Stands alone well	(11½-14 months)
GM.72	Walks alone two to three steps	(11½-13½ months)

© 1993 by Hawaii Early Learning Partners
Published by Communication Skill Builders, Inc./(602) 323-7500. This page may be reproduced for instructional use. (Catalog No. 7898)

Activities and Developmental Skills for 12-15 Months

Beginning to Feed Myself

Activities

I'm becoming so independent that I love to do things for myself! I'm still pretty messy as an eater, so keep putting old clothes and a bib on me and be sure the floor under me is easy to clean. I'll watch you while you get my food ready.

I like to eat with my family, and will learn from watching and listening to you. I can drink from a cup or glass. Put just a little in my cup and refill it for me. I'll spill less, and it's a good chance for me to practice nodding "Yes" when you ask me, "Want more?" or, "More juice?" I may even tell you, "More" or, "Juice."

Be sure to give me a spoon at meal-time so I can begin to use it to feed myself. I want to be like you, so show me how to hold it, then let me do my best. Maybe I'll pick up things to put in the spoon, then take it to my mouth. I'm likely to tip it over in my mouth.

I'm chewing better, but still am not ready for harder foods (like carrots, nuts, or popcorn). I'm interested in different tastes and temperatures of food. Notice what I prefer and enjoy my sometimes funny reactions to salty, sour, and sweet foods.

You'll still want to feed me at least sometimes, maybe to help me finish up a meal when I'm not so hungry and less motivated to feed myself. If you talk to me or I have the rest of the family to watch, I'll eat better. My appetite is decreasing, though, so sometimes I may not seem hungry at all.

Developmental Skills

Social and Emotional

S.37   Likes to be in constant sight and hearing of adult (12-13 months)

S.39   Displays independent behavior; is difficult to discipline (the "No" stage) (12-15 months)

S.41   Attempts self-direction; resists adult control (12-15 months)

S.45   Enjoys imitating adult behavior: responds well to the introduction of new tasks (12-18 months)

S.49   Tends to be quite messy (12-18 months)

Cognitive

C.59	Demonstrates drinking from a cup (10-15 months)
C.67	Hands toy back to adult (12-15 months)
C.73	Understands pointing (12-14 months)

Language

L.26	Shows understanding of words by appropriate behavior or gesture (9-14 months)
L.33	Omits final and some initial consonants (12-17 months)
L.36	Uses single-word sentences (12-14 months)
L.37	Uses expressive vocabulary of 1-3 words (12-15 months)
L.38	Vocalizes or gestures spontaneously to indicate needs (12-19 months)
L.40	Uses exclamatory expressions ("oh-oh," "no-no") (12½-14½ months)
L.41	Says "No" meaningfully (13-15 months)
L.42	Names one or two familiar objects (13-18 months)

Fine Motor

FM.54	Uses both hands freely; may show preference for one (11-13 months)
FM.60	Puts three or more objects into container (12-13 months)
FM.63	Points with index finger (12-16 months)

Self-Help

SH.31	Brings spoon to mouth; turns spoon over (12-15 months)
SH.32	Holds and drinks from cup with some spilling (12-18 months)
SH.33	Holds cup handle (12-15½ months)

Enjoying Bath Time II

Activities

I can begin to help with my bath if we both have a washcloth. I may try to wash my arm, leg, or tummy when you ask me to, or I may imitate what you've just done. I'm beginning to understand when you tell me what you're going to do and may offer you my arms or legs. I may close my eyes tight when you tell me, "Let's wash your face." Try pouring some warm water on my back and see if I like it.

After my bath, I'll enjoy time for water play. Give me several plastic containers and spoons and watch me pour and stir. Ice cubes in a cup are fun now, too. I'll try to pick up the slippery ice and will enjoy watching it melt in my hand.

Stay with me while I play. Either play with me or use this time to clean the bathroom, talking to me while you do it. Do not leave me alone—I am not safe alone in the water. Don't let me stay in the tub too long or I might get chilled.

I like to be in charge and may tell you "no" when you try to get me out of the tub, or I may decide I've had enough and try to climb out on my own. Recognize this as part of my growing independence.

Developmental Skills

Social and Emotional
S.37	Likes to be in constant sight and hearing of adult (12-13 months)
S.38	Gives toy to familiar adult spontaneously and upon request (12-15 months)
S.41	Attempts self-direction; resists adult control (12-15 months)
S.43	Needs and expects rituals and routines (12-18 months)

Cognitive
C.56	Responds to simple verbal requests (9-14 months)
C.67	Hands toy back to adult (12-15 months)

Language

L.26   Shows understanding of words by appropriate behavior
        or gesture (9-14 months)

L.30   Repeats sounds or gestures if laughed at (11-12½ months)

L.36   Uses single-word sentences (12-14 months)

L.38   Vocalizes or gestures spontaneously to indicate needs
        (12-19 months)

L.40   Uses exclamatory expressions ("oh-oh," "no-no")
        (12½-14½ months)

L.41   Says "No" meaningfully (13-15 months)

Gross Motor

GM.66   Stoops and recovers (10½-14 months)

GM.68   Stands a few seconds (11-13 months)

Fine Motor

FM.60   Puts three or more objects into container
        (12-13 months)

FM.67   Puts many objects into container without removing
        any (14-15 months)

Cutting My Hair

Activities

Most of us don't mind getting our hair cut, but some of us find it frightening. We could try my first haircut at home. Don't worry too much if the cut isn't perfect.

General Suggestions

Before starting, dust powder on my arms and legs and around my neck and a little on my face. With the powder, the hair that falls on me won't itch so much or stick to me.

Use a small piece of sheet-like material or a light plastic cape around my shoulders and pin or tie it at the back of my neck. Wet my hair, using a spray bottle, so that my hair won't fly loosely on me. If the hair falls on my face and I am bothered by this, use a small visor on my forehead to keep the hair from going past my eyes.

Try using a mirror in front of me so I can see what's happening. (The mirror might be distracting, though, if I keep wanting to reach and pat myself in the mirror or grab the mirror or scissors.) Scissors would be less scary than the electric hair-cutting tool.

After the haircut, dust me off with a light brush, towel, or fluffy powder puff. A bath after a haircut would feel nice.

At Home

Perhaps I could watch cartoons on TV to distract me or, in nice weather, sit outdoors.

At the Barber Shop or Hairdresser's

To make having my hair cut easier for me and you, think of ways to help me as well as the person cutting my hair. For my first haircut, I might feel more comfortable if I sat on your lap facing you. If I move around too much or become frightened, you could hold me or distract me by singing or reading to me.

When I am older, I could sit on a booster chair or high chair by myself. Remind the hairdresser or barber not to use the scissors close to my eyes because I might move suddenly. Let the haircutter know that holding my hair away from my face will make the haircut easier and safer for me.

Be positive, even if my haircut isn't perfect. Admire me and praise the way I look, saying, "Casey looks so grown up with his new haircut. Come on, let's go show Auntie Carol!"

Developmental Skills

Social and Emotional

S.29   May show fear and insecurity with previously accepted situations (6-18 months)

S.30   Shows like/dislike for certain people, objects, places (7-12 months)

S.31   Lets only mother meet needs (8-12 months)

S.37   Likes to be in constant sight and hearing of adult (12-13 months)

S.39   Displays independent behavior; is difficult to discipline (the "No" stage) (12-15 months)

S.40   Acts impulsively, unable to recognize rules (12-15 months)

S.41   Attempts self-direction; resists adult control (12-15 months)

S.42   Displays frequent tantrum behaviors (12-18 months)

S.45   Enjoys imitating adult behavior: responds well to the introduction of new tasks (12-18 months)

S.48   Displays distractible behavior (is easily distracted) (12-15 months)

S.55   Shows a wide variety of emotions: fear, anger, sympathy, modesty, guilt, embarrassment, anxiety, joy (18-24 months)

Cognitive

C.54   Listens to speech without being distracted by other sources (9-11 months)

C.56   Responds to simple verbal requests (9-14 months)

C.60   Enjoys looking at pictures in books (10-14 months)

Language

L.26   Shows understanding of words by appropriate behavior or gesture (9-14 months)

Playing with Objects and Containers

Activities

I am getting better and better at figuring out how to put small toys into containers. Give me some containers, such as a plastic peanut butter jar or an old plastic baby bottle, with smaller openings. I'll have to work harder to fill them with clothespins or spoons. When I can do this easily, use a margarine container or a coffee can with a circle cut out of the plastic cover. I can learn to match the object of the right size to the opening. Use spools, balls, or clothespins. Remember to comment on what I'm doing by using specific descriptive words like, "Put in," "Try the big hole," "You got the first ball in," or, "Can Auntie put the red spool in?"

Developmental Skills

Social and Emotional

S.38   Gives toy to familiar adult spontaneously and upon request (12-15 months)

S.47   Shows toy preferences (12-18 months)

Cognitive

C.56   Responds to simple verbal requests (9-14 months)

C.73   Understands pointing (12-14 months)

Language

L.26   Shows understanding of words by appropriate behavior or gesture (9-14 months)

L.36   Uses single-word sentences (12-14 months)

L.37   Uses expressive vocabulary of 1-3 words (12-15 months)

L.38   Vocalizes or gestures spontaneously to indicate needs (12-19 months)

L.42   Names one or two familiar objects (13-18 months)

Fine Motor

FM.54   Uses both hands freely; may show preference for one (11-13 months)

FM.60   Puts three or more objects into container (12-13 months)

FM.63   Points with index finger (12-16 months)

FM.64   Inverts small container to obtain tiny object after demonstration (12½-18 months)

FM.66   Inverts small container spontaneously to obtain tiny object (13½-19 months)

FM.67   Puts many objects into container without removing any (14-15 months)

Pointing and Naming

Activities

As we play with my favorite toys, ask me to point to them. You might ask me, "Where's your truck?" or, "Can you find your ball?" See if I can point to familiar things, like my bottle or blanket. I will also soon learn to point to familiar people when you ask me to find them.

Whenever I attempt to name things or people or just make sounds like I am talking about them, let me know you are listening. Repeat my words and add a few of your own. For example, if I see a baby and say, "Ba," say, "*Baby*, yes! That's another baby like you!"

Developmental Skills

Social and Emotional
S.38   Gives toy to familiar adult spontaneously and upon request (12-15 months)
S.47   Shows toy preferences (12-18 months)

Cognitive
C.56   Responds to simple verbal requests (9-14 months)
C.73   Understands pointing (12-14 months)
C.77   Recognizes several people in addition to immediate family (12-18 months)

Language
L.26   Shows understanding of words by appropriate behavior or gesture (9-14 months)
L.35   Experiments with communication; not frustrated when not understood (12-17½ months)
L.36   Uses single-word sentences (12-14 months)
L.37   Uses expressive vocabulary of one to three words (12-15 months)
L.38   Vocalizes or gestures spontaneously to indicate needs (12-19 months)
L.42   Names one or two familiar objects (13-18 months)

Fine Motor
FM.54   Uses both hands freely; may show preference for one (11-13 months)
FM.63   Points with index finger (12-16 months)

© 1993 by Hawaii Early Learning Partners
Published by Communication Skill Builders, Inc./(602) 323-7500. This page may be reproduced for instructional use. (Catalog No. 7898)

Finding a Hidden Toy

Activities

Play this game with me when I am in a good mood and well rested; I need to pay close attention to what you do to figure out how to play this game.

Find a small toy I really like, a container (such as a juice can), and a cloth diaper or washcloth. Show me the toy; while I am watching, put it into the juice container. Then, making sure I am watching, put the juice container under the cloth. Quickly shake the toy out of the can and under the cloth. I will not see the toy dropping under the cloth—just the container going under the cloth and then reappearing.

Give or show me the container and ask me to find the toy. Let me look into the container, since that is where I last saw the toy. See if I will then look under the cloth (the last place I saw the container). Give me time to figure out where to look, but if I seem to forget what I was looking for, quickly lift the cloth and show me the toy again. Try again for as long as I am interested. You can encourage me to keep looking and following your actions with your words and tone of voice. You may need to use a bigger toy or one that will make a sound as it falls from the container to help me be successful.

Developmental Skills

Cognitive
C.62   Hidden displacement one screen (11-13 months)

Language
L.26   Shows understanding of words by appropriate behavior or gesture (9-14 months)

Singing Action Songs

Activities

What are some of the songs you have been singing to me? I like all kinds of songs, but now that I'm older, I can begin to join you more actively with motions and a word or two in songs that describe actions, like "Pat-a-Cake." Sometimes I may try to sing familiar songs, or to sing when I hear music.

I like songs like "Twinkle, Twinkle, Little Star," which lets us put our hands up and use our fingers or wrists to make twinkling stars. Another fun song is "Row, Row, Row Your Boat," which has us hold hands and pretend to row by rocking forward and back. Doing the motions as you sing the songs helps me learn and remember them. It also allows me to let you know I want to play because I can start the motions and you'll know to join in!

We can make up our own songs to some of my favorite actions, like bouncing on my feet or looking through my legs. We can also add our own actions, like clapping and swaying, to our favorite songs. Maybe you can sing me songs that your mom or grandmother sang to you.

Developmental Skills

Cognitive
- C.56   Responds to simple verbal requests (9-14 months)
- C.66   Imitates several new gestures (11-14 months)

Language
- L.26   Shows understanding of words by appropriate behavior or gesture (9-14 months)
- L.36   Uses single-word sentences (12-14 months)
- L.38   Vocalizes or gestures spontaneously to indicate needs (12-19 months)
- L.43   Attempts to sing sounds to music (13-16 months)

Gross Motor
- GM.82   Bends over and looks through legs (14½-15½ months)

Fine Motor
- FM.54   Uses both hands freely; may show preference for one (11-13 months)

Stacking Toys

Activities

Show me how you stack rings by putting them on the pole. I can help take them off. Help me put them back on the pole. It might be easier at first if all of the rings and the pole are the same size. If the stacking toy is graduated, help me by giving me the largest one first, and so on. We can stack small boxes, plastic containers with lids on, small books, and large blocks.

While I'm learning to stack blocks, I might place the second block on top of the first without releasing it, but that shows you I have the idea. Gradually, I will learn to balance one block on top of the other, which will lead to building a tower of blocks. Learning to stack toys helps me improve my eye-hand coordination and teaches me about balance and spatial relationships. I can start to learn about colors, too, as you name the colors for me while we play together.

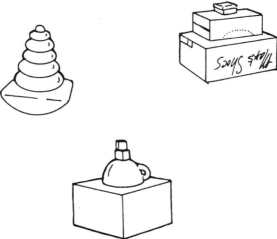

Developmental Skills

Cognitive
C.56   Responds to simple verbal requests (9-14 months)
C.64   Stacks rings (11-12 months)
C.70   Shows understanding of color and size (12-18 months)

Fine Motor
FM.54   Uses both hands freely; may show preference for one
          (11-13 months)
FM.61   Builds tower using two cubes (12-16 months)

Visiting the Zoo

Activities

A trip to the zoo is always fun! You may want to take a stroller or backpack if the zoo is large, but let me walk some of the time, too. I might enjoy practicing some new skills, such as walking sideways on a bench.

Take along a favorite snack (one example might be fruit or crackers and a cup with a handle for juice or milk carried in a small insulated container). Paper towels used for cleanup are fun to throw into large rubbish containers.

Remember that I may get very excited and run away to see something, so you will need to watch me closely if there are any dangerous areas, such as traffic or ponds. I may resist your efforts to control me in these circumstances, but, if it is a safety issue, act quickly and matter-of-factly. Give me other choices, such as which animal to visit first, and find a safe area for free exploration. I may show some anxiety in this new setting, so accept this as okay and reassure me with your presence and support.

The animals I'm most likely to enjoy are the ones that are large and easy to see. It's best if they move or make noise. We can imitate their sounds and you can remind me of the book we read at home where we saw pictures of these animals. Don't worry if I'm more interested in the other people or children than in the animals; I may want to chase the pigeons in the grass more than anything else. For someone my age, everything new and different is fascinating.

Developmental Skills

Social and Emotional
S.29   May show fear and insecurity with previously accepted situations (6-18 months)
S.40   Acts impulsively, unable to recognize rules (12-15 months)
S.41   Attempts self-direction; resists adult control (12-15 months)

Gross Motor
GM.71   Stands alone well (11½-14 months)
GM.79   Walks without support (13-15 months)
GM.80   Walks sideways (14-15 months)
GM.81   Runs—hurried walk (14-18 months)

Fine Motor
FM.60   Puts three or more objects into container (12-13 months)

Self-Help
SH.24   Chews food with munching pattern (8-13½ months)
SH.32   Holds and drinks from cup with some spilling (12-18 months)
SH.33   Holds cup handle (12-15½ months)

Learning about Zoo Animals

Activities

As I get older and more familiar with the zoo animals, I'll spend more time looking at them. Give me the names for the animals and the sounds they make; simple sounds, such as "s-s-s" for snake, and "grrrrr" for tiger. Point to different sights in the cages that you want me to see and encourage me to point also.

Talk about the colors and sizes of the animals you see. Be enthusiastic with your language; for example, say something like, "Uh-oh, the monkey just dropped the peanut!" I may use some single-word sentences, such as, "Come," "Eat," or, "Help" as part of exploring this different environment. Always respond verbally to my statements, saying something like, "Yes, the monkey is eating a banana. You like to eat bananas, too."

Developmental Skills

Cognitive
C.70   Shows understanding of color and size (12-18 months)
C.73   Understands pointing (12-14 months)

Language
L.22   Produces these sounds frequently in babbling: /b/, /m/, /p/, /d/, /t/, /n/, /g/, /k/, /w/, /h/, /f/, /v/, /th/, /s/, /z/, /l/, /r/ (7-15 months)
L.36   Uses single-word sentences (12-14 months)
L.40   Uses exclamatory expressions ("oh-oh," "no-no") (12½-14½ months)

Fine Motor
FM.63   Points with index finger (12-16 months)

Understanding Tantrum Behavior

Activities

This is about the age when I've had all I can stand. I scream, fall to the floor, kick my feet, bang my head against the wall or floor. It's not pretty to watch, and it's very uncomfortable for most parents.

There are a number of reasons why I have temper tantrums: I may be overtired, hungry, reacting badly to certain foods, overexcited, or feel overcontrolled. At any rate, I can no longer tolerate the feelings of frustration and must react.

What can you do?

- To prevent me from having a tantrum, you can try to keep me from getting overtired or overexcited, or try to find out whether certain foods affect me negatively. Helping me relax and introducing quiet activity may be some of the ways to reduce tantrums.

- Try to be consistent in the way you handle me. Don't let me touch your music tapes sometimes and scold me other times.

- Childproof the house. This will mean you don't have to keep saying, "No, no, no!" when I'm exploring, until I can't stand it and start to scream.

- Don't give in to my tantrum. Just wait till I run out of steam and comfort me. Stay calm and collected; this may be difficult, but if you don't learn this, we're in for lots more trouble. Be firm about the boundaries you've set. It'll help me define my limits.

Developmental Skills

Social and Emotional
S.42   Displays frequent tantrum behaviors (12-18 months)
S.56   Desires control of others: orders, fights, resists (18-24 months)
S.57   Feels easily frustrated (18-24 months)

Protecting Me from Danger

Activities

Mommies and daddies and other adults tend to think that I'm grown up because I'm beginning to walk or talk. They expect me to remember that they said, "No, don't touch," or, "You mustn't throw things," or, "You'll get a shock if you put your finger there." I need to hear these phrases, but the words alone are not enough to keep me safe.

Remember, I'm still only a year old. If the house isn't childproofed, I'm going to get into unsafe places, break things, explore, and play with things that I shouldn't.

I'm not trying to be bad or to upset you; I'm learning about the world and about your responses to my behavior. I'm trying out new skills like throwing things, which includes throwing food.

What can you do to help me handle this period of poor impulse control and limited verbal memory?

- Keep me away from forbidden areas.

- Stop me if I'm throwing things by removing them from me, saying, "Food is for eating," "Balls are for throwing."

- Childproof the home so you don't have to keep saying "No."

- Don't let me wander outside alone. I may explore something that is a danger to me.

- Don't expect me to understand that you're punishing me for breaking rules. Physical punishment won't work very well at this age.

- Find things for me to do so I can use my energy doing things that are fun and safe.

- Keep rules simple.

- Tell me what to *do,* rather than a series of *don'ts.*

- Don't leave my safety to a child, especially at places like the beach. I'm so active and curious that I need an adult to keep me safe.

Developmental Skills

Social and Emotional

S.36	Explores environment enthusiastically; safety precautions important (9-12 months)
S.39	Displays independent behavior; is difficult to discipline (the "No" stage) (12-15 months)
S.40	Acts impulsively, unable to recognize rules (12-15 months)

Helping Me through the "No" Stage

Activities

I'm learning about the word "No" and its remarkable effect on others as well as on myself. I find myself wanting to practice saying, "No, no, no" and shaking my head back and forth in rhythm.

Don't be upset by this, and don't discourage me from saying it. It's another move toward independence for me. It makes me feel like I'm in charge.

How should you help me through this "No" stage?

- Reinforce my positive, cooperative behavior and ignore my "No's" even if you let me practice saying it. If I get more points for being cooperative, I'll learn that that's the way to go.

- Give me opportunities to make real choices so I'll know that you respect my decisions. Don't ask me, though, if I want to choose to do something if I don't really have a choice.

- Distraction is a great technique to help me focus on the positive. For example, if I'm fighting with my brother, show me a toy I like.

- Reduce the need to say "No" to me by making my environment safe to explore.

- Even if I say "No," I may not mean it, so you must be firm but relaxed and get me to do what needs to be done.

- Don't punish me if I keep saying "No" and refuse to do as you ask. The effectiveness of the suggested techniques, such as distraction, firmness, routines, real choices, and reinforcement of positive behavior, grows during this phase.

Developmental Skills

Social and Emotional
S.27	Struggles against supine position (6-12 months)
S.33	Tests parental reactions during feeding (9-12 months)
S.34	Tests parental reactions at bedtime (9-12 months)
S.39	Displays independent behavior; is difficult to discipline (the "No" stage) (12-15 months)
S.40	Acts impulsively, unable to recognize rules (12-15 months)
S.41	Attempts self-direction; resists adult control (12-15 months)
S.42	Displays frequent tantrum behaviors (12-18 months)
S.43	Needs and expects rituals and routines (12-18 months)
S.56	Desires control of others; orders, fights, resists (18-24 months)

Being Messy

Activities

Most of us learn about the world by touching, feeling, moving things, and getting messy. We learn about textures and temperatures of things from things like sand that has gotten hot from the sun, from the cold snow, or the dewy grass.

You can provide me with things for messy play in the house. For example, I could finger paint in the bathtub. I probably will also try finger painting in my high chair with my food. I don't do it to upset you—it's one of the ways I learn.

You may not like to see me so dirty and messy, but I feel like a free spirit when I can play outside without worrying about my clothes or about dirty hands and feet. Just be sure I'm dressed in play clothes or wearing a big apron if you don't want me to dirty my clothes when I'm playing outside or with finger paints or clay.

Messy play is part of my growing up and learning about things. I can learn, too, about being clean and careful when I need to do so. But don't cramp my style or let me become someone who can't stand to be dirty.

Developmental Skills

Social and Emotional
S.49   Tends to be quite messy (12-15 months)

Cognitive
C.68   Enjoys messy activities, such as finger painting (12-15 months)
C.69   Reacts to various sensations, such as extremes in temperature and taste (12-15 months)

Self-Help
SH.38   Scoops food, feeds self with spoon with some spilling (15-24 months)

Riding Safely in a Car

Activities

I can use a convertible car seat until I am around four years old. When I was an infant, my seat faced the rear of the car. Now that I am able to sit up alone, the seat can be raised and turned around to face the front.

A toddler seat can also be used when I weigh 17 pounds. I will be safest if the seat is placed in the middle of the back seat. Do not put my car seat on a seat that can fold forward unless the seat has a lock. The shade screen you've placed on the window helps lessen the glare from the sun.

Since you have been consistent about putting me into my car seat ever since I was an infant, I have become accustomed to sitting in it whenever we go for a ride. You've always been careful about buckling me in and keeping me in the car seat, even when I resisted. When I was very fussy and cried a lot, or tried to unbuckle my belt or climb out of the seat, you would pull over and stop the car to try to calm me and be sure that I was safe. It helps me to have my special toy with me in the car. We also have fun when we talk, sing, or listen to music as we ride in the car.

Developmental Skills

Social and Emotional
S.39   Displays independent behavior; is difficult to discipline (the "No" stage) (12-15 months)
S.41   Attempts self-direction; resists adult control (12-15 months)
S.42   Displays frequent tantrum behaviors (12-18 months)
S.43   Needs and expects rituals and routines (12-18 months)
S.48   Displays distractible behavior (12-15 months)

Cognitive
C.56   Responds to simple verbal requests (9-14 months)

Language
L.43   Attempts to sing sounds to music (13-16 months)

Teething

Activities

My molars are starting to come through and I may be really cranky. My appetite may be poor for several days at a time. Let me chew on safe objects, such as a teething ring or washcloth (a teething biscuit or piece of hard, dry toast would be nice). Watch that I don't chew or gnaw on the furniture.

Developmental Skills

Self-Help
SH.23   Drools less except when teething (7-12 months)
SH.30   May refuse foods; appetite decreases (12-18 months)

Checking on My Hearing

Activities

If you are concerned about my hearing, let my doctor know. There are hearing tests that can be given to infants and children to detect any hearing problems. Some signs of hearing loss include:

- Not turning or looking up when you call me by my name.
- Not noticing sounds, such as the television, a knock on the door, the telephone ringing, or a dog barking.
- Not listening to people talking.
- Not babbling as much as I used to or not using inflection (pitch changes) that sound like talking.
- Consistently favoring one ear when listening.
- Having a poor reaction or response after having a high or prolonged fever, or after an illness, such as meningitis or measles.

Developmental Skills

Social and Emotional
S.09	Vocalizes in response to adult talk and smile (3-5 months)

Cognitive
C.03	Responds to sounds (0-1 month)
C.07	Listens to voice for 30 seconds (1-3 months)
C.10	Searches with eyes for sound (2-3½ months)
C.12	Watches speaker's eyes and mouth (2-3 months)
C.16	Turns eyes and head to sound of hidden voice (3-7 months)
C.18	Awakens or quiets to mother's voice (3-6 months)
C.19	Localizes sound with eyes (3½-5 months)
C.27	Distinguishes between friendly and angry voices (5-6½ months)
C.41	Turns head and shoulders to find hidden sound (7-10 months)
C.48	Listens selectively to familiar words (8-12 months)
C.54	Listens to speech without being distracted by other sources (9-11 months)
C.56	Responds to simple verbal requests (9-14 months)
C.65	Moves to rhythms (11-14 months)

Language
L.07	Coos open vowels (aah), closed vowels (ee), diphthongs (oy as in boy) (2-7 months)
L.08	Disassociates vocalizations from body movement (2-3 months)
L.13	Babbles consonant chains ("bababababa") (4-6½ months)
L.15	Reacts to music by cooing (5-6 months)
L.16	Looks and vocalizes to own name (5-7 months)
L.18	Babbles to people (5½-6½ months)
L.20	Says "dada" or "mama" nonspecifically (6½-11½ months)
L.24	Babbles with inflection similar to adult speech (7½-12 months)
L.26	Shows understanding of words by appropriate behavior or gesture (9-14 months)
L.27	Babbles in response to human voice (11-15 months)
L.28	Babbles monologue when left alone (11-12 months)

Activities and Developmental Skills for 15-18 Months

Making Choices for Dressing

Activities

My desire for independence can be frustrating at times. When I'm getting dressed and having my diapers changed, you can let me make some decisions and participate a little.

In the morning, choose two outfits and ask me which one I want to wear ("Do you want the blue shirt or the red shirt?"). Another choice you can give me is, "What should we put on next, your shirt or your pants?" I am developing likes and dislikes, and this gives me some control.

As you dress me, I can help by extending my arm or leg. I can learn to undress by pulling my socks off or taking off my hat.

Developmental Skills

Social and Emotional
S.43   Needs and expects rituals and routines (12-18 months)
S.45   Enjoys imitating adult behavior: responds well to the introduction of new tasks (12-18 months)

Cognitive
C.75   Makes detours to retrieve objects (12-18 months)
C.87   Indicates two objects from a group of familiar objects (15-18 months)
C.88   Brings objects from another room on request (15-18 months)
C.91   Identifies one body part (15-19 months)
C.102   Points to several clothing items on request (18-20 months)

Language
L.38   Vocalizes or gestures spontaneously to indicate needs (12-19 months)
L.42   Names one or two familiar objects (13-18 months)
L.44   Uses voice in conjunction with pointing or gesturing (14-20 months)
L.45   Uses 10-15 words spontaneously (15-17½ months)

Gross Motor
GM.83   Demonstrates balance reactions in standing (15-18 months)
GM.89   Stands on one foot with help (16-17 months)

Fine Motor
FM.63   Points with index finger (12-16 months)
FM.68   Uses both hands in midline; one holds, other manipulates (16-18 months)

Self-Help
SH.39   Removes socks (15-18 months)
SH.40   Removes hat (15-16½ months)
SH.41   Places hat on head (16½-18½ months)

Pulling and Pushing Toys

Activities

Now that I can walk by myself, I *love* to practice. I like games that involve my new skill. I will discover that I can move my toys to different places by pushing them as I walk or by pulling them if there is a handle or string.

It would be fun if you could make a *wagon* by tying a short piece of yarn, shoelace, or clothesline to a cardboard box. I could take my special bear or doll for a ride. I'll probably enjoy doing little jobs for you. For example, if you ask me to get a diaper or a book from another room, I can put it in my *wagon* and bring it to you. You may be surprised to find out that I know the names of lots of things you ask for even if I can't say them yet.

You might find some special toy for me at the store, such as a duck that quacks as I pull it behind me. There is also a popper that makes wonderful sounds when it is pushed. We can have fun imitating those sounds as we move our toy around the house.

It would be fun if we played together sometimes. You might try to get in my *wagon* and ask me to pull you! I'll probably enjoy the joke because I'll understand that's not possible.

I like to imitate what you do and practice being grown up. When you vacuum, I could push my little popper toy around and pretend to help you.

Developmental Skills

Social and Emotional
S.44   Begins to show a sense of humor; laughs at incongruities (12-18 months)
S.45   Enjoys imitating adult behavior; responds well to the introduction of new tasks (12-18 months)

Cognitive
C.88   Brings objects from another room on request (15-18 months)
C.93   Understands most noun objects (16-19 months)

Language
L.35   Experiments with communication; not frustrated when not understood (12-17½ months)

Gross Motor
GM.87   Pulls toy behind while walking (15-18 months)
GM.92   Pushes and pulls large toys or boxes around the floor (17-18½ months)

© 1993 by Hawaii Early Learning Partners
Published by Communication Skill Builders, Inc./(602) 323-7500. This page may be reproduced for instructional use. (Catalog No. 7898)

Nesting Toys

Activities

I enjoy nesting toys and objects (the shape is the same but the size varies). They're called *nesting* because the smaller ones can be placed inside the larger ones. These toys teach me about sizes, shapes, and colors.

You can find many household items that I can nest, such as plastic food containers, measuring cups, aluminum plates, plastic mixing bowls, small pots, and pans. Colorful nesting toys (cups, barrels, eggs, drums) are fun, too.

It would be easier for me if you let me play with just two sizes at first, then three, then more as I become good at nesting. I learn by trial and error, so let me try. Talk to me about the size (for example, big and small), the shape, and the colors of my nesting toys as I play with them.

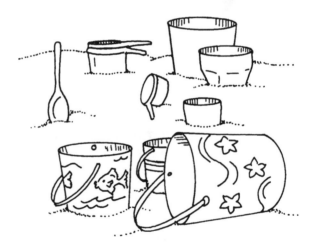

Developmental Skills

Cognitive
    C.56   Responds to simple verbal requests (9-14 months)
    C.66   Imitates several new gestures (11-14 months)
    C.72   Nests two, then three cans (12-19 months)

Language
    L.26   Shows understanding of words by appropriate behavior or gesture (9-14 months)

Fine Motor
    FM.54   Uses both hands freely; may show preference for one (11-13 months)

Learning about Sameness

Activities

Many familiar objects come in pairs (two of the same). When I use things that come in pairs, tell me and show me they are the same. Use the word "same" because I want to learn the concept even if I am not able to name everything.

My socks, shoes, feet, ears, and eyes come in twos or pairs, and each pair is the same. Talk with me about things that are the same as we play with them together. When I'm holding a spoon, give me another one and tell me it's the same. Later, when I have a spoon again, show me a spoon and a cup. Ask me to pick up the one that is the same. When I can choose correctly between two, you really know that I understand the concept.

It can also be fun if you purposefully make a mistake and pick the wrong object when you are searching for the second part of a pair, like the doll's other shoe. Try putting the doll's hat on her foot and see if I think it's funny. Your face and intonation will help me and encourage my developing sense of humor. Then we can find the doll's other shoe, confirm that they are the same, and finish dressing the doll. The more you describe to me the things that make an object the same or not, the more I learn about color, shape, and functions.

I can learn to match objects whenever I play with my toys, stack cubes, or put pegs into a peg board. I can tell you what I know by pointing to (or sometimes naming) a familiar object and looking for another one like it. When I name something I know, find another one in my environment and show it to me, too!

Developmental Skills

Social and Emotional
S.44   Begins to show a sense of humor; laughs at incongruities (12-18 months)

Cognitive
C.70   Shows understanding of color and size (12-18 months)
C.85   Matches objects (15-19 months)
C.93   Understands most noun objects (16-19 months)

Language
L.38   Vocalizes or gestures spontaneously to indicate needs (12-19 months)
L.42   Names one or two familiar objects (13-18 months)
L.44   Uses voice in conjunction with pointing or gesturing (14-20 months)
L.45   Uses 10 to 15 words spontaneously (15-17½ months)
L.49   Echoes prominent word or last word spoken (17-19 months)
L.50   Uses expressive vocabulary of 15 to 20 words (17½-20½ months)

Fine Motor
FM.63   Points with index finger (12-16 months)
FM.69   Builds tower using three cubes (16-18 months)
FM.70   Places six round pegs in peg board (16-19 months)

Playing Make-Believe with Toy Animals and Dolls I

Activities

Come play with me with my toy animals or dolls. Since I am usually the one being helped in undressing and feeding, it is fun for me to be in charge of helping my bear or doll. Let me undress my bear as we pretend it's bath time. Some of my old baby clothes will fit my bear, or we could find other clothes (hat, socks, shoes) around the house.

We can use a small box for our bathtub and a small cloth to pretend to wash my bear. Ask me to point to my bear's body parts or name each part as I wash it. We can do this as I dry or diaper my bear, too! A small cup, spoon, and bowl let me feed my bear. With a toy bottle and blanket, I can rock my bear to sleep.

Another time, we might play in front of a mirror. Using the mirror, we could sing and clap our hands and do other motions to songs we know. I can help Bear clap hands. We can also try imitating gestures that are hard to see on ourselves but easy to see when Bear does them (like patting my head or scratching my nose). How many of these gestures can I imitate? Can I identify myself in the mirror? Ask me!

The small box we used for a bathtub can become our wagon with a short rope (about 12 inches) attached in the front. Then I can take my bear for a make-believe ride to the store or beach. We would need to get ready by packing a bag for our wagon. You might suggest I get something from another room to take along. Another way for you to play is to get a few things and ask me to name them or to hand them to you when you name them so you can put them into the wagon. Then, let me pull the wagon around inside the house.

I like to imitate the things you do, so think of other make-believe games we can play with a few simple objects. Remember, I learn a great deal when you describe the things we do with simple but specific words.

Developmental Skills

Social and Emotional
S.44   Begins to show a sense of humor; laughs at incongruities (12-18 months)

S.45   Enjoys imitating adult behavior; responds well to the introduction of new tasks (12-18 months)

S.47   Shows toy preferences (12-18 months)

S.52   Imitates doing housework (15-18 months)

Cognitive
C.70   Shows understanding of color and size (12-18 months)

C.75   Makes detours to retrieve objects (12-18 months)

C.84   Imitates "invisible" gesture (14-17 months)

C.87   Indicates two objects from a group of familiar objects (15-18 months)

C.88   Brings objects from another room on request (15-18 months)

C.90   Identifies self in mirror (15-16 months)

C.91   Identifies one body part (15-19 months)

C.93   Understands most noun objects (16-19 months)

C.96   Imitates several "invisible" gestures (17-20 months)

Language
L.34   Babbles intricate inflection (12-18 months)

L.35   Experiments with communication; not frustrated when not understood (12-17½ months)

L.38   Vocalizes or gestures spontaneously to indicate needs (12-19 months)

L.42   Names one or two familiar objects (13-18 months)

L.43   Attempts to sing sounds to music (13-16 months)

L.44   Uses voice in conjunction with pointing or gesturing (14-20 months)

L.45   Uses 10 to 15 words spontaneously (15-17½ months)

L.46   Vocalizes wishes and needs at the table; names desired items (15-17½ months)

L.48   Jabbers tunefully at play (17-19 months)

L.49   Echoes prominent word or last word spoken (17-19 months)

L.50   Uses expressive vocabulary of 15 to 20 words (17½-20½ months)

Gross Motor
GM.76   Walks backwards (12½-21 months)

GM.87   Pulls toy behind while walking (15-18 months)

GM.91   Carries large toy while walking (17-18½ months)

GM.92   Pushes and pulls large toys or boxes around the floor (17-18½ months)

Fine Motor
FM.63   Points with index finger (12-16 months)

FM.68   Uses both hands in midline; one holds, other manipulates (16-18 months)

Self-Help
SH.39   Removes socks (15-18 months)

SH.40   Removes hat (15-16½ months)

SH.41   Places hat on head (16½-18½ months)

Enjoying Water Play

Activities

Fill a bucket with water and small plastic toys. Let me gather all the small objects and put them in another container. Show me how to scoop up toys by reaching for them with a long-handled scoop net or a plastic ladle. Remember: Never leave me alone with a bucket of water.

Another game we can play is to find the hidden toy in one of three empty buckets. Let me put a small toy in your hand. Close your hand to hide the toy. Then hide your hand under each of the three upside-down buckets, one at a time. Leave it in the third bucket and show me your empty hand. I should then go to the last bucket to find the toy. If I don't, help me find it and play the game again.

I'll enjoy pouring water from bucket to bucket and on myself while I'm in the tub. Learning that some things will float and others sink will keep my attention. Maybe you can find plastic spoons and metal spoons with which I can experiment. I'll also have fun squeezing water with a clean sponge into containers and onto you.

Developmental Skills

Cognitive
C.94   Series of hidden displacements: object under last screen (17-18 months)
C.95   Solves simple problems using tools (17-24 months)

Gross Motor
GM.85   Throws ball forward (15-18 months)

Fine Motor
FM.67   Puts many objects into container without removing any (14-15 months)
FM.68   Uses both hands in midline; one holds, other manipulates (16-18 months)

Playing in Water Outdoors

Activities

I like sitting in the inflatable pool or large plastic tub of water that you prepare. I also like playing with toys or objects in my pool, such as a doll, washcloth, containers or buckets, a ball, and small plastic floating toys. Take me out to my pool dressed, including socks and a hat, so that I have a chance to practice taking them off. Always stay with me while I do this in case I slip and fall. Never leave me around a pool or bucket of water by myself.

Encourage me to sit in the tub. If I insist on standing, be sure there is a sturdy edge for me to hold. Put nonslip adhesive strips on the bottom of the tub to make it safer.

Let's pretend to bathe the doll. Tell me about the doll's arms and legs, and ask me to point to my own arms and legs. Move the doll's arms, then ask me to move my arms the same way. Encourage me to hug and kiss my doll. As I play, expect some spontaneous use of language, familiar simple words, and jabbering. Reinforce my attempts to communicate by talking to me, repeating words I use, and adding more words.

When I go outside for water play, be careful about my exposure to the sun and remember that it's strongest between 10 a.m. and 3 p.m. Please check with my doctor about using a sunscreen to protect my skin. If you put sunscreen on me, try a small dab on my arm the day before we plan to use it to see if I react with a rash. If there is a rash, check back with my doctor.

If I do get a sunburn, cool me off by applying a washcloth soaked in cool water. Remove the cloth and let the water evaporate before putting on another cool washcloth. If there are blisters from the burn, do not break them because they protect my skin; call the doctor for advice.

Playing ball is another fun activity in the water. Throwing the ball between us will make fun splashes. Reach for the ball with the scoop net. Throw the ball into a bucket if the bucket's large enough. Help me be successful by moving the bucket so that it's under the ball when it lands. Cheer for me when I am successful.

Developmental Skills

Social and Emotional

    S.51   Hugs and kisses parents (14-15½ months)

Cognitive

    C.84   Imitates "invisible" gesture (14-17 months)

    C.91   Identifies one body part (15-19 months)

    C.96   Imitates several "invisible" gestures (17-20 months)

Language

    L.45   Uses 10 to 15 words spontaneously (15-17½ months)

    L.48   Jabbers tunefully at play (17-19 months)

Gross Motor

    GM.83   Demonstrates balance reactions in standing
                (15-18 months)

Self-Help

    SH.39   Removes socks (15-18 months)

    SH.40   Removes hat (15-16½ months)

    SH.41   Places hat on head (16½-18½ months)

Helping in the Yard

Activities

I like being outdoors when you work in the yard. You know that I should have a head covering if it's very sunny or very cold outside (luckily, I like to put on hats now). When you ask me to put on my hat, I'll know that it signals a special outdoor activity.

Give me a small wagon or box to pull so I can pick up leaves, put them in the wagon, and pull them to you. I'll understand your request if you ask me to find sticks, flowers, and so forth. You might want to show me a sample of what you want me to pick up; this will help me find more of the same.

I may try to talk as I point out things I see in the yard. I like it when you respond by talking back and trying to understand what I'm saying. My *help* might make it slower for you now, but I really will be able to help later.

Developmental Skills

Social and Emotional
S.45   Enjoys imitating adult behavior; responds well to the introduction of new tasks (12-18 months)

Cognitive
C.85   Matches objects (15-19 months)
C.88   Brings objects from another room on request (15-18 months)

Language
L.44   Uses voice in conjunction with pointing or gesturing (14-20 months)

Gross Motor
GM.87   Pulls toy behind while walking (15-18 months)

Fine Motor
FM.68   Uses both hands in midline; one holds, other manipulates (16-18 months)

Self-Help
SH.41   Places hat on head (16½-18½ months)

Wanting to Be Like You

Activities

I want to be like you and do what you do. I like to play with pots and pans because you use them. I like banging them, and I like to put one pot into another as you do.

I also want to water the plants as you do. A small plastic cup and a bucket of water to dip from will keep me busy in the back-yard as I help water the garden. Just re-member, I'll probably get myself as wet as I get the plants.

I like playing with dishes because you use them all the time. I use them when I feed my bear. My bear eats anything but is pretty messy so I have to help feed the bear. After we eat, I like to take the dishes off the table and put them in a basket so I can wash them. Washing dishes is fun, especially when I use real water and soap bubbles.

When you read me a story, I like to sit with my bear, show the bear my picture book, and tell Bear about the pictures. It's just great to have such nice models as Daddy and Mommy to imitate.

Developmental Skills

Social and Emotional
S.32   Extends toy to show others, not for release (9-12 months)
S.45   Enjoys imitating adult behavior; responds well to the
        introduction of new tasks (12-18 months)
S.47   Shows toy preferences (12-18 months)
S.52   Imitates doing housework (15-18 months)

Cognitive
C.72   Nests two, then three cans (12-19 months)
C.89   Turns two or three pages at a time (15-18 months)

Language
L.43   Attempts to sing sounds to music (13-16 months)

Being Safe in the Car

Activities

There are lots of things you have to think about when you have me in the car. You have to be sure to put me in a safe car seat and use the seat belts (you, too!). I see by this that *everyone* in the car uses seat belts, and learn why I also must be in a car seat with a safety belt.

Please be careful about metal parts in the car that are exposed to the sun, such as the seat-belt buckles, because these can get hot enough to burn me. Take me with you whenever you leave the car, even for a short period of time. If I'm left alone, I may suffer from heat exhaustion in a hot car, or I could be kidnapped. If I am left with other children in the car, we may accidentally put the car in motion or fall out the window.

Developmental Skills

Social and Emotional

S.36   Explores environment enthusiastically; safety precautions important (9-12 months)

S.39   Displays independent behavior; is difficult to discipline (the "No" stage) (12-15 months)

S.40   Acts impulsively, unable to recognize rules (12-15 months)

S.41   Attempts self-direction; resists adult control (12-15 months)

S.45   Enjoys imitating adult behavior; responds well to the introduction of new tasks (12-18 months)

Fine Motor

FM.54   Uses both hands freely; may show preference for one (11-13 months)

© 1993 by Hawaii Early Learning Partners

Published by Communication Skill Builders, Inc./(602) 323-7500. This page may be reproduced for instructional use. (Catalog No. 7898)

Detecting Ear Infections

Activities

A number of symptoms may mean that I have an ear infection: if you see me pulling or rubbing my ear a lot, if I'm fussy, crying in pain, or not as active as usual, or if I have diarrhea or vomit. If these things happen, especially after I've had a cold for a few days, call the doctor.

With an ear infection, fluid gets trapped in the middle ear, puts pressure on the ear drum, and can affect my hearing. Ear infections that are not treated may cause some hearing loss and become a serious problem, even affecting how well I learn to talk. I am learning many new words at this age so, when I cannot hear clearly, I may learn incorrect words and become inattentive to new words. This may discourage me and interfere with my language learning.

Be sure to take me to the doctor if you suspect I have an ear infection. If my earache goes away, tell my doctor about it anyway because the infection may still be there. Whenever the doctor gives me medicine, be sure I take it according to the doctor's instructions.

Developmental Skills

Language

L.35	Experiments with communication; not frustrated when not understood (12-17½ months)
L.43	Attempts to sing sounds to music (13-16 months)
L.48	Jabbers tunefully at play (17-19 months)
L.49	Echoes prominent or last word spoken (17-19 months)

Activities and Developmental Skills for 18-21 Months

Feeling Good about Clean Diapers

Activities

You may notice that I sometimes become very quiet, act uncomfortable, or even walk funny. This behavior may be a sign of wet or dirty diapers. Ask me if I need to be changed or if I'm wet. If I am (and I won't always admit it), invite me to go get a clean diaper. Be sure to change me promptly when I am wet or dirty so that I know how it feels to be dry. Knowing this will help me when I am ready to be toilet trained. If I'm comfortable being wet, I may not be motivated to use the toilet!

After a diaper change, you might tell me, "Go throw the diaper away." Help me so I get the diaper in the right place. Praise me for helping and remark how good it must feel to be dry. Afterwards, help me wash my hands, using soap and water. Talk about what we're doing as we do it.

Developmental Skills

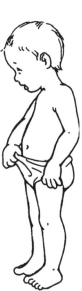

Social and Emotional
S.55   Shows a wide variety of emotions: fear, anger, sympathy, modesty, guilt, embarrassment, anxiety, joy (18-24 months)
S.62   Experiences a strong sense of self-importance (18-24 months)

Cognitive
C.91   Identifies one body part (15-19 months)
C.111   Identifies three body parts (19-22 months)
C.112   Understands personal pronouns, some action verbs, and adjectives (20-24 months)

Language
L.38   Vocalizes or gestures spontaneously to indicate needs (12-19 months)
L.49   Echoes prominent word or last word spoken (17-19 months)
L.50   Uses expressive vocabulary of 15 to 20 words (17½-20½ months)
L.52   Uses own name to refer to self (18-24 months)
L.53   Imitates environmental sounds (18-21 months)

Gross Motor
GM.90   Walks upstairs with one hand held (17-19 months)
GM.102   Picks up toy from floor without falling (19-24 months)
GM.103   Squats in play (20-21 months)
GM.110   Walks with legs closer together (23-25 months)

Self-Help
SH.48   Sits on potty chair or on adaptive seat on toilet with assistance (18-24 months)
SH.49   May be toilet-regulated by adult (18-24 months)
SH.51   Washes and dries hands partially (19-24 months)
SH.57   Puts shoes on with assistance (21-30 months)

Settling Down for Bedtime

Activities

The bedtime routines we've been following help me settle down for sleep. It's time to think about perhaps changing them to fit what I'm doing now.

Be sure you use a soft toothbrush when you brush my teeth every night. I may object sometimes, but my teeth are important and I like to have you admire them.

After I'm all clean and in my pajamas, I'm nice to cuddle. I like to tell people goodnight, and give and get a hug. I can even say "Night-night." Instead of just pointing or waving "Night-night" to people, I might throw a kiss to my toys or pictures on my walls, or even use two or three words together to say, "Night-night, Teddy" or, "Go to sleep, Teddy."

As you tuck me in my bed, talk to me about what we did today and what we will do in the morning. "Did you like going to the grocery store today? We bought crackers. Maybe tomorrow we'll play outside if the weather's nice." This is a start on a bedtime story that stars my favorite people—you and me.

You know the routines that are important to me, such as having a drink or getting my favorite stuffed animal or blanket. If you forget, I'll try to tell you with words or actions. When you are consistent and remember what's important to me, I learn to trust and count on people.

Developmental Skills

Social and Emotional
S.53   Expresses affection (18-24 months)
S.55   Shows a wide variety of emotions: fear, anger, sympathy, modesty, guilt, embarrassment, anxiety, joy (18-24 months)
S.56   Desires control of others; orders, fights, resists (18-24 months)

Cognitive

C.92   Recognizes and points to four animal pictures (16-21 months)
C.104   Matches sounds to animals (18-22 months)
C.106   Enjoys nursery rhymes, nonsense rhymes, finger plays, poetry (18-30 months)
C.110   Recognizes self in photograph (19-24 months)
C.112   Understands personal pronouns, some action verbs, and adjectives (20-24 months)

Language

L.38   Vocalizes or gestures spontaneously to indicate needs (12-19 months)
L.44   Uses voice in conjunction with pointing or gesturing (14-20 months)
L.49   Echoes prominent word or last word spoken (17-19 months)
L.50   Uses expressive vocabulary of 15 to 20 words (17½-20½ months)
L.52   Uses own name to refer to self (18-24 months)
L.54   Imitates two-word phrases (18-21 months)
L.56   Names two pictures (19-21½ months)

Gross Motor

GM.90   Walks upstairs with one hand held (17-19 months)
GM.91   Carries large toy while walking (17-18½ months)
GM.102   Picks up toy from floor without falling (19-24 months)

Self-Help

SH.46   Removes shoe when laces undone (18-24 months)
SH.47   Unzips, zips large zipper (18-21 months)
SH.51   Washes and dries hands partially (19-24 months)

Exploring Our Home

Activities

Our home is a wonderful place to explore. Because I can climb and move independently, I find exploring cabinets, drawers, closets, and every part of our home fun.

Let me know which cabinets and drawers I can explore. Fill bottom bureau drawers and low cabinets with old, safe, interesting things for me to take out. If you name some of the clothes and familiar things you put in the drawers, I should be able to pick them out.

For safety, the drawers should have stops; otherwise they may come all the way out and land on my toes. Keep safety locks on other low cabinets where you keep cleaning agents or other harmful objects.

Try putting some toys out of reach under a chair or sofa. Put another, long-handled toy near the chair. See what I do to get the toys. If I ignore the long-handled toy, show me how to use it to get the toys that are out of reach, then let me try.

Help me to walk down stairs. Help me slide or back into my small chair and climb and sit on your chair. I may sometimes want to climb onto a chair near the window so I can look out and see what is going on, as well as locate and imitate sounds I hear. Encourage me to tiptoe to peek outside. Sometimes play a game of pointing to familiar things that we like.

Let me look at pictures of myself and others in my family that are displayed in the house. Ask me to point to myself, others, or even familiar details like body parts. Ask me to identify myself by name. I will want to look at some pictures again and again. If I point and use a word like "ba" or "baby," expand on it: "You want to see baby Chad's picture?" or, "Baby Casey's picture, shall we look at baby Casey swimming?" Tell me what the picture shows and what people are doing in it.

© 1993 by Hawaii Early Learning Partners
Published by Communication Skill Builders, Inc./(602) 323-7500. This page may be reproduced for instructional use. (Catalog No. 7898)

Developmental Skills

Cognitive

C.93	Understands most noun objects (16-19 months)
C.95	Solves simple problems using tools (17-24 months)
C.97	Points to distant objects outdoors (17½-18½)
C.102	Points to several clothing items on request (18-20 months)
C.103	Explores cabinets and drawers (18-24 months)
C.110	Recognizes self in photograph (19-24 months)
C.111	Identifies three body parts (19-22 months)
C.112	Understands personal pronouns, some action verbs, and adjectives (20-24 months)

Language

L.38	Vocalizes or gestures spontaneously to indicate needs (12-19 months)
L.44	Uses voice in conjunction with pointing or gesturing (14-20 months)
L.52	Uses own name to refer to self (18-24 months)
L.53	Imitates environmental sounds (18-21 months)
L.58	Uses nouns, verbs, modifiers (20½-24 months)

Gross Motor

GM.95	Backs into small chair or slides sideways (17½-19 months)
GM.100	Climbs forward on adult chair, turns around, and sits (18-21 months)
GM.101	Walks downstairs with one hand held (19-21 months)
GM.109	Stands on tiptoes (23-25½ months)

Riding around the House

Activities

I can sit on a four-wheeled ride-on toy and make it go when I push it with my feet! You'll have to be there at first to hold on to the toy while I try to climb on to it. Be sure it's not too high for me so my feet can touch the floor firmly and that I can hold on to the handles securely. Tell me you will help me move, then give me a gentle push forward while you hold me steady so I can get the feel of the movement.

I may push backwards with my feet before I learn to push forward. At first, my feet may move together, but then you'll see me moving one leg at a time as I learn to enjoy my toy. This toy will prepare me for a tricycle, which I'll be able to ride when I am about 3 years old.

Keep me away from slopes, especially driveways that slope down into a street. You'll need to childproof the area for riding by blocking off steps and stairs that go down.

I don't need a new ride-on toy. Swap meets or secondhand toy stores are good places to get one. Just be sure that it is a safe toy.

Developmental Skills

Cognitive
C.112   Understands personal pronouns, some action verbs, and adjectives (20-24 months)

Gross Motor
GM.83   Demonstrates balance reactions in standing (15-18 months)
GM.89   Stands on one foot with help (16-17 months)
GM.92   Pushes and pulls large toys or boxes around the floor (17-18½ months)
GM.95   Backs into small chair or slides sideways (17½-19 months)
GM.98   Moves on ride-on toys without pedals (18-24 months)
GM.100   Climbs forward on adult chair, turns around, and sits (18-21 months)

© 1993 by Hawaii Early Learning Partners
Published by Communication Skill Builders, Inc./(602) 323-7500. This page may be reproduced for instructional use. (Catalog No. 7898)

Matching Sounds to Animals

Activities

Like most children, I probably am fascinated by animals. If we have a dog or a cat at home or if you have been pointing them out to me in books and outdoors, I probably recognize them and can even tell you their sounds. Find out by asking me. When we see a dog or a picture of a dog, say, "Look! A dog! Do you know what a dog says?" If I don't answer, say, "Does it say 'woof woof' or 'meow?'" If I still don't answer, tell me, "It says 'woof woof'!"

Tell me about all the animals we see: don't stop at dog and cat! Help me discover cows, horses, sheep, pigs and goats. Make their sounds and encourage me to imitate. Name the animals too. While we're playing with animal sounds, tell me how a *little* dog sounds ("woof woof") and how a *big* dog sounds ("Woof! Woof!").

I'd enjoy a picture book or scrapbook of animal pictures. Sometimes when we look at the pictures together, give me the book upside down. Do I fix it so it's right side up? When I point to an animal picture, entertain me by making the sound that animal makes. Then, let me have a turn to make the sounds while you point.

This is a great time to start to teach me "Old McDonald Had a Farm." You sing the words and I'll try to join you for the sounds. Maybe I have stuffed animals we can use for props.

If we have real animals around, help me touch them gently. Tell me how they feel and what part I'm reaching for or touching. Help me be gentle. I don't mean to be cruel, but I might try to touch eyes or squeeze too tight. I would enjoy a trip to the zoo, a petting zoo, or even just to a pet store to look.

Developmental Skills

Social and Emotional
S.53   Expresses affection (18-24 months)
S.55   Shows a wide variety of emotions: fear, anger, sympathy, modesty, guilt, embarrassment, anxiety, joy (18-24 months)
S.56   Desires control of others; orders, fights, resists (18-24 months)

Cognitive
C.92   Recognizes and points to four animal pictures (16-21 months)
C.104   Matches sounds to animals (18-22 months)
C.105   Rights familiar picture (18-24 months)
C.111   Identifies three body parts (19-22 months)

Language
L.44   Uses voice in conjunction with pointing or gesturing (14-20 months)
L.49   Echoes prominent word or last word spoken (17-19 months)
L.50   Uses expressive vocabulary of 15 to 20 words (17½-20½ months)
L.53   Imitates environmental sounds (18-21 months)
L.54   Imitates two-word phrases (18-21 months)
L.56   Names two pictures (19-21½ months)
L.57   Uses two-word sentences (20½-24 months)
L.58   Uses nouns, verbs, modifiers (20½-24 months)

Gross Motor
GM.76   Walks backwards (12½-21 months)
GM.99   Runs fairly well (18-24 months)

Enjoying Play Dough Together

Activities

Let's make some play dough! We will need 2 cups of flour, 1 cup of salt, and enough water (about 1 cup) to make our play dough pliable so that it can be shaped easily. Adding a few drops of food coloring will brighten up the things we make with our play dough. The dough will keep for about a week in the refrigerator.

At first I may just want to poke, pinch, pull, and pound my dough. Sit with me and roll and squeeze your dough, too. Make interesting faces and animals. Tell me what body part you are making and what the animal will need next. Occasionally check to see how I'm doing; encourage me to do whatever I can. When we make things, take the time to stop and play with them; pretend to eat the cookies we made, or make the dog I made bark and run.

If I'm interested, let me help you make things. For example, you could let me put one of my small pieces on your pumpkin's face to be the eyes or nose. After you make a car, let me make it zoom and crash, then fix it with you!

We can match or sort things we make, stack pieces on top of each other, put our *fruits* inside a bowl, or line up our *snakes.* Whatever we make, we can have lots of fun together.

Later, we can use tools such as craft sticks to cut or flatten our dough.

Developmental Skills

Social and Emotional

S.60   Enjoys solitary play (coloring, building, looking at picture books) for a few minutes (18-24 months)

Cognitive

C.85   Matches objects (15-19 months)
C.91   Identifies one body part (15-19 months)
C.93   Understands most noun objects (16-19 months)
C.99   Uses play dough and paints (18-24 months)
C.108   Sorts objects (19-24 months)
C.111   Identifies three body parts (19-22 months)
C.112   Understands personal pronouns, some action verbs, and adjectives (20-24 months)

Language

L.38   Vocalizes or gestures spontaneously to indicate needs (12-19 months)
L.44   Uses voice in conjunction with pointing or gesturing (14-20 months)
L.58   Uses nouns, verbs, modifiers (20½-24 months)

Learning Nursery Rhymes

Activities

Nursery rhymes are fun to say and sing because they have nice rhythms and sounds.

Tell me a rhyme when I am doing something that the person in the nursery rhyme is doing. For instance, if I am jumping, you might chant, "Jack be nimble, Jack be quick, Jack jump over the candlestick." When I am playing with my toy sheep or looking at one in my picture book, you might sing, "Baa, Baa, Black Sheep." "Twinkle, Twinkle Little Star" would be a good one to sing when we see stars at night.

Use lots of gestures and facial expressions to accompany the rhyme. Motions can easily be added to rhymes such as "Humpty Dumpty." We can do just a line or two at a time, but don't be surprised if I want you to say it over and over; that's the way I learn.

There are lots of nursery rhyme books for us to enjoy together, especially after I learn many of them. Let me point to the different animals, objects, and people in the books. Let's see if I can bring or point to some objects around the house that I see pictured in the book.

Developmental Skills

Social and Emotional
S.60   Enjoys solitary play (coloring, building, looking at picture books) for a few minutes (18-24 months)

Cognitive
C.92   Recognizes and points to four animal pictures (16-21 months)
C.96   Imitates several "invisible" gestures (17-20 months)
C.106   Enjoys nursery rhymes, nonsense rhymes, finger plays, poetry (18-30 months)
C.107   Matches objects to pictures (19-27 months)
C.112   Understands personal pronouns, some action verbs, and adjectives (20-24 months)

Language
L.55   Attempts to sing songs with words (18-23 months)
L.56   Names two pictures (19-21½ months)
L.58   Uses nouns, verbs, modifiers (20½-24 months)

Throwing Games for Indoors

Activities

Sometimes I need active indoor games. I can learn how to play throwing games indoors if you will show me what things you consider appropriate to throw inside, such as balls of paper, foam balls, or beanbags. These balls usually won't cause damage if they hit the wrong thing. I can learn that random throwing is *not* okay, but that aiming for a target such as a box is. When I miss my target, let me pick up the beanbags (or foam balls or whatever I'm throwing) and try again.

When I can get most of my balls into a box, you might show me a variation of the game. Attach a string to the box so that I can pull it to me to get the balls. You will need to put the box back in its original spot so I can use it again as a target.

It would be nice to have a friend to play with me. Be sure to give each of us our own balls and boxes. We will enjoy playing beside each other, but don't expect us to share toys until we're older.

Developmental Skills

Social and Emotional
  S.59   Engages in parallel play (18-24 months)

Cognitive
  C.95   Solves simple problems using tools (17-24 months)

Language
  L.54   Imitates two-word phrases (18-21 months)

Gross Motor
GM.97   Throws ball into a box (18-20 months)
GM.102   Picks up toy from floor without falling (19-24 months)

Having Fun at the Beach I

Activities

A trip to the beach holds many special experiences. I'll *help* by pulling a beach mat or bag along the sand as we look for our spot. Let me do the things I can by myself, such as removing my shoes or unzipping a beach bag to get out a towel and sunscreen.

Help me do somersaults and wheelbarrow in the sand—great fun because the surface is soft. This kind of play may encourage me to use some of my favorite words and to ask you to "Do it again."

While I'm sitting on the sand, you could cover one of my feet with sand, then ask me to wiggle my toes to get my foot out. Cover my hand and talk about the body part you're covering. If I don't like sand on my body, let me cover your hand or foot. You can search for your foot and act surprised when you *find* it. Never cover my whole body with sand—the weight can be too heavy on my chest and make it hard for me to breathe.

A large beach ball is fun for rolling, kicking, and throwing with you.

Help me identify special sounds at the beach. Let's imitate the noise of waves, birds, and wind. Show me distant objects, such as boats, airplanes, and clouds. I like to point to things that are far away.

Developmental Skills

Social and Emotional

S.59 Engages in parallel play
(18-24 months)
S.61 Enjoys rough-and-tumble play
(18-24 months)

Cognitive

C.97 Points to distant objects
outdoors (17½-18½ months)

Language

L.50 Uses expressive vocabulary of
15 to 20 words (17½-20½ months)
L.53 Imitates environmental sounds (18-21 months)

Gross Motor

GM.88 Throws ball overhand landing within 3 feet of target (16-22 months)
GM.92 Pushes and pulls large toys or boxes around the floor (17-18½ months)
GM.96 Kicks ball forward (18-24½ months)

Self-Help

SH.46 Removes shoe when laces undone (18-24 months)
SH.47 Unzips, zips large zipper (18-21 months)

Having Fun at the Beach II

Activities

Let's take buckets and shovels to the beach. There are lots of fun things we can do together. I can help you carry things from the car. We can squat to dig holes in the sand. Then it's fun to collect water in the bucket and bring it back to fill the hole. If there are big shells on the beach, it's fun to use them for digging.

Have enough buckets and shovels for all the children who are with us. Don't expect us to share the toys yet.

If I seem afraid of the water, don't rush me. Let me say "No." We might sit near the water, or I might need to be carried as we both get wet. Sometimes it's easier for me if we do something like splashing the water or pouring water from a cup, and I don't notice that we sat down in the water on the sand.

It's fun to try walking backward, running, jumping, and standing on tiptoe in the sand because it feels different than the harder surfaces I'm used to. If the sand is hot, I will need something to wear on my feet.

Remember that I need some protection from the sun. Sunscreen will keep me from burning, and we should avoid being out when the sun is strongest (10 a.m. to 3 p.m.).

Developmental Skills

Social and Emotional

S.55   Shows a wide variety of emotions: fear, anger, sympathy, modesty, guilt, embarrassment, anxiety, joy (18-24 months)

S.59   Engages in parallel play (18-24 months)

Cognitive

C.95   Solves simple problems using tools (17-24 months)

C.97   Points to distant objects outdoors (17½-18½ months)

Language

L.53   Imitates environmental sounds (18-21 months)

Gross Motor

GM.76   Walks backwards (12½-21 months)

GM.91   Carries large toy while walking (17-18½ months)

GM.99   Runs fairly well (18-24 months)

GM.103   Squats in play (20-21 months)

GM.107   Jumps in place both feet (22-30 months)

GM.109   Stands on tiptoes (23-25½ months)

Managing Tantrums

Activities

I still have tantrums when I feel frustrated—frustrated because I can't get my toys to do what I want them to, because I can't get people to understand me, or for any one of a number of reasons related to my age limitations. I know I will gradually learn to figure out how to do things and to communicate more effectively.

If you reward my tantrum behavior by giving me lots of attention, I will begin to have tantrums on purpose. It's one of the ways I can get what I want. Tantrums like that usually don't occur until I'm older, about two years old.

Ways to handle attention-seeking tantrums are:

- Ignore the tantrum and me, which means that you shouldn't try to comfort or talk to me.

- Don't get angry or tense. Try to learn to be as matter-of-fact as possible. If this is hard for you, leave the room.

- Don't punish me, especially if I'm under 2 years of age. Punishment is attention for negative behavior, and I like attention.

- Be sure I'm in a safe place so that I don't hurt myself while raving and ranting and throwing myself around.

Another form of tantrum I might try is holding my breath. Don't panic. Even if I turn blue and lose consciousness, I will begin immediately to breathe hard and rapidly, and I will resume normal breathing.

If I hold my breath as a way of having a tantrum, you may want to consult your physician about this behavior. I know that doctors say that those observing my breath-holding may become terrified, allowing toddlers like me to rule the roost and make everybody, including me, miserable. After all, I need limits, and you're the one I depend on to set them for me.

At this age, I'm not trying to exert control with this behavior. However, if you respond anxiously and give me too much attention, I'll be inclined to get your attention this way in the future.

Developmental Skills

Social and Emotional
S.42   Displays frequent tantrum behaviors (12-18 months)
S.56   Desires control of others; orders, fights, resists (18-24 months)
S.57   Feels easily frustrated (18-24 months)

Expressing My Feelings

Activities

I'm growing up. I'm beginning to have lots of different feelings:

- I tend to become very aggressive and want to control other people by fighting, resisting, giving orders.

- I'm easily frustrated because I can't seem to do certain things. This may be a peak time for me to have tantrums.

- I may suddenly become afraid of my bath or of the toilet flushing.

- I may push and grab others' toys. I'm certainly not ready to share *my* toys.

- I may not want to be dressed or undressed in front of others.

As these new feelings and behaviors occur and old feelings become more intense, it's important that you let me have these feelings and not embarrass or tease me. You can help me by:

- Not scolding or correcting me in front of others.

- Not making me feel guilty about toilet accidents, masturbation, or my body in general.

- Allowing me to feel that it's okay to have my own things and to feel important. You can try to help me exchange toys, but don't expect me to learn to share yet.

- Showing me pictures of children with different facial expressions and telling me about them. Be sure to show me happy faces, as well as sad and angry faces.

- Being affectionate so I learn to be affectionate, listening to me, understanding why I may cry when another child cries. It's my way of empathizing, and I'll show my sympathy by trying to console my friend. Don't laugh or be amused at my attempts to be grown up; I may feel that you are laughing at me.

- Labeling or naming some of the emotions you or I show. Use these words when I see other people acting angry, sad, helpful, happy, or afraid.

Respect my right to be angry, and teach me appropriate ways to express my anger. Remember that I learn by watching you and the people around me. I've noticed that when you're angry, you talk to yourself about what made you angry, take a walk, or hit a pillow.

Developmental Skills

Social and Emotional

S.50	Enjoys being center of attention in family group (12-18 months)	
S.53	Expresses affection (18-24 months)	
S.54	Shows jealousy at attention given to others, especially other family members (18-24 months)	
S.55	Shows a wide variety of emotions: fear, anger, sympathy, modesty, guilt, embarrassment, anxiety, joy (18-24 months)	
S.56	Desires control of others; orders, fights, resists (18-24 months)	
S.57	Feels easily frustrated (18-24 months)	
S.58	Interacts with peers using gestures (18-24 months)	
S.62	Experiences a strong sense of self-importance (18-24 months)	
S.63	Attempts to comfort others in distress (22-24 months)	
S.64	Defends possessions (23-24 months)	

Feeling Jealous

Activities

About this time in my life, I seem to resent the attention that anyone else gets, especially from Mommy. In response to this strange feeling, I find myself becoming aggressive and angry. I want to break things, and I begin to act like I haven't grown up at all.

Ways to help me reduce my negative behavior might be to:

- Give me a lot more attention, especially for any positive or helping behavior I show.

- If there's going to be a new baby, be sure that you talk to me about the baby, give me lots of extra attention, and reinforce my grown-up behavior. Do not shame me or laugh if I imitate the baby's behavior.

- If I hit the new baby, firmly tell me "No hitting," and teach me how I can touch the baby gently. Let me pat the baby's feet or arms gently and say "Hi" to the baby, then hug me and pat my feet and arms gently and tell me you love me.

  We will need to do this many times. It is very hard for me to share you with a small baby that everyone else likes to talk to and hold. Plan a special time or activity each day or as often as you can when you and I can be alone, with no baby around to distract you from me.

- Don't get upset with me if I seem to be going backwards as far as using the toilet or feeding is concerned. You may find that I want the bottle more often, or seem to have my thumb in my mouth all the time, or want to be carried a lot. Humor me and let me indulge myself. I really won't find these regressive behaviors that interesting, so you should take every opportunity to commend me for being big, strong, and smart.

Developmental Skills

Social and Emotional

S.37	Likes to be in constant sight and hearing of adult (12-13 months)	
S.50	Enjoys being center of attention in family group (12-18 months)	
S.53	Expresses affection (18-24 months)	
S.54	Shows jealousy at attention given to others, especially other family members (18-24 months)	
S.55	Shows a wide variety of emotions: fear, anger, sympathy, modesty, guilt, embarrassment, anxiety, joy (18-24 months)	

Playing Independently

Activities

While you work building houses or cooking for a big party, I work by building blocks or scribbling with my crayons. My job is to learn through play. I want you to play with me, and I like to play with other children. But to feel independent and extend my imagination, I also need to play on my own for short periods of time.

To help me learn to do this, you might:

- Begin by playing with me, but then gradually withdrawing into just watching. You could continue to talk to me and tell me how nicely I'm playing. Then you may want to go about your business for brief periods, returning to make a suggestion or reinforcing my work.

- Be sure that the toys I have around me are fun and colorful, but that I don't have too many different toys. I could feel overwhelmed if there are too many to choose from or become frustrated because I can't handle them. All your efforts to help me learn to play independently could go down the drain because I'll get fussy and may start to have a tantrum because I'm frustrated. Always remember how old I am when you get me new toys: the simpler, the better. What's fun for you may be too hard for me.

- Television is okay, but should be limited. Some families don't have one, and their children learn to do things rather than just watch.

  As I get closer to 2 years of age, learning by imitation becomes my way of life. I want to imitate you getting dressed, sweeping, getting ready to go outside to work, washing dishes, cooking with pots and pans.

I'm also ready for rough-and-tumble play with you. It's fun to be swung around (when you swing me around, hold me around my chest, not by my hands). Help me stand on my head or touch the ceiling. The park is a great place to run around, to get on the swing, and to climb the monkey bars. Be sure I use the play equipment that's the right size for me.

Remember, though, a little goes a long way, so don't overdo it. Let me have fun without becoming overtired and fussy.

Developmental Skills

Social and Emotional

S.59   Engages in parallel play (18-24 months)
S.60   Enjoys solitary play (coloring, building, looking at picture books) for a few minutes (18-24 months)
S.61   Enjoys rough-and-tumble play (18-24 months)

© 1993 by Hawaii Early Learning Partners
Published by Communication Skill Builders, Inc./(602) 323-7500. This page may be reproduced for instructional use. (Catalog No. 7898)

Activities and Developmental Skills for 21-24 Months

Enjoying Bath Time III

Activities

Let me help get ready for bath time by getting my toys and putting them in the tub. Have me help undress myself by asking me to, "Take off your shoes and socks" or, "Take off your pants." Give me a chance to sit on my potty chair. While I sit on the potty, you can run the water for my bath. Then let me climb into the tub holding your hand or shoulder. Talk to me about what I'm doing and praise my efforts.

Name my body parts as you wash me and encourage me to say what you say: "Wash Darcy's hands. Wash Darcy's face." If I use my name, then try using pronouns to see if I'll do the same: "My hands, your hands"; "My nose, your nose."

I still enjoy water play with my toys for pouring and stirring. An old, well-rinsed squirt bottle, like the ones used to hold liquid soap, will be a fun toy. But remember that I probably can't resist drinking from it and squirting water out of the tub! Help me learn limits by patiently telling me, "No, not *out* of the tub, *inside* the tub!"

It's still not safe to leave me alone in the tub, so don't leave me, not even to answer the phone.

When my bath time is over, help me stand up and climb out. Give me a small towel to help dry myself while you use a big one. Talk about what we are doing together and what we'll do after I'm dressed.

Developmental Skills

Social and Emotional

S.55   Shows a wide variety of emotions: fear, anger, sympathy, modesty, guilt, embarrassment, anxiety, joy (18-24 months)

S.59   Engages in parallel play (18-24 months)

S.60   Enjoys solitary play (coloring, building, looking at picture books) for a few minutes (18-24 months)

S.64   Defends possessions (23-24 months)

Cognitive

C.108	Sorts objects (19-24 months)
C.111	Identifies three body parts (19-22 months)
C.112	Understands personal pronouns, some action verbs, and adjectives (20-24 months)
C.115	Remembers where objects belong (21-24 months)
C.119	Identifies six body parts (22-24 months)

Language

L.52	Uses own name to refer to self (18-24 months)
L.57	Uses two-word sentences (20½-24 months)
L.58	Uses nouns, verbs, modifiers (20½-24 months)
L.59	Tells experiences using jargon and words (21-24 months)
L.63	Imitates four-word phrases (22-24 months)

Gross Motor

GM.102	Picks up toy from floor without falling (19-24 months)
GM.104	Stands from supine by rolling to side (20-22 months)

Self-Help

SH.51	Washes and dries hands partially (19-24 months)

Beginning to Use the Potty Chair

Activities

If you don't feel that toilet training is important at this time, we can wait until I'm older (say, two-and-a-half or three years old), when I may eventually train myself. But if the following signs suggest to you that I'm ready to begin toilet training, let's give it a try:

- I've been able to stay dry for about two hours at a time.
- I can understand simple directions.
- I am proud of myself when I can do things by myself.
- I enjoy imitating my older brother or sister or you.
- I am happy when I please you.
- I am beginning to notice when I have wet or dirty diapers.

I need you to be calm, casual, and relaxed about toilet training. You might start by letting me watch my brother, sister, or you use the toilet. When you buy my potty chair or seat, let me become familiar with it by looking at it, touching it, and sitting on it before I actually use it. When I first start sitting on the seat, just leave me on it for a few minutes at a time (not more than 5 minutes).

Try to keep me as relaxed and as comfortable as possible when I am sitting on the seat. Help me on the seat and keep your hands on me until I become used to sitting on the toilet. While I'm on the seat, we can sing a song or do finger play games.

If I'm not successful at using the potty, do not scold or embarrass me. Praise me when I am successful, though! Use the same words each time so I will learn the terms (for example, "shi-shi," "pee-pee," "tinkle," "b.m.,"or "doo-doo"). A good time for success would be if I'm dry after a nap or a night's sleep. Try to *catch* me by putting me on the potty when I give you signs of wanting to use the potty, or try putting me on it every two hours or so.

It helps me if you take me to the potty casually, rather than rushing me off to it. You can expect that it may take a while before I am potty trained, and that for awhile I'll continue to have accidents.

There are several books for children about using the potty. I might enjoy having you read one to me or look at it with me. Go to the library and ask the librarian to help you find one.

Praise me when I am successful on the potty. Let me know who is proud of me for being so grown-up—you, Grandma, Grandpa, even my favorite TV people and Santa!

Please be patient with me; this can be a trying time for both of us. If this experience becomes too frustrating, let's stop for now and try again in a month or so.

Developmental Skills

Social and Emotional

S.60   Enjoys solitary play (coloring, building, looking at picture books) for a few minutes (18-24 months)

S.62   Experiences a strong sense of self-importance (18-24 months)

S.65   Distinguishes self as a separate person; contrasts self with others (24-36 months)

S.69   Displays dependent behavior; clings and whines (24-30 months)

S.71   Says "No," but submits anyway (24-30 months)

S.73   Enjoys experimenting with adult activities (24-30 months)

S.74   Frustration tantrums peak (24-30 months)

S.82   Takes pride in clothing (24-30 months)

S.83   Becoming aware of sex differences (24-30 months)

Cognitive

C.111   Identifies three body parts (19-22 months)

C.112   Understands personal pronouns, some action verbs, and adjectives (20-24 months)

Language

L.44   Uses voice in conjunction with pointing or gesturing (14-20 months)

L.61   Names three pictures (21½-24 months)

Gross Motor

GM.95   Backs into small chair or slides sideways (17½-19 months)

Self-Help

SH.48   Sits on potty chair or on adaptive seat on toilet with assistance (18-24 months)

SH.49   May be toilet-regulated by adult (18-24 months)

SH.51   Washes and dries hands partially (19-24 months)

SH.52   Anticipates need to eliminate; uses same word for both functions (19-24 months)

SH.64   Pulls pants down with assistance (24-26 months)

SH.66   Washes hands (24-30 months)

SH.68   Anticipates need to eliminate in time (24-36 months)

SH.69   Uses toilet with assistance; has daytime control (24-36 months)

SH.70   Undresses with assistance (26-32 months)

SH.71   Pulls pants up with assistance (26-28 months)

Happy Birthday! I'm Two!

Activities

Wow! Another birthday already! It's been another busy, growing year for me. Think of all the things you've helped me learn. You should be proud of me and yourself for all we've accomplished.

Small family parties are often planned for this birthday. The people I live with, and maybe grandparents or a favorite aunt or uncle, may join in the celebration.

The important parts of this birthday are the people, the cake, and the happy birthday song! Sing it to me the week before and encourage me to sing along. This may be the first song I learn to sing. After my birthday, we can sing happy birthday to my toys.

I'll probably want to try to blow out my birthday candles, but be ready for anything—don't let me burn my fingers, clothes, or hair! I'll eat some cake and ice cream, but you know how messy I can be when I feed myself. Have a bib and a change of clothes available!

Birthday presents are fun. Any wrapping paper, including newspaper, is fine with me. Let me try to unwrap things. If I'm having trouble, a little help with ribbons and with starting to tear paper is appropriate. Unwrapping and playing with the paper and ribbons may be as much fun to me as getting the present.

Some ideas for gifts for me are a toy telephone, pyramid stacking rings, large blocks, a ride-on toy, a doll, a teddy bear, sand toys, books, or a special trip to an interesting place, like the zoo.

It's okay to remind me to say thank you, but don't get upset with me if I don't. My smiles and your thank you will be enough for our guests. Don't forget to take a picture of your cute little toddler, me!

Developmental Skills

Social and Emotional
S.53   Expresses affection (18-24 months)
S.55   Shows a wide variety of emotions: fear, anger, sympathy, modesty, guilt, embarrassment, anxiety, joy (18-24 months)
S.56   Desires control of others; orders, fights, resists (18-24 months)
S.57   Feels easily frustrated (18-24 months)
S.62   Experiences a strong sense of self-importance (18-24 months)
S.64   Defends possessions (23-24 months)
S.77   Dramatizes using a doll (24-30 months)
S.81   Values own property; uses word "mine" (24-30 months)

Cognitive
C.106   Enjoys nursery rhymes, nonsense rhymes, finger plays, poetry (18-30 months)
C.110   Recognizes self in photograph (19-24 months)

Language
L.54   Imitates two-word phrases (18-21 months)
L.55   Attempts to sing songs with words (18-23 months)
L.63   Imitates four-word phrases (22-24 months)
L.64   Sings phrases of songs (23-27 months)

Gross Motor
GM.98   Moves on ride-on toys without pedals (18-24 months)
GM.111   Catches large ball (24-26 months)
GM.112   Rides tricycle (24-30 months)

Self-Help
SH.43   Distinguishes between edible and inedible objects (18-23 months)
SH.50   Plays with food (19-23 months)
SH.54   Holds small cup in one hand (20-30 months)
SH.58   May have definite food preferences (23-25 months)
SH.59   Unwraps food (23-25 months)

Playing with Blocks and Spools

Activities

Let's play with shapes that are different instead of just with ones that are all the same. I'm getting better at figuring out how to put small shapes into matching holes. Sometimes shape sorters with circles, squares, triangles, and other simple shapes can be found in a store, but we can make our own if necessary.

To make a shape sorter, first we collect objects such as spools or film containers, square blocks or film boxes. We'll also need a container with a plastic cover (such as a coffee can or large margarine container).

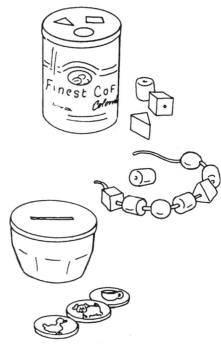

Cut shapes in the cover that match the size and shape of our objects. For example, cut a rectangle that matches the size of the film box container, or a narrow rectangle that lets me slip the metal jar covers through when I turn the container on its side.

Let me experiment; you can give helpful verbal clues about what I am doing right. If I need more help, point or touch the correct place on the cover.

We can take turns putting different shapes into our container. If we decorate our shapes with stickers of animals or objects, we will have more to talk about and do, such as making the sounds of the animals or singing "Old MacDonald."

We might be able to find a store that sells large wooden stringing beads that are round, square, and triangular. If we use these with our containers, we can stack or string them sometimes.

Developmental Skills

Social and Emotional
S.57	Feels easily frustrated (18-24 months)	
S.59	Engages in parallel play (18-24 months)	
S.60	Enjoys solitary play (coloring, building, looking at picture books) for a few minutes (18-24 months)	
S.62	Experiences a strong sense of self-importance (18-24 months)	

Cognitive

C.104   Matches sounds to animals (18-22 months)

C.105   Rights familiar picture (18-24 months)

C.106   Enjoys nursery rhymes, nonsense rhymes, finger plays, poetry (18-30 months)

C.112   Understands personal pronouns, some action verbs, and adjectives (20-24 months)

C.117   Points to five to seven pictures of familiar objects and people (21-30 months)

C.118   Matches sounds to pictures of animals (22-24 months)

Language

L.52   Uses own name to refer to self (18-24 months)

L.55   Attempts to sing songs with words (18-23 months)

L.56   Names two pictures (19-21½ months)

L.57   Uses two-word sentences (20½-24 months)

L.58   Uses nouns, verbs, modifiers (20½-24 months)

L.59   Tells experiences using jargon and words (21-24 months)

L.60   Uses intelligible words about 65% of the time (21½-24 months)

L.61   Names three pictures (21½-24 months)

L.62   Uses elaborate jargon (22-24 months)

L.63   Imitates four-word phrases (22-24 months)

L.64   Sings phrases of songs (23-27 months)

Gross Motor

GM.102   Picks up toy from floor without falling (19-24 months)

GM.104   Stands from supine by rolling to side (20-22 months)

Fine Motor

FM.72   Builds tower using four cubes (18-22 months)

FM.74   Strings one 1-inch bead (20-23 months)

FM.77   Builds tower using six cubes (22-24 months)

FM.79   Imitates three-block train using cubes (23-26 months)

FM.80   Strings three 1-inch beads (23-25 months)

Playing with Mechanical Toys

Activities

Play with me as I discover how to make mechanical toys move. Find toys that start by winding, pressing a switch, or some means I can accomplish once I figure out that this is what will make my toy move.

Sometimes when I see a mechanical toy I am very cautious, especially if it jumps suddenly or makes loud noises. But if I am allowed to take my time and play with it when it is not moving, I can learn how to make it move in a variety of ways.

First, start the toy. Enjoy the toy and its actions with me. Tell me about the toy and its movements, especially when you see me inspect and handle it.

When the toy stops, wait to see what I will do. As I explore ways of making the toy move, make suggestions, using gestures and words. Show me how to start the toy when I have had a chance to try.

Some mechanical toys are objects, such as cars; others are animals or people. While playing with animal or people toys, pause occasionally to look at the features of the toys. It would be particularly appropriate to name or ask me to point to common body parts on the toy. Making the sounds of the animals would also be fun, since I have been learning to identify animals and their sounds.

Developmental Skills

Social and Emotional
S.62   Experiences a strong sense of
        self-importance (18-24 months)

Cognitive
C.95   Solves simple problems using tools (17-24 months)
C.98   Attempts and then succeeds in activating mechanical
        toy (18-22 months)
C.104   Matches sounds to animals (18-22 months)
C.111   Identifies three body parts (19-22 months)
C.112   Understands personal pronouns, some action verbs,
        and adjectives (20-24 months)

Language

L.51	Uses jargon with good inflection (18-22 months)
L.52	Uses own name to refer to self (18-24 months)
L.53	Imitates environmental sounds (18-21 months)
L.54	Imitates two-word phrases (18-21 months)
L.58	Uses nouns, verbs, modifiers (20½-24 months)

Gross Motor

GM.99	Runs fairly well (18-24 months)
GM.102	Picks up toy from floor without falling (19-24 months)
GM.103	Squats in play (20-21 months)
GM.104	Stands from supine by rolling to side (20-22 months)

Acting Out Nursery Rhymes, Songs, and Stories

Activities

Now that I have been singing and saying nursery rhymes, it would be fun to act out the rhymes.

Let's start with a simple one, like "Little Boy Blue." We can both be Little Boy Blue. When he blows his horn, we can pretend to blow our horns and make "tooting" sounds. We can look for the sheep with a hand above our eyebrows and look shocked that the cows are in our corn. Then, we go to sleep very quietly under the haystack.

Some rhymes will make us jump; others will give us a chance to hold hands and run, as the dish and spoon do in "Hey Diddle Diddle." You can ask me to identify objects from around the house, such as a paper plate and spoon, that look like ones in the nursery rhyme book; then we can use them as props.

I also enjoy imitating the characters in my favorite books. I like to be a mouse that yawns, laughs, or squeaks, a bear that coughs or cries, or a monkey that winks or dances on her toes. I can do all of these when you read these books to me over and over again. Sometimes I will look at the books all by myself.

Developmental Skills

Social and Emotional
S.55   Shows a wide variety of emotions: fear, anger, sympathy,
        modesty, guilt, embarrassment, anxiety, joy (18-24 months)
S.60   Enjoys solitary play (coloring, building, looking at picture
        books) for a few minutes (18-24 months)

Cognitive

C.106   Enjoys nursery rhymes, nonsense rhymes, finger plays, poetry (18-30 months)

C.107   Matches objects to pictures (19-27 months)

C.112   Understands personal pronouns, some action verbs, and adjectives (20-24 months)

C.116   Turns pages one at a time (21-24 months)

C.117   Points to five to seven pictures of familiar objects and people (21-30 months)

C.118   Matches sounds to pictures of animals (22-24 months)

Language

L.55   Attempts to sing songs with words (18-23 months)

L.56   Names two pictures (19-21½ months)

L.58   Uses nouns, verbs, modifiers (20½-24 months)

L.61   Names three pictures (21½-24 months)

L.63   Imitates four-word phrases (22-24 months)

L.64   Sings phrases of songs (23-27 months)

Gross Motor

GM.99   Runs fairly well (18-24 months)

GM.107   Jumps in place both feet (22-30 months)

GM.109   Stands on tiptoes (23-25½ months)

Getting Ready to Go to a Family Party

Activities

A few days before the party, tell me a little bit about the party we're going to and what will happen. Let's look at a few family pictures and talk about who will be there. I will recognize myself in pictures, but may not yet recognize others. I can say my own name now when I see my picture. I will also enjoy pointing out other objects in the photos, such as doll, tree, dog, and so forth.

I may be jealous if I see you holding another baby at the party, but it will help me if I'm prepared for this ahead of time. I know you'll also try to give me some special attention at the party.

When you get things ready to take to the party, include a change of clothes, a few toys, and a blanket or stuffed animal if I'm likely to get tired.

Please remember that I may not be able to get involved readily in play with other children at the party. I may need to come back to you periodically for security. This is very appropriate for my age, and I'll be okay if you allow this and help me gradually join the other children by staying near me for a while.

Developmental Skills

Social and Emotional
S.54　Shows jealousy at attention given to others, especially other family members (18-24 months)
S.62　Experiences a strong sense of self-importance (18-24 months)

Cognitive
C.110　Recognizes self in photograph (19-24 months)
C.117　Points to five to seven pictures of familiar objects and people (21-30 months)

Language
L.52　Uses own name to refer to self (18-24 months)
L.61　Names three pictures (21½-24 months)

Gross Motor
GM.106　Walks upstairs holding rail, both feet on step (22-24 months)

Self-Help
SH.55　Opens door by turning knob (21-23 months)

Having Fun at Parties

Activities

You know my eating habits. If I need to eat at certain hours or need special types of food, you might feed me something before the party so I won't have to wait long hours for a meal. This early meal may also keep me from filling up on snacks before the party meal is served.

Be sure to give the home we're visiting a quick look for safety hazards for a toddler like me. This quick survey will also give me a chance to see the area where I will be playing so I can get familiar with it. Although I may be playing with my cousins or with adults, be sure to check on me occasionally. No one knows me like you do, so I depend on you for safety and security.

I'm glad if you have brought along a few activities from home. Blocks or a special animal are easy things for me to carry in my own bag. I will feel the need to identify these toys as my own; I may not be ready to share them, and this is okay. If there are going to be other children at the party, you could bring some paper and crayons for all of us.

You might spend some time with me building with the blocks and making pictures to help me get adjusted and give me some special attention. This special time will help me deal with the attention you will be paying to others.

If there are stairs to climb at the home we visit, let me try it myself, holding the rail, while you supervise. I'll be proud to show off my new skills.

As food is being prepared, I may show a lot of interest. I have some definite food preferences right now, so it's best not to make an issue of having me try something that's new to me or that you know I don't like. Allow me some choice of what goes on my plate. I will do my best to eat with a spoon by myself. Remember, though, that I still am likely to have some spills, so you might have me sit in a place where cleanup is easy.

Developmental Skills

Social

S.54   Shows jealousy at attention given to others, especially other family members (18-24 months)

S.62   Experiences a strong sense of self-importance (18-24 months)

S.64   Defends possessions (23-24 months)

Fine Motor

FM.73   Imitates circular scribble (20-24 months)

FM.75   Imitates horizontal stroke (21-24 months)

FM.77   Builds tower using six cubes (22-24 months)

FM.78   Holds crayon with thumb and fingers (23-25 months)

Self-Help

SH.56   Helps with simple household tasks (21-23 months)

SH.58   May have definite food preferences (23-25 months)

Feeling Good about Myself

Activities

You may think me selfish and demanding, but I really feel good about being me. I feel like I'm on top of the world (and maybe own it, too!). You may feel like something has come over me because I won't share, I may grab my friends' toys, I sometimes get into fights. But I want you to know what a great feeling it is to know that I'm a person, that I have my own space, that I have my own things.

How can you help me maintain this feeling?

- It's important for you to know that I am too young to share, that sharing occurs usually after 3 years of age, and that even then there are some things I may never want to share. Nevertheless, even at this age, I may lend someone a toy (preferably an old used one) if I'm asked nicely. Don't get upset or scold me if I still refuse to share; praise me if I do.

- It's also important that I know that things are *mine*, that I can play with them any way I want to. To help me establish this sense of *mine* and respect for my property, give me a special place that's all my own to keep my toys, my clothes, my shoes, and so forth. Don't be upset, however, if I'm not always sure that *your* things belong to you.

- For me to grow up, I need to know how to protect my property. You shouldn't interfere too much if you see me fight for my toys or protect them from someone else. Intervene only if it looks like we're going to hurt each other. We should learn to settle our differences ourselves, and I'll be more likely to share if there is an even exchange or if it's with someone I like.

- While it's important for me to be able to claim what's mine, it also helps me to know that others feel the same way about their toys. Labeling my toys with a marking pen, or telling me ahead of time, "This car belongs to Bruce" or, "This is Regan's yellow truck" helps me learn what's mine and what's someone else's.

Developmental Skills

Social and Emotional

S.41	Attempts self-direction; resists adult control	(12-15 months)
S.50	Enjoys being center of attention in family group	(12-18 months)
S.62	Experiences a strong sense of self-importance	(18-24 months)
S.64	Defends possessions	(23-24 months)
S.65	Distinguishes self as a separate person; contrasts self with others (24-36 months)	

Comforting Others

Activities

Just as you have cried with others because you feel as sad as they do, you will notice that sometimes I cry when another child does. You may also find me patting and consoling my friend. You've shown me how to be sympathetic by your understanding and comforting ways when I've been hurt or unhappy.

I know some grown-ups think they shouldn't console me if I'm to become strong and fearless; instead, they think they should ignore my being hurt. I know some grown-ups think that if I cry and you try to comfort me, I'm going to be a *sissy. Not true.* If you don't show sympathy for me, I'll feel that you don't care how I feel. In fact, ignoring me might make me cry or scream and *really* become a crybaby.

Usually, if I'm treated with sympathy, I'll be more inclined to be brave rather than to cry as a way of feeling *big* and grown-up. Anyway, kids cry more often because of hurt feelings than of physical hurt, which is why it's important to sympathize.

If Dad and Mom yell at each other and are very angry, I get upset too and feel I have to do something about what's happening. Please don't get mad at me for trying to help. I'm scared and I don't understand. If you get mad at me too, I'll really become a problem. This is a time when I need to have you cuddle me and reassure me more than ever. I also need to know that we all get angry sometimes, and that it's okay.

Developmental Skills

Social and Emotional
    S.53   Expresses affection (18-24 months)
    S.55   Shows a wide variety of emotions: fear, anger, sympathy, modesty, guilt, embarrassment, anxiety, joy (18-24 months)
    S.63   Attempts to comfort others in distress (22-24 months)

Activities and Developmental Skills for 24-27 Months

Learning More at Snack and Mealtime

Activities

I'm beginning to enjoy make-believe and doing what you do. Take advantage of this by letting me share snack time with my doll or teddy bear! I'll offer a drink, cereal, cookies, or cracker. If you've been telling me "just one," I probably understand that and will give you or my teddy bear "just one" on request. If I don't understand "just one" yet, snack time is an enjoyable time to practice taking "just one" bite, cookie, or sip.

I like to try adult activities with you; I do best if it's just the two of us working together. I'm beginning to recognize common dangers, like the hot stove, and to avoid them. My curiosity can still overcome me, though, so remind me of dangers and keep an eye on me. I'm more careful with breakable things and will handle them gently. I can carry a breakable dish to the table but, in case I stumble, don't give me a favorite one. Given crayons and paper, I'll make place mats while you cook. Let me hear how proud you are of your *helper*.

Watch me stand on my tiptoes to try to see what you are doing in the kitchen. I'm so curious! I'm beginning to understand complex sentences such as, "After you wash your hands you can have a taste." I'm even beginning to follow two-part commands such as, "Put this away and then tell Daddy to come eat." Listen to see how I tell Dad to come. I may use pronouns like "you" or three-word sentences such as, "Daddy come eat."

At the table, you'll notice I'm getting better at lots of things. I hold my spoon with my fingers and with palm up. I hold a small cup in one hand. I can chew things like raisins and dried fruits. Although I may have strong food preferences, keep offering me a variety of things to eat.

Developmental Skills

Social and Emotional
S.73   Enjoys experimenting with adult activities (24-30 months)
S.75   Relates best to one familiar adult at a time (24-36 months)
S.77   Dramatizes using a doll (24-30 months)

Cognitive

C.122	Demonstrates awareness of class routines (24-27 months)
C.123	Understands concept of one (24-30 months)
C.124	Identifies rooms in own house (24-28 months)
C.125	Demonstrates use of objects (24-28 months)
C.130	Engages in simple make-believe activities (24-30 months)
C.133	Obeys two-part commands (24-29 months)
C.134	Understands complex and compound sentences (24-27 months)
C.135	Gives one out of many (25-30 months)

Language

L.66	Uses pronouns (24-30 months)
L.67	Uses three-word sentences (24-30 months)
L.71	Imitates spontaneously or requests new words (24-27 months)
L.73	Relates experiences using short sentences (24-34 months)
L.74	Answers questions (24-36 months)
L.76	Uses size words (25-30 months)

Gross Motor

GM.109	Stands on tiptoes (23-25½ months)

Fine Motor

FM.78	Holds crayon with thumb and fingers (23-25 months)
FM.82	Imitates a cross (24-36 months)
FM.83	Makes first designs or spontaneous forms (24-35 months)
FM.84	Puts tiny objects into small container (24-30 months)

Self-Help

SH.54	Holds small cup in one hand (20-30 months)
SH.58	May have definite food preferences (23-25 months)
SH.60	Understands and stays away from common dangers (stairs, glass, strange animals) (24-30 months)
SH.61	Handles fragile items carefully (24-26 months)
SH.62	Helps put things away (24-29½ months)
SH.63	Holds spoon in fingers palm up (24-30 months)
SH.66	Washes hands (24-30 months)

Playing Make-Believe with Toy Animals and Dolls II

Activities

Remember when we played with my stuffed animals and dolls? I still like to play these pretend games, but now I can put more ideas together and do more.

Undressing my bear is easier than dressing it, and I can even unbutton a few buttons on a shirt or dress. The buttons and buttonholes need to be large so I can be successful. I might be able to put a boot on my bear with your help (for example, help me hold the foot). Saying something like, "Turn the shoe over, try pushing from the top of the shoe" will help me learn words as well as dress the bear. Ask me, "What shall we put on Bear to go swimming? . . . yes, these nice swimming shorts."

Let me show you that I understand what common objects are for by using them correctly with my doll. I can comb or brush my doll's hair, or use a cup to give the doll a drink. Occasionally ask me to tell you what I am doing and encourage me to use the words I know. I can also learn to point to more body parts, such as neck and elbow, if you help me learn them on your body, mine, and my doll's.

We can make a few familiar props to play with from shoe boxes and things around the house. A piece of cloth in a shoe box makes a good bed for my doll so I can sing "Rock-A-Bye, Baby" as I put the doll to sleep. A milk carton with one side cut out can be a boat. Sometimes I'll try to get into the box or sit on it, too!

Developmental Skills

Social and Emotional
S.73 Enjoys experimenting with adult activities (24-30 months)
S.75 Relates best to one familiar adult at a time (24-36 months)
S.76 Engages best in peer interaction with just one older child, not a sibling (24-36 months)
S.77 Dramatizes using a doll (24-30 months)
S.78 Initiates own play, but requires supervision to carry out ideas (24-36 months)

Cognitive

C.125   Demonstrates use of objects (24-28 months)
C.126   Identifies clothing items for different occasions (24-28 months)
C.130   Engages in simple make-believe activities (24-30 months)
C.131   Knows more body parts (24-28 months)
C.133   Obeys two-part commands (24-29 months)
C.134   Understands complex and compound sentences (24-27 months)

Language

L.64   Sings phrases of songs (23-27 months)
L.66   Uses pronouns (24-30 months)
L.67   Uses three-word sentences (24-30 months)
L.68   Uses past tense (24-30 months)
L.69   Uses expressive vocabulary of 50 or more words (24-30½ months)
L.71   Imitates spontaneously or requests new words (24-27 months)
L.72   Experiments with communication; frustrated when not understood (24-28½ months)
L.73   Relates experiences using short sentences (24-34 months)

Self-Help

SH.54   Holds small cup in one hand (20-30 months)
SH.65   Unbuttons large buttons (24-25 months)

Creating with Boxes, Cans, and Things

Activities

There are many things around the house that we can use to make airports, highways with tunnels, bridges, and ramps, or other interesting places. Collect potential *construction* material such as milk cartons, cans, toilet or paper towel rolls, rolls from ribbon or sturdy boxes, cardboard from boxes, oatmeal containers, empty wax paper or foil boxes, and shoe boxes.

Some of these materials can be used as they are; others may need some cutting or some pounding to be safe (for example, vegetable or coffee cans should have edges pounded smooth). Metal edges from foil or wax paper boxes must be removed.

We could start with something like a wide piece of masking tape on the floor to mark our *roads*. We can line our cars up to make a parade. Depending on the sizes of our cars, we can cut our paper towel rolls in half for tunnels or use our wax paper box as a square tunnel. If we want to add ramps, we can tape together cardboard pieces so that one end is slightly higher than the other. Watch—cars can roll down the incline!

We can pretend that some of our other boxes are markets, restaurants, gasoline stations, or other familiar places that we visit. If we have pictures of these places that I'll recognize, we can glue the pictures to the box. We could also draw a symbol for the gas stations, like an orange ball with a 76 on it or a yellow shell. We can attach any symbol I recognize to make our play more enjoyable.

Remember to use lots of words when we talk about our play and where we're going on our make-believe trips: *over* the *grassy* hill, *under* the bridge, *through* the big *dark* tunnel, *sliding* fast down the *ramp, park* the red car *next* to the *dump* truck, *follow* the *yellow* bus, *first* in line for gas, or *last* airplane to land at the *airport.*

Introduce me to the idea of grouping some of my toys by size or type even if I won't be able to do this by myself until I'm closer to three. When we put our toys away, you might suggest that we put all the cars into a can for cars first or that we "drive our trucks into the big box."

Developmental Skills

Social and Emotional
S.75   Relates best to one familiar adult at a time (24-36 months)
S.76   Engages best in peer interaction with just one older child, not a sibling (24-36 months)
S.78   Initiates own play, but requires supervision to carry out ideas (24-36 months)

Cognitive
C.125   Demonstrates use of objects (24-28 months)
C.130   Engages in simple make-believe activities (24-30 months)
C.133   Obeys two-part commands (24-29 months)
C.134   Understands complex and compound sentences (24-27 months)
C.135   Gives one out of many (25-30 months)

Language
L.66   Uses pronouns (24-30 months)
L.67   Uses three-word sentences (24-30 months)
L.68   Uses past tense (24-30 months)
L.69   Uses expressive vocabulary of 50 or more words (24-30½ months)
L.71   Imitates spontaneously or requests new words (24-27 months)

Fine Motor
FM.79   Imitates three-block train using cubes (23-26 months)

Self-Help
SH.62   Helps put things away (24-29½ months)

Having Fun at the Park

Activities

I'm at a wonderful age to take to the park. I will stay with you and hold your hand as we walk around exploring the sights. I understand and will avoid common dangerous situations, such as broken glass and large animals. I have good control when I run and can avoid obstacles. I love to be active and, if there's a tricycle available to take with us, I can practice my new skill. A large ball is also great fun because I can catch the ball now.

If I'm starting to be toilet trained and we're gone a long time, we may want to use a rest room. I will, of course, need some help from you. Our trip to the rest room can provide a break I need, since I do tire easily. If I'm still in diapers, that's okay; just bring a supply for changes.

If we can find a sandbox, this would give me time for a quiet activity. It would be fun to make circles and crosses in the sand with my finger. I also love to play imaginary games; we could, perhaps, pretend to be Easter bunnies and form *eggs* with the damp sand. This is also a wonderful time for conversation. I can answer questions and respond to requests, and I love trying out new words that I've heard.

Developmental Skills

Social and Emotional
S.68   Feels strongly possessive of loved ones (24-36 months)
S.79   Fatigues easily (24-30 months)

Cognitive
C.120   Plays with water and sand (24-36 months)
C.130   Engages in simple make-believe activities (24-30 months)
C.131   Knows more body parts (24-28 months)
C.132   Selects pictures involving action words (24-30 months)
C.133   Obeys two-part commands (24-29 months)

Language
L.71   Imitates spontaneously or requests new words (24-27 months)
L.74   Answers questions (24-36 months)

Gross Motor
GM.112   Rides tricycle (24-30 months)
GM.118   Runs; stops without holding and avoids obstacles (24-30 months)

Fine Motor
FM.82   Imitates a cross (24-36 months)
FM.86   Copies a circle (25-36 months)

Self-Help
SH.60   Understands and stays away from common dangers (stairs, glass, strange animals) (24-30 months)
SH.69   Uses toilet with assistance; has daytime control (24-36 months)

Continuing the "No" Stage

Activities

I'm still saying "No," and I'm saying it perhaps even more strongly than before because now my "No" expresses my need to become independent. I want to be in charge, and don't like to be bossed. I feel that I have to decide things for myself, yet you'll see that I'm really not sure what I want. You will notice that I keep changing my mind, then get angry and frustrated.

How can you help me assert my independence, even if I seem to be very negative, while we both keep our cool?

- Be understanding (we babies expect a lot from you, don't we?) and allow me to assert myself comfortably. Don't hurry me to make or act on my decisions. Instead, make preparations for an activity early so I can move into it at my own pace.

- Be cheerful and relaxed. Direct me by your actions, rather than by talking.

- Don't expect me to remember and follow a whole bunch of rules. I'll only get frustrated, and then so will you.

- Remember to rely on your sense of humor; then I won't take myself too seriously, and we'll both feel okay.

Because you convey your expectations in an easy, understanding way, I am better able as I grow a little older to learn about my limits and feel that I'm in control.

Developmental Skills

Social and Emotional

S.39   Displays independent behavior; is difficult to discipline (the "No" stage) (12-15 months)

S.41   Attempts self-direction; resists adult control (12-15 months)

S.56   Desires control of others; orders, fights, resists (18-24 months)

S.71   Says "No," but submits anyway (24-30 months)

Spending Time with One Adult at a Time

Activities

You may think it's strange if I get upset when I have the best of everything—both Mommy and Daddy together wanting to spend time with me. But I can feel overwhelmed and overstimulated when I think I have to please both of you at the same time. Sometimes I think I have to choose between you; I also can feel jealous when you're *lovey dovey* toward each other while you're with me. Two years old can be a tough time for everybody: for me and for those I love.

How can you make things easier for me *and* you?

- Let me play with Daddy alone sometime during the day and do the same with Mommy.

- If I'm more used to one parent and a little afraid of the other because that parent's not home very much, let me spend time with the second parent just having fun.

- When I'm tired, which usually is near the end of the day, it's important for us to spend time in a quiet and relaxed fashion.

- It's a good idea for me to spend time with adults other than Daddy or Mommy.

- Activities I can enjoy with each of you can include looking at books together, playing ball, fixing a snack, or collecting leaves.

Developmental Skills

Social and Emotional

S.30	Shows like/dislike for certain people, objects, places (7-12 months)
S.31	Lets only mother meet needs (8-12 months)
S.45	Enjoys imitating adult behavior; responds well to the introduction of new tasks (12-18 months)
S.50	Enjoys being center of attention in family group (12-18 months)
S.54	Shows jealousy at attention given to others, especially other family members (18-24 months)
S.68	Feels strongly possessive of loved ones (24-36 months)
S.70	Enjoys a wide range of relationships; meets more people (24-36 months)
S.75	Relates best to one familiar adult at a time (24-36 months)

Developing Sudden Fears

Activities

At about this age, some of us feel frightened of many different things. Animals, water, going to bed, lightning, thunder—all these and others may scare us. Don't force me into any of these feared situations. Let me know that you care about me and how I feel.

For example, if I'm afraid of dogs, you might take these steps:

- Let me play with a toy puppy, something I can control and play with any way I want.

- Next, have me look at a dog at a pet store or at a neighbor's friendly dog from a safe distance.

- Ask me to do what you do as you gently pat the neighbor's dog.

- Show me a picture book of dogs, talk about them, and have me name the pictures.

You should always be relaxed when you talk to me about my being scared. If I tell you about those features of the dog that scare me and we talk about them together, I may be able to handle my fears better. You can repeat the words I use in a relaxed fashion or use them in a pleasant context such as, "The dog is *big* (fear word); Daddy is "big" and "nice" (or "fun," and so on).

Most of my other fears can be handled the same way as with the pet dog.

Developmental Skills

Social and Emotional

S.55   Shows a wide variety of emotions: fear, anger, sympathy, modesty, guilt, embarrassment, anxiety, joy (18-24 months)

S.84   May develop sudden fears, especially of large animals (24-30 months)

Becoming My Own Person

Activities

It was fun having a lot of friends at my second birthday, and I felt really grown up. But two years old is also a scary time. That's because I'm realizing that I'm separate from Mom and everybody else. I'm my own person, and Mom and Dad will expect me to be more independent and grown up. Just thinking about this makes me feel dependent and need to cling to Mommy and be sure that she's around.

It's also kind of frightening to know that I'm responsible for myself and my body. What's going to happen if I get a cut or hurt myself?

I have all kinds of other fears, too, such as getting lost or worrying whether you'll be around after I fall asleep.

What can you do to help me ease into this critical time?

- Most important is that you be aware that I'm reacting to this new separate role and am frightened by it. You shouldn't make fun of me or call me names. Instead, be sympathetic and, at the same time, calm and relaxed.

- It may be important to avoid any great changes during this period, such as a move or one of you taking a trip.

- You may have to indulge me somewhat by not leaving me until I'm really fast asleep at bedtime. It's important for you to be casual and relaxed, as if my behavior is "no big thing." If you become upset or seem tense or disgusted, I'll feel really bad and think that I'm going to lose you.

- Please try to remember also that both boys and girls need to cling and hug their *loveys*. If I know that it's okay to be dependent, I am more likely to be *in*dependent and able to handle my fears, rather than be ashamed and pretend I'm not afraid.

- If I know that you're there when I need you, I can strike out on my own. I must feel, though, that when I return I'll find you ready to give me a hug. What seems like such a little thing will help give me the reassurance and confidence to go off again.

Developmental Skills

Social and Emotional

S.37	Likes to be in constant sight and hearing of adult (12-13 months)
S.39	Displays independent behavior; is difficult to discipline (the "No" stage) (12-15 months)
S.41	Attempts self-direction; resists adult control (12-15 months)
S.50	Enjoys being center of attention in a family group (12-18 months)
S.53	Expresses affection (18-24 months)
S.55	Shows a wide variety of emotions: fear, anger, sympathy, modesty, guilt, embarrassment, anxiety, joy (18-24 months)
S.56	Desires control of others; orders, fights, resists (18-24 months)
S.62	Experiences a strong sense of self-importance (18-24 months)
S.65	Distinguishes self as a separate person; contrasts self with others (24-36 months)
S.66	Displays shyness with strangers and in outside situations (24-30 months)
S.67	Holds parent's hand outdoors (24-30 months)
S.68	Feels strongly possessive of loved ones (24-36 months)
S.69	Displays dependent behavior; clings and whines (24-30 months)

© 1993 by Hawaii Early Learning Partners
Published by Communication Skill Builders, Inc./(602) 323-7500. This page may be reproduced for instructional use. (Catalog No. 7898)

Visiting the Dentist

Activities

You'll be happy to know that my teething period will end when I am between 24 and 30 months of age. When it ends, I probably will have all 20 of my primary teeth, including my molars. This would be a great time to make my first appointment with the dentist. Check with the dentist about procedures for my introductory visit so you can describe it to me.

To prepare me for my first visit to the dentist, show me a picture book on visiting the dentist. Some role playing or pretending can be fun, such as sitting in a chair, placing a napkin under my chin, and asking me to open my mouth so you can count my teeth.

If you set a good example about dental care, I probably will imitate you. Help me to brush and floss my teeth regularly. Give me nutritious foods and snacks to eat. Don't let me get into the habit of going to sleep with a bottle of milk or juice in my mouth because this can cause tooth decay. I should rinse my mouth or brush my teeth after eating to prevent tooth decay.

Developmental Skills

Social and Emotional

S.43   Needs and expects rituals and routines (12-18 months)

S.45   Enjoys imitating adult behavior; responds well to the introduction of new tasks (12-18 months)

Self-Help

SH.45   Gives up bottle (18-24 months)

SH.67   Brushes teeth with assistance (24 months and above)

Activities and Developmental Skills for 27-30 Months

Adjusting Bedtime Routines

Activities

I enjoy the comfort and security of my bedtime routine, but I'm ready for some adjustments. I'm ready to help by undressing myself and will work a little at getting on my pajamas. Don't make me try too hard, though, before offering help. It's bedtime, and I'm tired.

If you help me get started and stay with me, I'll work at picking up my toys. I may tell you "mine" if it's a favorite toy.

When you brush my teeth, I'll help pick out my toothbrush and put the toothpaste on, maybe telling you "mine" again. I might like tucking in my favorite toy animal or doll. It's fun to pretend that I'm the parent and telling my bear, "Time for bed."

As we are getting ready for bed, talk about our day. Ask me questions and I'll answer as best I can. If you ask me what I did today, I'll try to tell you. You may hear me use past tense ("I saw," not "I see") and plurals (dogs, cats).

Developmental Skills

Social and Emotional
S.72	Tends to be physically aggressive (24-30 months)
S.81	Values own property; uses word "mine" (24-30 months)

Cognitive
C.117	Points to five to seven pictures of familiar objects and people (21-30 months)
C.119	Identifies six body parts (22-24 months)
C.123	Understands concept of one (24-30 months)
C.130	Engages in simple make-believe activities (24-30 months)
C.133	Obeys two-part commands (24-29 months)
C.134	Understands complex and compound sentences (24-27 months)
C.136	Matches shapes—circle, triangle, square (toys) (26-30 months)
C.140	Listens to stories (27-30 months)
C.142	Identifies objects with their use (28-34 months)
C.143	Identifies body parts with their function (28-34 months)
C.144	Matches primary colors (29-33 months)

Language

L.66	Uses pronouns (24-30 months)
L.67	Uses three-word sentences (24-30 months)
L.68	Uses past tense (24-30 months)
L.70	Names five pictures (24-29 months)
L.73	Relates experiences using short sentences (24-34 months)
L.74	Answers questions (24-36 months)
L.75	Formulates negative reasoning (24-36 months)
L.77	Uses plurals (27-36 months)
L.78	Refers to self using pronoun (27-40 months)
L.80	Verbalizes one preposition (28-33 months)
L.83	Names eight or more pictures (29-36 months)

Self-Help

SH.66	Washes hands (24-30 months)
SH.67	Brushes teeth with assistance (24 months and above)
SH.68	Anticipates need to eliminate in time (24-36 months)
SH.70	Undresses with assistance (26-32 months)
SH.71	Pulls pants up with assistance (26-28 months)
SH.72	Dresses self with assistance (28-32 months)

© 1993 by Hawaii Early Learning Partners
Published by Communication Skill Builders, Inc./(602) 323-7500. This page may be reproduced for instructional use. (Catalog No. 7898)

Building with Blocks or Boxes

Activities

I like to remember the places I have visited and the things we did there. When we play with toy animals, we can pretend we are at the zoo, farm, circus, or a parade! If would be even more fun to make barns and houses and other things that go with our animals.

If we cut out the bottom of a big rectangular box, we can make a corral for farm animals. We might even make a gate to open and close for our animals. We can use a bigger box for a barn or the farmhouse. Peg people or toy people will add to our fun.

Wooden, plastic, or foam blocks or blocks made out of milk cartons are inexpensive and will let us build just about anything.

We can make our own props by cutting out pictures of trees, houses, animals, and so forth from magazines, advertisements, pamphlets, or old books. (If you use old books, do this while I'm sleeping so I don't think that books are for cutting.) Paste the pictures onto small film boxes, spools, pieces of wood, and similar things that can stand alone and be moved around easily.

Developmental Skills

Cognitive
C.117   Points to five to seven pictures of familiar objects
          and people (21-30 months)
C.121   Pastes on appropriate side (24-30 months)
C.123   Understands concept of one (24-30 months)
C.130   Engages in simple make-believe activities (24-30 months)
C.133   Obeys two-part commands (24-29 months)
C.135   Gives one out of many (25-30 months)
C.139   Matches identical simple pictures of objects (27-30 months)

Language
L.76   Uses size words (25-30 months)
L.77   Uses plurals (27-36 months)
L.80   Verbalizes one preposition (28-33 months)
L.83   Names eight or more pictures (29-36 months)

Making Mobiles and Touch-and-Feel Books

Activities

On a visit to the park or a walk, we can collect all kinds of interesting objects, like leaves, seeds, flowers, twigs, or bird feathers. Our house and yard are also fascinating places to find bottle caps, wooden spoons, and even dead insects!

We can paste some of our treasures onto cardboard squares cut from boxes or construction paper and cover them with clear contact paper. Another idea is to put them between two pieces of wax paper and iron them together, putting a towel or cloth between the wax paper and iron. Using clear plastic sandwich bags also makes a good book.

If we put one object on each square, we can make a mobile for my room or the living room. Use string or yarn to tie one end to the square and the other to a hanger. Vary the lengths of the strings for different objects. Attaching bells to the mobile will add sounds as the wind blows it around.

If we paste several objects on a paper plate or construction paper and attach them with metal rings, brads, or just yarn sewn through holes in each, we can put together our own touch-and-feel book. You might write names for our objects; I could add a few colorful touches of my own with crayons or felt pens. Be sure that we make up titles for our books, such as "What's in Regan's Yard?" and that you write on the book that you and I made it.

We can make all kinds of books! We can make a book of different flowers, or one of different sizes or colors of leaves. Before we put a book together, we can plan it by naming our objects and matching objects by shape, color, or size. We can decide whether to put just one object on each page, or maybe two.

Making books is so much fun that you might want to make some, too. You can share your books with me.

Published by Communication Skill Builders, Inc./(602) 323-7500. This page may be reproduced for instructional use. (Catalog No. 7898)

Developmental Skills

Cognitive

C.121	Pastes on appropriate side (24-30 months)
C.123	Understands concept of one (24-30 months)
C.127	Enjoys tactile books (24-29 months)
C.135	Gives one out of many (25-30 months)
C.136	Matches shapes—circle, triangle, square (toys) (26-30 months)
C.137	Matches colors (black, white) (26-29 months)
C.144	Matches primary colors (29-33 months)

Language

L.76	Uses size words (25-30 months)

Fine Motor

FM.82	Imitates a cross (24-36 months)
FM.83	Makes first designs or spontaneous forms (24-35 months)
FM.85	Folds paper in half (24-30 months)
FM.86	Copies a circle (25-36 months)
FM.89	Holds pencil with thumb and finger; adult-like grasp (29-31 months)

Visiting the Shopping Center

Activities

A *short* shopping center trip can be fun. If you have a lot of shopping to do, it's better to leave me at home because I will tire easily. If you do take me along, I can be involved in decisions and I'll enjoy being included in the conversation. I'll be able to tell you about different types of clothes for different occasions if you say, for example, "There's a swimsuit and there's a dress. Which one do I wear to the beach?" You may notice my more mature language as I talk about *my* dress or what *I* want to buy. I don't use my name as much anymore.

As we look in different stores, you can keep me interested by pointing out objects and asking me what they are used for, such as a brush, vacuum cleaner, spoon, or purse.

I'll want some active play as part of our shopping trip, also. Perhaps you can challenge me to try walking on tiptoe or walking backwards for a short distance. Walking on a low curb is also a great way to try my balancing skills.

If we need to wait for someone or to rest, we can have fun looking at the people at the shopping center. We can see a boy, girl, lady, grandpa, big people, short people, man with red shirt, or baby in stroller.

If I need a visit to a rest room during our shopping trip, I may be able to indicate my need to you. I won't be able to wait very long, though, so it would be wise for you to know where the bathroom facilities are. If I have an accident, it's no big deal. Help me clean up as quickly as possible and don't make me feel ashamed.

Let me try to identify the rest room appropriate for my sex. I'm old enough to have some understanding of the difference. However, point out to me that small children always go to the rest room with an adult, so it's okay for a little boy to go in the lady's rest room. I may need to be reminded to wash my own hands after using the toilet, but I can do it. If I am still in diapers, that's okay, too.

If we meet friends of yours along the way, remember that they are probably strangers to me and that I'll be shy. Don't push me to respond the same way I would with familiar family members.

A special treat at the shopping center will be a snack or meal. Since I can hold a spoon to feed myself, there are more choices in what I can eat. Ice cream with a spoon may be a better choice than a cone, which is hard to control.

Point out the signs that show the names of stores so I'll learn that the letters have meaning.

Developmental Skills

Social and Emotional
S.66   Displays shyness with strangers and in outside situations (24-30 months)
S.82   Takes pride in clothing (24-30 months)
S.83   Becoming aware of sex differences (24-30 months)

Cognitive
C.126   Identifies clothing items for different occasions (24-28 months)
C.141   Understands many action verbs (27-30 months)
C.142   Identifies objects with their use (28-34 months)

Gross Motor
GM.124   Walks on tiptoes a few steps (25½-30 months)
GM.126   Attempts step on 2-inch balance beam (27½-28½ months)
GM.127   Walks backward 10 feet (28-29½ months)

Self-Help
SH.62   Helps put things away (24-29½ months)
SH.63   Holds spoon in fingers, palm up (24-30 months)
SH.66   Washes hands (24-30 months)
SH.68   Anticipates need to eliminate in time (24-36 months)
SH.69   Uses toilet with assistance; has daytime control (24-36 months)
SH.70   Undresses with assistance (26-32 months)
SH.71   Pulls pants up with assistance (26-28 months)
SH.72   Dresses self with assistance (28-32 months)

Being Safe Outdoors

Activities

I am becoming quite independent now. I'm also usually full of energy and quick in my movements, which means that you will need to anticipate accidents before they happen.

Keep me from going out to the driveway, sidewalk, or street without you. Always hold my hand when we walk across the street. When I'm playing with older children, please be cautious of rough play and play equipment such as bicycles, bats, balls, and swings. If you need to have an older child watch me, select someone who is at least 13 years old and known to be mature and responsible.

Developmental Skills

Social and Emotional
- S.67   Holds parent's hand outdoors (24-30 months)
- S.71   Says "No," but submits anyway (24-30 months)
- S.72   Tends to be physically aggressive (24-30 months)
- S.73   Enjoys experimenting with adult activities (24-30 months)
- S.74   Frustration tantrums peak (24-30 months)
- S.78   Initiates own play, but requires supervision to carry out ideas (24-36 months)
- S.79   Fatigues easily (24-30 months)
- S.84   May develop sudden fears, especially of large animals (24-30 months)
- S.86   Shows independence; runs ahead of mother outdoors, refuses to have hand held (30-36 months)

Gross Motor
- GM.108   Goes up and down slide (23-26 months)
- GM.112   Rides tricycle (24-30 months)
- GM.118   Runs; stops without holding and avoids obstacles (24-30 months)
- GM.125   Jumps backwards (27-29 months)
- GM.126   Attempts step on 2-inch balance beam (27½-28½ months)
- GM.129   Jumps on trampoline with adult holding hands (29-31 months)
- GM.133   Hops on one foot (30-36 months)

Self-Help
- SH.60   Understands and stays away from common dangers (stairs, glass, and strange animals) (24-30 months)
- SH.61   Handles fragile items carefully (24-26 months)
- SH.75   Insists on doing things independently (30 months and above)

Published by Communication Skill Builders, Inc./(602) 323-7500. This page may be reproduced for instructional use. (Catalog No. 7898)

Activities and Developmental Skills for 30-33 Months

Eating with My Family

Activities

Mealtimes have changed so much in the past year! I can eat nearly all table foods, though I might have trouble with some meats. I still need you to cut my meat and help me serve myself (not too much; I'll let you know if I want more). I can feed myself with a spoon and want to try a fork. I hope there's a small not-too-pointed fork for me to use.

Eating with my family is an important way for me to learn acceptable table behaviors. I learn by watching others and will imitate what I see, especially things you notice and comment on, such as using a napkin or serving myself. Be sure to praise me so that I know what I'm doing right.

Before a meal, remind me to wash and dry my hands. I can do it myself (or with just a little help). Be sure there's a step stool so I can reach. I like to be grown up and will *help* you set the table or clear my plate if you encourage and praise me. Help me find a big spoon for serving and a little or regular spoon for eating. I am beginning to know where things belong, so I can find things you tell me to get. When I help you carry or get things, be sure to give me nonbreakable things that are not too heavy, just in case. When I do spill or drop something, remind yourself it was an accident. I'm learning, and I do want to please you!

I may try to tell you things, such as, "Spoons not there." I'm really trying to communicate important information. You'll notice that I'm using less jargon and get frustrated when I'm not understood.

Developmental Skills

Social and Emotional
S.86   Shows independence; runs ahead of adult outdoors, refuses to have hand held (30-36 months)
S.87   Demonstrates extreme emotional shifts and paradoxical responses (30-36 months)
S.88   Begins to obey and respect simple rules (30 months and above)
S.91   Resists change; is extremely ritualistic (30-36 months)
S.94   Takes pride in own achievements; resists help (30-36 months)

Cognitive
C.149   Points to larger or smaller of two spoons (30-36 months)
C.150   Understands concept of two (30-36 months)
C.153   Plays house (30-36 months)
C.155   Understands more adjectives (30-33 months)

Language
L.77   Uses plurals (27-36 months)
L.78   Refers to self using pronoun (27-40 months)
L.80   Verbalizes one preposition (28-33 months)
L.81   Frustrated if not understood; utterances have communicative intent (28½-36 months)
L.82   Replaces jargon with sentences (29-31 months)
L.84   Repeats words and sounds (29-36 months)
L.85   Talks intelligently to self (29½-36 months)
L.88   Vocalizes for all needs (30-31½ months)

Self-Help
SH.75   Insists on doing things independently (30 months and above)
SH.76   Knows proper place for own things (30-36 months)
SH.78   Uses fork (30-36 months)
SH.79   Uses napkin (30-36 months)
SH.82   Dries hands (30-36 months)
SH.85   Serves self at table with little spilling (31 months and above)
SH.86   Shows interest in setting table (31 months and above)

Playing Make-Believe

Activities

Going to the Restaurant
Let's have a tea party or play restaurant! A pencil and pad of paper can be used to "write orders down." A few pots, dishes, large spoons, and tongs can be used to cook and serve.

We can make our own play food using crumpled tin foil, food pictures pasted on cardboard (cut from food magazines or canned food labels), or other things around the house (plastic film containers, plastic pen caps, baby-food jar caps, spools, and so forth). Real napkins can be used or pretend ones made, and we can use paper for pretend money if I am familiar with its use. Often I can just pretend I have money in my hand and put it in yours if you show me first.

This is a good time to ask me to do several things: to tell you my full name (so you can write it on my order); to point to the big spoon from a choice of two (to go with my soup); to order just *two* eggs or *one* cup of milk; and to tell you whether I like my hot dog *with* or *without* ketchup.

Ask me to sit *between* my doll and teddy bear. When it's my turn or my doll's turn to order food, encourage me to name what I want. Play food or pictures of food would help. A play menu with words and pictures will help me give you my order.

Going on a Trip
If I have traveled on a bus or train, I might enjoy playing bus or train trip. We can line up a few chairs or boxes for our "bus" or just use a large box for me and my dolls to get into. Again, pretend money or tickets can be used. I might also like to dress up in a cap or clothes.

Other Ideas
Using pretend or plastic tools for gardening, building, or fixing things around the house might also be fun. The books we read together will give us lots of ideas for things to do and also introduce me to lots of new words.

Developmental Skills

Social and Emotional

S.78   Initiates own play, but requires supervision to carry out ideas (24-36 months)

S.88   Begins to obey and respect simple rules (30 months and above)

Cognitive

C.142   Identifies objects with their use (28-34 months)

C.149   Points to larger or smaller of two spoons (30-36 months)

C.150   Understands concept of two (30-36 months)

C.153   Plays house (30-36 months)

C.155   Understands more adjectives (30-33 months)

Language

L.77   Uses plurals (27-36 months)

L.80   Verbalizes one preposition (28-33 months)

L.83   Names eight or more pictures (29-36 months)

L.84   Repeats words and sounds (29-36 months)

L.88   Vocalizes for all needs (30-31½ months)

L.89   Gives full name on request (30-33 months)

L.92   Uses expressive vocabulary of 200 or more words (30½-35 months)

Fine Motor

FM.83   Makes first designs or spontaneous forms (24-35 months)

FM.89   Holds pencil with thumb and finger; adult-like grasp (29-31 months)

Playing with Puzzles

Activities

I can now begin to learn to put together three- and four-piece puzzles. Sturdy wooden puzzles are easiest for me to handle. Some come with small knobs attached; we can also glue on small spools or beads to make our own handles.

Good puzzles to start with are ones in which each piece is a picture of a whole object. Examples of simple puzzles are ones of farm animals, fruits, vegetables, toys, or other familiar objects.

I may need help fitting the puzzle pieces in at first, but let me try. Wait to see what I do to try to get in the puzzle pieces.

Give me suggestions such as, "Turn the horse so the feet are on the ground," "The banana is long. Look for the long hole," or, "That was a good idea, to take out just one piece and put it back again."

You can also help me by suggesting which pieces are easiest to start with, arranging pieces so each is near its correct hole, pointing to the correct place, or tilting the board (if that's easier for me).

I can also help *you* do puzzles. Let me tell you which pieces to use. When it's your turn to tell me what to put in, don't just name the pieces. Instead, sometimes describe one by saying something like, "Put in your favorite fruit," "Put in the one that bounces," or, "Put in the one that says 'oink, oink.'"

I'll enjoy it more if you tell me about the animals or objects shown in the puzzle: what they say, eat, do, are used for, or where I've seen them before.

We can also play with the pieces without the board. We can sing songs about animals, make up short stories, recite poems or rhymes, and pretend to make the puzzle pieces move.

Developmental Skills

Social and Emotional
S.75   Relates best to one familiar adult at a time (24-36 months)

Cognitive
C.142   Identifies objects with their use (28-34 months)
C.144   Matches primary colors (29-33 months)
C.146   Sorts shapes—circle, triangle, square (toys) (30-36 months)
C.147   Completes 3- or 4-piece puzzle (30-36 months)
C.155   Understands more adjectives (30-33 months)

Language
L.83   Names eight or more pictures (29-36 months)
L.84   Repeats words and sounds (29-36 months)
L.88   Vocalizes for all needs (30-31½ months)
L.90   Participates in storytelling (30-36 months)
L.91   Recites a few nursery rhymes (30-36 months)

Shopping at the Toy Store

Activities

A trip to the toy store is fascinating because I see so many things I would love to play with. I may show my enthusiasm by running ahead of you to something that looks especially appealing. It's a good idea for you to prepare me with a few simple rules, such as, "Ask Mommy if you want to touch the toys."

Take me to the toy store when you are going to buy something for me; it would be hard for me to leave empty-handed. If we're shopping for a special event, put my favorite item on your list to buy later, but let me get something small today.

I'll probably ask you for toys as we walk around. You don't have to stop or buy what I want, but you could look at or touch what I'm talking about and say, "Another time," "That is a big truck," or, "Yes, that looks like a fun toy."

If I insist on having more than you think I should, just be firm and calm and remind me that I was allowed just one toy. When it's time to go, just move quickly out the door. Don't worry about what other people think if I cry and throw a tantrum.

If the store has some big things that children can play with, I will want to do that. I love hopping, jumping, and sliding activities, but I need close supervision, so stay nearby.

Other good activities for me to try right now are playing with large cardboard blocks, with pegs and pegboards, or riding large toys. See if you can find toys like this at the toy store that are available for me to try.

As we look at the boxes toys come in, I can identify pictures on the boxes (even if I can't play with the toys) and point out two similar colors. Ask me, "Can you find something that's the same as this green color?"

© 1993 by Hawaii Early Learning Partners
Published by Communication Skill Builders, Inc./(602) 323-7500. This page may be reproduced for instructional use. (Catalog No. 7898)

Developmental Skills

Social and Emotional
S.86   Shows independence; runs ahead of adult outdoors, refuses to have hand held (30-36 months)

S.88   Begins to obey and respect simple rules (30 months and above)

Cognitive
C.144   Matches primary colors (29-33 months)

C.150   Understands concept of two (30-36 months)

C.153   Plays house (30-36 months)

Language
L.83   Names eight or more pictures (29-36 months)

L.88   Vocalizes for all needs (30-31½ months)

Gross Motor
GM.129   Jumps on trampoline with adult holding hands (29-31 months)

GM.133   Hops on one foot (30-36 months)

GM.134   Jumps a distance of 14 to 24 inches (30-34½ months)

Fine Motor
FM.84   Puts tiny objects into small container (24-30 months)

FM.87   Builds a tower using eight cubes (28-31 months)

FM.90   Places six square pegs in pegboard (29-31 months)

Making Transitions

Activities

I think most of us experience some difficulty when we move into a new situation: when we change jobs, change schools, or meet new people, for example.

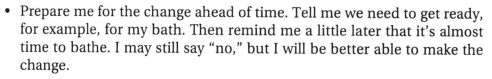

It's the same with me as I become more aware of beginnings and endings, of the need to complete projects, of all kinds of changes. If I'm enjoying what I'm doing, it's very hard to stop playing just to eat lunch, or to have to get up to go to school. It's also more fun to play with one of you than to have to go to bed. I guess when I'm older, about three or four years old, I'll find these changes easier to accept.

What can you do to help me ease into these changes?

- Prepare me for the change ahead of time. Tell me we need to get ready, for example, for my bath. Then remind me a little later that it's almost time to bathe. I may still say "no," but I will be better able to make the change.

  Just before it's time, remind me again and don't hesitate to get me going. Look to see what I'm doing so that what you need to do won't start in the middle of something very important to me. If you rush me, I may have a tantrum, even if I don't want to have one.

- If it's time to go to school, a day-care center, or the baby sitter's, be sure we follow a regular ritual as we get ready to leave the house.

- If I insist on dawdling, don't just keep talking to me—tell me you are going to help me and just pick me up bodily to move to the next activity.

- Remember what we said earlier about firmness and having a routine at bedtime.

- As thoughtful and careful as you may be, I may still have tantrums. Don't worry; just ignore them, and remain calm and relaxed.

Developmental Skills

Social and Emotional
S.34   Tests parental reactions at bedtime (9-12 months)
S.41   Attempts self-direction; resists adult control (12-15 months)
S.92   Experiences difficulty with transitions (30-36 months)

Managing My Emotions

Activities

Growing up isn't easy, is it? Sometimes it seems like I don't know my own mind. I keep contradicting myself, and I find myself getting angry and frustrated very easily. I'm sure I must jar your nerves when I talk loudly and impatiently. I'm sure you also find it hard to get used to my demanding behavior, or-dering people around and being irritated about so many things. There are times (though not very many, I admit) that I surprise you by being compliant and pleasant. Most of the time, I feel I'm between a rock and a hard place, and you must feel the same.

How can you help me go through this period of wanting to comply but also wanting to assert my independence? It won't be easy, but here are some suggestions that may help.

- Don't expect me to stick with my decisions. Since I don't know what I want, it's almost better to go ahead and make the decision for me.

- Don't get too upset because I'm so emotional. Try to be calm and re-laxed; you can even ignore my protests.

- If you know that I'm going to have a hard time making a choice, don't give me the option to decide. If I said no and didn't get to go to the park, for example, I'd feel miserable and make you feel the same.

- Avoid saying, "Do you want to?" I still tend to say "No" almost auto-matically, so if you give me such a choice, I may say "No" and have a tantrum because I'm furious at you and myself.

- Another expression to avoid is "or." I have problems understanding what that means.

- Keep your sense of humor and take things in stride.

- Limit your demands. Don't expect me at this difficult age to learn man-ners, follow orders, or be cooperative.

- Set limits and keep them, but keep them at a minimum. Accept most of my behaviors; I *will* outgrow them.

- In response to my loud demanding voice, speak quietly and in low tones. Don't respond in the usual manner of raising your voice. The louder I speak, the softer your voice.

Remember, as strange as it sounds, this is a very important time in my life. I'm learning to be an assertive and independent person, but I'm also trying to be like you, and that's confusing.

Developmental Skills

Social and Emotional

S.39	Displays independent behavior; is difficult to discipline (the "No" stage) (12-15 months)
S.40	Acts impulsively, unable to recognize rules (12-15 months)
S.55	Shows a wide variety of emotions: fear, anger, sympathy, modesty, guilt, embarrassment, anxiety, joy (18-24 months)
S.56	Desires control of others—orders, fights, resists (18-24 months)
S.57	Feels easily frustrated (18-24 months)
S.62	Experiences a strong sense of self-importance (18-24 months)
S.71	Says "No," but submits anyway (24-30 months)
S.72	Tends to be physically aggressive (24-30 months)
S.74	Frustration tantrums peak (24-30 months)
S.87	Demonstrates extreme emotional shifts and paradoxical responses (30-36 months)
S.89	Tends to be dictatorial and demanding (30-36 months)
S.90	Talks with a loud, urgent voice (30-36 months)

Riding Safely in the Car

Activities

Please continue to have me securely placed in a child's car seat whenever we go for a ride in the car, no matter how short the distance we travel. I will need to use the car seat until I weigh about 40 pounds. If I sit on the regular seat without a car seat, the seat belt could put too much pressure on my body if an accident occurs.

If I protest the use of the car seat, you can make it very clear that the car won't start until I'm safely seated. Be sure to demonstrate the use of seat belts by everyone else in the car so I will see that I need to be safe, too. Remind me that when I sit in my car seat I can see lots of things out the window.

Developmental Skills

Social and Emotional
S.69   Displays dependent behavior: clings and whines (24-30 months)
S.71   Says "No," but submits anyway (24-30 months)
S.88   Begins to obey and respect simple rules (30 months and above)
S.91   Resists change; is extremely ritualistic (30-36 months)

Cognitive
C.134   Understands complex and compound sentences (24-27 months)

Self-Help
SH.75   Insists on doing things independently (30 months and above)
SH.76   Knows proper place for own things (30-36 months)

Activities and Developmental Skills for 33-36 Months

Dressing

Activities

I can do it! I can get dressed all by myself (except for fasteners). It takes me longer than if you do it, of course, but I'm so proud of my accomplishments! By giving me simple loose clothing, you can let me dress myself. Give me a choice of two outfits if what I wear is important to you. Otherwise, I can pick out my own play clothes if they are in a drawer I can reach.

Be with me to help me dress in case I get frustrated. Offer encouragement and help me learn concepts like front, back, and right side out. Encourage me to put my clothes on hooks that are at a good height for me. If there's a routine for dressing and undressing, I'll do my best. The routine can include where clothes are kept and when I get dressed, but don't insist that I always dress myself. Sometimes you're in a rush and I'm not very fast. Other times, I just need you to help me.

Dressing is a great time for talking about colors, textures, stripes, dots, and other words we use to describe clothes. As I learn these words, I'll be able to tell you what I want to wear and even comment on what other people are wearing.

Developmental Skills

Social and Emotional
S.86	Shows independence; runs ahead of adult outdoors, refuses to have hand held (30-36 months)
S.91	Resists change; is extremely ritualistic (30-36 months)
S.94	Takes pride in own achievements; resists help (30-36 months)

Cognitive
C.155	Understands more adjectives (30-33 months)
C.156	Sorts colors and points to several colors when named (33 months and above)
C.157	Identifies longer stick (33 months and above)
C.158	Begins to pick longer of two lines (33-36 months)

Language
L.94	Begins to respond to opposite analogies (33-36 months)
L.96	Relates experiences more frequently using short sentences (34 months and above)

Self-Help
SH.75	Insists on doing things independently (30 months and above)
SH.76	Knows proper place for own things (30-36 months)
SH.80	Hangs clothing on hook (30 months and above)
SH.81	Buttons large buttons (30-36 months)
SH.92	Dresses with supervision, requires assistance with fastenings (32 months and above)

Helping with Cooking

Activities

I like it when we spend time together preparing a snack or cooking. Let's do this when we have lots of time because accidents are more likely to occur when we are in a hurry. We should wash our hands with soap and water and dry them well before we cook.

I enjoy helping to prepare simple snacks, like putting cheese slices on crackers or making a simple sandwich. Help me organize my actions with chants like, "First the cracker, then the cheese." I can do lots of things with your help. Rolling out cookie dough with a rolling pin and using cookie cutters to press out shapes are fun.

Use action words to describe what we are doing, such as stirring, mixing, and pouring. While we are cooking together, name the ingredients and utensils we are using. Don't allow me to handle anything hot, sharp, or heavy, but show me how careful you are while cooking. Use unbreakable things, such as plastic bowls and measuring cups, to make cooking a safe and fun experience. Of course, the best part is to eat and enjoy what we prepared together.

Developmental Skills

Social and Emotional
S.73	Enjoys experimenting with adult activities (24-30 months)
S.94	Takes pride in own achievements; resists help (30-36 months)

Cognitive
C.149	Points to larger or smaller of two spoons (30-36 months)
C.153	Plays house (30-36 months)

Self-Help
SH.54	Holds small cup in one hand (20-30 months)
SH.56	Helps with simple household tasks (21-23 months)
SH.62	Helps put things away (24-29½ months)
SH.63	Holds spoon in fingers, palm up (24-30 months)
SH.66	Washes hands (24-30 months)
SH.77	Pours liquid from small container (30-36 months)
SH.82	Dries hands (30-36 months)
SH.85	Serves self at table with little spilling (31 months and above)
SH.86	Shows interest in setting table (31 months and above)

Happy Birthday to Me!

Activities

Do you remember your third birthday? You might, or you might remember pictures or stories from it. This is a birthday *I* might remember. It's one where you might include some of my friends or cousins my age. Three of my friends plus me is plenty for this year. Remember, my friends, like me, are pretty young, so their parents might want to stay, too.

A party at a park with simple activities and simple, easy-to-eat refreshments is fine. Games and activities could include follow the leader (led by an adult and including running, jumping, climbing, swinging arms, clapping), ball rolling, beanbag tossing, listening to a story, and coloring a party hat. A party where you visit the zoo, a farm, or even the local fire station can be fun at this age, too. This kind of party doesn't require you to entertain, only make the arrangements.

One to one-and-a-half hours is plenty for us, but if the parents are staying, you might plan for a little longer. It's difficult for us to give a present at this age, so don't be surprised if my guests want to help open or play with the presents. Be flexible so my friends and I enjoy the party. A small present for each of my friends to take home will help.

Whether the party is just my family or includes friends, don't forget to take pictures, admire me and all my accomplishments, and know what an important part you play in my development and my life. We've come a long way in the past three years.

Developmental Skills

Social and Emotional

S.65	Distinguishes self as a separate person; contrasts self with others (24-36 months)
S.68	Feels strongly possessive of loved ones (24-36 months)
S.70	Enjoys a wider range of relationships; meets more people (24-36 months)
S.75	Relates best to one familiar adult at a time (24-36 months)
S.76	Engages best in peer interaction with just one older child, not a sibling (24-36 months)
S.85	Separates easily from parent in familiar surroundings (30-36 months)
S.86	Shows independence; runs ahead of adult outdoors, refuses to have hand held (30-36 months)
S.89	Tends to be dictatorial and demanding (30-36 months)
S.90	Talks with a loud, urgent voice (30-36 months)
S.92	Experiences difficulty with transitions (30-36 months)
S.93	Participates in circle games; plays interactive games (30 months and above)

Cognitive

C.152	Enjoys being read to and looks at books independently (30-36 months)
C.159	Understands all common verbs, most common adjectives (33-36 months)

Language

L.92	Uses expressive vocabulary of 200 or more words (30½-35 months)
L.93	Verbalizes two prepositions (33-35½ months)
L.95	Repeats five-word sentences (33½-36 months)
L.96	Relates experiences more frequently using short sentences (34 months and above)
L.98	Uses intelligible words about 80% of the time (35 months and above)
L.99	Uses expressive vocabulary of 300-1,000 words (35 months and above)

Gross Motor

GM.113	Imitates simple bilateral movements of limbs, head, and trunk (24-36 months)
GM.132	Jumps over string 2 to 8 inches high (30-36 months)
GM.133	Hops on one foot (30-36 months)
GM.134	Jumps a distance of 14 to 24 inches (30-34½ months)
GM.136	Stands on one foot 1 to 5 seconds (30-36 months)
GM.137	Walks on tiptoes 10 feet (30-36 months)
GM.141	Climbs jungle gyms and ladders (34½-36 months)
GM.142	Catches an 8-inch ball (35 months and above)
GM.143	Jumps a distance of 24 to 34 inches (34½-36 months)
GM.144	Avoids obstacles in path (34½-36 months)
GM.145	Runs on toes (34½-36 months)
GM.146	Makes sharp turns around corners when running (34½-36 months)

Fine Motor

FM.82	Imitates a cross (24-36 months)
FM.83	Makes first designs or spontaneous forms (24-35 months)

Self-Help

SH.68	Anticipates need to eliminate in time (24-36 months)
SH.69	Uses toilet with assistance; has daytime control (24-36 months)

Enjoying Books and Stories with You

Activities

Now that I'm almost three, I like to look at familiar books by myself. I am able to listen to short stories about familiar animals or boys and girls. My favorite stories usually have words that rhyme or phrases that repeat, which lets me begin to join in and help tell the story. Sometimes you can pause before you turn the page and ask me what will happen next. Encourage me to tell you and then we can turn the page to check the picture and read the text.

The library has books with a variety of artwork as well as stories of children from many cultures. Good artwork helps me to figure out the story as well as retell it. Some pictures are worth stopping to examine in detail; we can find objects we know about, and I can learn about new things you name.

Now that I can snip with my scissors, I can help cut pictures from magazines, advertisements, or catalogues to make my own books and tell my own stories.

Help me paste one or two pictures on construction paper or any sturdy material. Then ask me to tell you about the picture; write what I say or try to say. I will learn I can "tell stories" and that writing is putting my words down. We can also use photographs or drawings to make our storybooks. If we read the books we make often enough, I'll learn them by heart.

Another fun way to remember and tell stories is to make and use puppets. An old glove with a hook-and-loop fastener sewn on each fingertip is an instant stage. Pictures, objects, felt cut-outs, and the like with a hook-and-loop fastener sewed or glued on can be used to recite finger plays, nursery rhymes, poems, and short stories that are attached in the correct sequence onto the glove. Paper-bag, finger, sock, or store-bought puppets can all be fun. Be careful not to use scary puppets with scary voices.

Developmental Skills

Cognitive
- C.145   Matches similar pictures of objects (30-36 months)
- C.150   Understands concept of two (30-36 months)
- C.152   Enjoys being read to and looks at books independently (30-36 months)

Language
- L.83   Names eight or more pictures (29-36 months)
- L.84   Repeats words and sounds (29-36 months)
- L.90   Participates in storytelling (30-36 months)
- L.91   Recites a few nursery rhymes (30-36 months)
- L.92   Uses expressive vocabulary of 200 or more words (30½-35 months)
- L.95   Repeats five-word sentences (33½-36 months)
- L.96   Relates experiences more frequently using short sentences (34 months and above)

Fine Motor
- FM.88   Snips on line using scissors (28-35 months)

Sorting Again

Activities

A fun activity for me is sorting. I like to put all the pennies into the piggy bank, then all the nickels, then the dimes.

At first it will be easier for me to sort just two kinds of things (about five of each). Place a penny in one box and a nickel in another. Then give me a penny and ask me to put it in the box with the same thing. Show me if I seem puzzled. Pass me the coins one at a time so I can concentrate on just one at a time.

As I get better, I will be able to sort more objects into different containers or piles. Sometimes it is fun if we take turns sorting the objects. Be sure to tell me, "Your turn . . . now it's my turn to put the red block in . . ." You might also pretend to forget and ask me whose turn it is.

Other fun things to sort are colorful buttons and poker chips that I can slip through a slit in a box or put into a transparent container. I might like to clip clothespins on the rim of the can I use for blocks. How about flowers and leaves for lei making?

Sometimes after we sort things we can use them for building or for making pictures. After sorting some cubes, we can stack them to make a tall building. Stringing the beads we sorted would be fun to do; then we can wear them on head or wrist. We can snip paper, sort the paper by color, then paste them on paper to make a cat or a paper-bag puppet or a decoration for a holiday.

Developmental Skills

Social and Emotional
S.75   Relates best to one familiar adult at a time (24-36 months)
S.76   Engages best in peer interaction with just one older child, not a sibling (24-36 months)
S.78   Initiates own play, but requires supervision to carry out ideas (24-36 months)
S.87   Demonstrates extreme emotional shifts and paradoxical responses (30-36 months)
S.88   Begins to obey and respect simple rules (30 months and above)
S.89   Tends to be dictatorial and demanding (30-36 months)
S.90   Talks with a loud, urgent voice (30-36 months)
S.91   Resists change; is extremely ritualistic (30-36 months)
S.92   Experiences difficulty with transitions (30-36 months)
S.94   Takes pride in own achievements; resists help (30-36 months)

Cognitive
C.142   Identifies objects with their use (28-34 months)
C.146   Sorts shapes—circle, triangle, square (toys) (30-36 months)
C.148   Stacks rings in correct order (30-36 months)
C.156   Sorts colors and points to several colors when named (33 months and above)
C.157   Identifies longer stick (33 months and above)
C.159   Understands all common verbs, most common adjectives (33-36 months)

Language
L.77   Uses plurals (27-36 months)
L.78   Refers to self using pronoun (27-40 months)
L.84   Repeats words and sounds (29-36 months)
L.86   Uses most basic grammatical structures (30-36 months)
L.87   Over-regulates and systematizes plurals and verbs (foots, doed) (30-36 months)
L.92   Uses expressive vocabulary of 200 or more words (30½-35 months)
L.93   Verbalizes two prepositions (33-35½ months)
L.96   Relates experiences more frequently using short sentences (34 months and above)
L.97   Asks questions beginning with "what," "where," "when" (34½ months and above)
L.98   Uses intelligible words about 80% of the time (35 months and above)

Fine Motor
FM.91   Imitates three-block bridge using cubes (31 months and above)
FM.92   Builds tower using nine cubes (32-36 months)
FM.93   Strings ½-inch beads (33½ months and above)

Self-Help
SH.75   Insists on doing things independently (30 months and above)
SH.76   Knows proper place for own things (30-36 months)

Making Holiday Cards

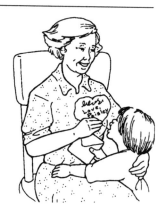

Activities

Let's make holiday cards to send to friends and family! It's a wonderful way for me to practice my pasting, cutting, and drawing skills. I also learn that reading and writing are fun and important ways to communicate my ideas and feelings.

We can use plain white envelopes and typing paper, index cards, or construction paper from the store. Our card does not have to fit the envelope perfectly; the important part is that we do it together and have fun.

Let me write (scribble) my own messages on the cards. Join me and add a message, too! Explain to me that you will write the address on the front of the envelope, and I can help paste on the stamp. If we hand deliver our letters, we can draw our own stamps. When I see you write in our card and on the envelope and hear you read our card aloud, I am learning about the importance of communicating through writing.

Sometimes I may want to tell you a story to record in our card or message. You might like to ask me what I've drawn on a card and write those words or sentences down near the object or picture. This teaches me that printed words have meaning and that I can be the *author*.

Christmas

- Cut Christmas shapes (such as bells, stars, and balls) from colorful wrapping paper or from Christmas advertisements. Let me choose the ones I'd like for a card to Grandmother, and then let me paste them onto the card.

- Show me how to fold a piece of paper in half. Then cut it into a Christmas shape, being careful to leave part of the folded portion so I have a card to open rather than two separate pieces. Together we can tear some pieces of colorful tissue paper. Show me how to use a large child-size paintbrush to spread diluted liquid glue onto the front of our card. Then encourage me to put pieces of tissue paper on the card while it is wet with the glue.

Thanksgiving

- Trace my hand onto the card with a crayon or felt pen. Help me make my thumb into a turkey face by adding two eyes, a wattle, and so forth. The outline of my fingers will be the turkey's feathers, so let's color them! Add some turkey legs at the bottom, with grass, flowers, and other pretty things.

- Let me cut some strips of colorful construction paper about 1 inch by 2 inches. We can use these as feathers to paste onto a round circle. Then draw or trace a turkey head, or paste on one from a magazine picture.

© 1993 by Hawaii Early Learning Partners
Published by Communication Skill Builders, Inc./(602) 323-7500. This page may be reproduced for instructional use. (Catalog No. 7898)

Developmental Skills

Social and Emotional

S.65 Distinguishes self as a separate person; contrasts self with others (24-36 months)

S.75 Relates best to one familiar adult at a time (24-36 months)

S.76 Engages best in peer interaction with just one older child, not a sibling (24-36 months)

S.88 Begins to obey and respect simple rules (30 months and above)

S.94 Takes pride in own achievements; resists help (30-36 months)

Cognitive

C.150 Understands concept of two (30-36 months)

C.156 Sorts colors and points to several colors when named (33 months and above)

Language

L.78 Refers to self using pronoun (27-40 months)

L.84 Repeats words and sounds (29-36 months)

L.90 Participates in storytelling (30-36 months)

L.92 Uses expressive vocabulary of 200 or more words (30½-35 months)

L.95 Repeats five-word sentences (33½-36 months)

L.96 Relates experiences more frequently using short sentences (34 months and above)

L.98 Uses intelligible words about 80% of the time (35 months and above)

L.99 Uses expressive vocabulary of 300-1,000 words (35 months and above)

Fine Motor

FM.82 Imitates a cross (24-36 months)

FM.83 Makes first designs or spontaneous forms (24-35 months)

FM.86 Copies a circle (25-36 months)

FM.88 Snips on line using scissors (28-35 months)

Self-Help

SH.75 Insists on doing things independently (30 months and above)

Learning about My Environment

Activities

Let's go outside to explore my environment. I can learn a lot in my own backyard, a park, or a beach. We should take along a bag for collecting things. A magnifying glass or colored cellophane will let us look at the world with different eyes.

I'll want some running time outdoors, so first we might play some active games. Good games include running on tiptoes and jumping across natural obstacles, such as sticks on the ground or cracks in the pavement. I may also just want to run around by myself.

When we're ready for our *treasure hunt*, we can go slowly and look for leaves, sticks, seed pods, flowers, shells, stones, and other fun things. Using the magnifying glass, we can examine each *treasure* very closely, or we can look through the colored cellophane and talk about what we see. I might ask you some questions, such as, "What is that?" or "Where is my bag?" I'll enjoy gathering many items to take home. I like to do things myself, so I may not want your help in collecting or carrying my bag.

After we've collected a lot of items, let's find a table or a mat and spread out my *treasures*. If you show me how to sort them, I can place all the leaves in one place, for example, or all the sticks in another place. I can also identify basic colors, putting all the red items (flowers, leaves, stones) together and all the green items together (leaves, moss, sticks). If you ask, I can probably tell you which is the longer of two sticks, or you can help by showing me the difference between short and long.

Another game I might enjoy is to show me several of my items, then place them in my bag where I can't see them. Ask me to find a specific item (a stone, for example) and see if I can reach into the bag and find the stone by feel alone.

When we get home, I might enjoy making a collage or picture using some of my *treasures*. We can use a paper plate and paste. Let me make my own design; I'll want to do this all by myself, and I'll be very proud of my accomplishment. Working on my picture is a good time for me to tell another family member about our excursion. Let me help pick a special place to hang my picture in my room or in a family area where all can admire it.

Developmental Skills

Social and Emotional
S.94   Takes pride in own achievements; resists help (30-36 months)

Cognitive
C.151   Identifies familiar objects by touch (30-36 months)
C.156   Sorts colors and points to several colors when named (33 months and above)
C.157   Identifies longer stick (33 months and above)
C.158   Begins to pick longer of two lines (33-36 months)
C.159   Understands all common verbs, most common adjectives (33-36 months)

Language
L.93   Verbalizes two prepositions (33-35½ months)
L.95   Repeats five-word sentences (33½-36 months)
L.96   Relates experiences more frequently using short sentences (34 months and above)
L.97   Asks questions beginning with "what," "where," "when" (34½ months and above)

Gross Motor
GM.143 Jumps a distance of 24 to 34 inches (34½-36 months)
GM.144 Avoids obstacles in path (34½-36 months)
GM.145 Runs on toes (34½-36 months)
GM.146 Makes sharp turns around corners when running (34½-36 months)

Fine Motor
FM.83   Makes first designs or spontaneous forms (24-35 months)

Self-Help
SH.75   Insists on doing things independently (30 months and above)

Dining Out

Activities

Dinner at a restaurant can be fun if I'm properly prepared. I like to be told ahead of time about changes in activities so that I can make gradual shifts in what I'm doing. I'm also very proud of my achievements and will like it if you'll allow me to use my skills (for example, going up and down stairs with alternating feet) as we enter the restaurant. Ask for a booster seat or high chair to help me reach the table.

Please realize that I won't have much patience waiting for food to be served, so either have a few crackers to hold me until the meal comes or pick a buffet-type restaurant where food is available immediately.

If we do have to wait, let's carry on a conversation. I can use sentences and I like to tell you about some of my activities. However, I can also get bored quickly, so perhaps you could have some crayons, pencils, or pens for me to draw with or have some paper available in your purse. I can be challenged with making designs, copying circles or crosses, or playing a simple game such as tic-tac-toe. You might draw sets of pictures and ask me, "Which one is longer?" or "Which one is smaller?" Another way to occupy me while we wait for the meal is to take a trip to the bathroom.

Show me the menu and point to the choices I have. I'll enjoy the occasion more if I can select my own meal. A children's menu is nice if they have one because the choices and serving sizes are more to my scale.

Once the food arrives, I can show everybody how well I use a fork and napkin. I may still need some help in cutting large pieces of food. If there are large family-style dishes, please let me serve myself. I feel quite grown up when I can be so independent.

Developmental Skills

Social and Emotional
S.92   Experiences difficulty with transitions (30-36 months)
S.93   Participates in circle games; plays interactive games (30 months and above)
S.94   Takes pride in own achievements; resists help (30-36 months)

Cognitive
C.157   Identifies longer stick (33 months and above)
C.158   Begins to pick longer of two lines (33-36 months)

Language
L.95   Repeats five-word sentences (33½-36 months)
L.96   Relates experiences more frequently using short sentences (34 months and above)

Gross Motor
GM.140   Walks downstairs alternating feet (34 months and above)

Fine Motor
FM.82   Imitates a cross (24-36 months)
FM.83   Makes first designs or spontaneous forms (24-35 months)
FM.84   Puts tiny objects into small container (24-30 months)

Self-Help
SH.78   Uses fork (30-36 months)
SH.79   Uses napkin (30-36 months)
SH.85   Serves self at table with little spilling (31 months and above)

Talking to Me about Sex

Activities

I know I'm a boy and my baby sister's a girl. I'm beginning to wonder, though, why I'm different and why I look different from Mommy and Daddy. I worry that something may be wrong with me.

If I haven't asked questions, that doesn't mean I haven't been thinking about being different. I've been watching you bathe my sister and wondered why she looks the way she does; is that what's going to happen to me too?

I give many hints that indicate I'm very curious. You noticed that I said, "Baby's hurt" and how I touched her wee-wee and mine too.

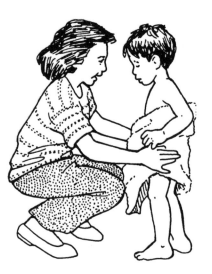

You can help me by explaining:

- That I'm like Daddy and baby's like Mommy. That's the way we were born. I need to be told that when I grow up I'm going to be a Daddy and baby Sarah is going to be a Mommy. It's reassuring to know that I'm made just right for a boy, and baby's made just right for a girl.

- I need to know too why daddy's penis is so much bigger than mine. I'm relieved when I'm told that's because I'm small all over, while Daddy is big all over.

- I'm sure baby Sarah needs to be told when she's older that she's okay the way she is.

Even if I'm satisfied now with your answers, I will probably be asking questions like these and about how babies are born every so often. Remember, don't bore me with long and complicated explanations. I just want a simple answer to satisfy my curiosity at that moment.

Developmental Skills

Social and Emotional
S.65   Distinguishes self as a separate person; contrasts self
          with others (24-36 months)
S.77   Dramatizes using a doll (24-30 months)
S.83   Becoming aware of sex differences (24-30 months)
S.94   Takes pride in own achievements; resists help (30-36 months)

Needing Rituals and Routines

Activities

I've just become used to order and routine, so I don't take to change kindly or easily. In fact, this is about the age when I seem to need to do the same things in the same way, to use the same utensils, to eat the same things, to listen to the same story by the same person at bedtime. I know I drive my family crazy because I can't seem to stand change. Don't worry; this too shall pass. It happens with some of us because it's important for us to have order in our lives.

Just humor me and allow me to keep these rituals. For the rest of my time, I'm adjusting to a lot of new and interesting changes. For me to be able to handle these changes, I need order for the more routine parts of my life.

Developmental Skills

Social and Emotional

S.43   Needs and expects rituals and routines (12-18 months)
S.91   Resists change; is extremely ritualistic (30-36 months)
S.92   Experiences difficulty with transitions (30-36 months)

Helping Me toward Independence

Activities

This is about the time when I want to begin to do things on my own. I want to dress myself as much as possible, I want to bathe myself, I want to be useful around the house.

I know I'm going to get angry and upset because I can't do certain things, such as know front from back or my right from my left shoe. But you can help me toward being independent.

How can you help?

- You can tell me specifically what I'm doing well on my own.

- You can arrange my clothes so I'll put them on correctly and help me with things I can't do, such as buttoning.

- You can tell me how much I'm growing up to be like Mom or Dad.

- If you see me struggling and ready to have a tantrum because I'm trying to do something that's beyond my skill at this age period, stop me, help me with it, or divert my interest to something else.

- Remember also that I need toys that are fun to play with, so you should help me choose things that are within my abilities. If I receive toys that are not appropriate, we can play with them together so I don't get frustrated, or they can be put away for me to play with alone at a later time.

What's important is that you should be close, aware of my anxiety about becoming independent, and helping me enjoy becoming a separate person.

Developmental Skills

Social and Emotional

S.33   Tests parental reactions during feeding (9-12 months)

S.34   Tests parental reactions at bedtime (9-12 months)

S.39   Displays independent behavior; is difficult to discipline (the "No" stage) (12-15 months)

S.40   Acts impulsively, unable to recognize rules (12-15 months)

S.41   Attempts self-direction; resists adult control (12-15 months)

S.45   Enjoys imitating adult behavior; responds well to the introduction of new tasks (12-18 months)

S.50   Enjoys being center of attention in family group (12-18 months)

S.56   Desires control of others—orders, fights, resists (18-24 months)

S.62   Experiences a strong sense of self-importance (18-24 months)

S.64   Defends possessions (23-24 months)

S.65   Distinguishes self as a separate person; contrasts self with others (24-36 months)

S.71   Says "No," but submits anyway (24-30 months)

S.73   Enjoys experimenting with adult activities (24-30 months)

S.78   Initiates own play, but requires supervision to carry out ideas (24-36 months)

S.79   Fatigues easily (24-30 months)

S.80   Dawdles and procrastinates (24-30 months)

S.81   Values own property; uses word "mine" (24-30 months)

S.82   Takes pride in clothing (24-30 months)

S.85   Separates easily from mother in familiar surroundings (30-36 months)

S.86   Shows independence; runs ahead of parent outdoors, refuses to have hand held (30-36 months)

S.93   Participates in circle games; plays interactive games (30 months and above)

S.94   Takes pride in own achievements, resists help (30-36 months)

© 1993 by Hawaii Early Learning Partners
Published by Communication Skill Builders, Inc./(602) 323-7500. This page may be reproduced for instructional use. (Catalog No. 7898)

Playing with Safe Toys

Activities

Please help me by eliminating toys that can be dangerous for me, such as sharp or pointed toys, electrical toys, shooting games, and flammable costumes. Be sure to check my tricycle and wagon periodically for parts that may be loose, missing, or broken, and to be sure that the wheels are balanced.

You will need to be there with me to teach me to be careful when riding near driveways, sidewalks, and streets. Caution me never to ride in the street.

Developmental Skills

Social and Emotional
S.72   Tends to be physically aggressive (24-30 months)
S.88   Begins to obey and respect simple rules (30 months and above)

Cognitive
C.159   Understands all common verbs, most common adjectives (33-36 months)

Gross Motor
GM.112   Rides tricycle (24-30 months)
GM.139   Uses pedals on tricycle alternately (32-36 months)
GM.141   Climbs jungle gyms and ladders (34½-36 months)

Fine Motor
FM.81   Snips with scissors (23-25 months)

© 1993 by Hawaii Early Learning Partners
Published by Communication Skill Builders, Inc./(602) 323-7500. This page may be reproduced for instructional use. (Catalog No. 7898)

Appendix

Definitions of Skills

Appendix

Definitions of Skills

Note: Definition not provided if skill description is self-explanatory. For editorial simplicity, the authors have used the masculine pronoun to include both genders in reference to the child. The feminine pronoun is used in reference to the adult.

Social and Emotional Skill Definitions

S.01   **Enjoys and needs a great deal of physical contact and tactile stimulation (0-3 months)**

S.02   **Regards face (0-1 month)**
The child momentarily and solemnly stares at the face of the person with whom he is interacting.

S.03   **Smiles reflexively (0-1½ months)**
The child's smiles are fleeting and rare at this time. They do not occur consistently.

S.04   **Establishes eye contact (0-2 months)**
The child looks the adult in the eye fairly consistently.

S.05   **Molds and relaxes body when held; cuddles (0-3 months)**
The child, when picked up and held, molds the body to the adult's and snuggles comfortably. It is very important that a child who actively rejects being held be helped to find a position that is comfortable and acceptable.

S.06   **Draws attention to self when in distress (0-3 months)**
The child may fuss, cry, or scream when exposed to unpleasant environmental situations, such as loud noises, or when internally upset (for example, hungry).

S.07   **Responds with smile when socially approached (1½-4 months)**
The child smiles fairly consistently when an effort is made to "see him smile."

S.08   **Stops unexplained crying (3-6 months)**
By the age of 3 months, a child has usually outgrown the fretful, colicky crying that often characterizes the early months. This condition can last as long as 5 or 6 months, but this is rare.

S.09   Vocalizes in response to adult talk and smile (3-5 months)
The child vocalizes, coos, or makes happy sounds in response to social interactions.

S.10   Discriminates strangers (3-6 months)
The child freezes, stares, quiets, or refuses to smile on sight of a stranger. The child discriminates between familiar and unfamiliar people.

S.11   Socializes with strangers/anyone (3-5 months)
The child can be exposed to any comfortable person and responds well.

S.12   Demands social attention (3-8 months)
The child becomes bored and fretful when left alone, and learns that crying brings attention. Crying for attention is a positive behavior and should be reinforced.

S.13   Vocalizes attitudes (pleasure and displeasure) (3-6 months)
The child no longer cries for everything, although crying is still the usual response. Sometimes the child whines, grunts, or makes an unhappy noise instead of crying. Pleasure may be indicated by a coo, chuckle, laugh, or any other sound. The child's vocalizations are not yet very consistent, especially those of displeasure.

S.14   Becomes aware of strange situations (3-6 months)

S.15   Enjoys social play (3-6 months)

S.16   Makes approach movements to mirror (3-5H months)
The child stares at and moves slightly toward the mirror. The child's arms may move. The stare is usually very solemn.

S.17   Recognizes mother visually (4-8 months)
The child may smile, move, quiet, or cry at the sight of the mother or primary caretaker.

S.18   Enjoys frolic play (4-8 months)

S.19   Repeats enjoyable activities (4-8 months)
The young child loves repetition and will repeat or attempt to repeat any "game" he enjoys.

S.20   Displays stranger anxiety (5-8 months)
The child who is stranger-anxious is evidencing real growth in discrimination and affection. Although difficult for parents and staff members, this is an important and positive stage.

S.21   Lifts arms to mother (5-6 months)

S.22   Explores adult features (5-7 months)

S.23   Smiles at mirror image (5H-8H months)

S.24   Distinguishes self as separate from mother (6-9 months)
The child probably considers himself a part of his mother and his environment at first. By this age, he has learned to distinguish himself from his environment, and knows he is a distinct individual, as is his mother or caretaker. This awareness fosters a real knowledge of the child's dependency on and love for the mother or caretaker. It is through this attachment to one primary caretaker that the child develops self-esteem and the ability to love others.

S.25 **Shows anxiety over separation from mother (6-9 months)**
The child's fear of being separated from his mother at this time is evidence of his emotional normality as well as his cognitive awareness and recognition of his great dependence on her. Although the eventual goal for every child includes the ability to separate and be independent, this is not the age at which to demand development of these skills. Separation takes a very long time, and the way in which we handle separation is quite dependent upon the child's developmental level. Working through separation fears is a gradual process that will probably start now but continue until the child is age two-and-a-half or three, or older.

S.26 **Cooperates in games (6-10 months)**
The child enjoys the give-and-take of simple games, such as "Pat-a-cake," and cooperates with any efforts to initiate the games. The games should be fun.

S.27 **Struggles against supine position (6-12 months)**
The child's activity level increases during the latter half of the first year. It is his increased need to explore and his enjoyment of an upright posture that cause him to resist lying down.

S.28 **Responds playfully to mirror (6-9 months)**
The child pats, points to, laughs at, "talks" to, or makes faces at his mirror image. Any positive response that is more than a smile is acceptable.

S.29 **May show fear and insecurity with previously accepted situations (6-18 months)**
The child's growing awareness of the environment and increased understanding of helplessness seem to trigger new fears and insecurities. These are positive signs, however, of increased cognitive ability. The child's most common fears include: the bathtub, hairwashing, vacuum cleaners, animals, things that move suddenly, or things that make loud noises. The child may fear only one thing or many different things. At the same time, the child may be frightened of strangers and fearful of separation from the mother. So much fear may disturb parents who see it as a serious personality change in their once outgoing and fearless child. It is, however, a perfectly normal phase, and one the child gradually outgrows. This is not a stage that lasts from six to 18 months. Rather, a sudden fear may crop up at any time within this age period and last for a few months. Long-lasting, stubborn fears require special psychological help.

There is also a period when stranger anxiety and suspicion may crop up again, especially at age 12 or 13 months. It is not a cause for concern and may be treated casually.

S.30 **Shows like/dislike for certain people, objects, places (7-12 months)**

S.31 **Lets only mother meet needs (8-12 months)**
The child refuses attention and caretaking from everyone except the mother. The child cries, fusses, or rejects, especially if the mother is in sight.

S.32 **Extends toy to show others, not for release (9-12 months)**
The child is physically capable of release but is not developmentally or socially ready to do so. Toys are offered as a means of socializing; the child does not intend to give them up.

S.33 **Tests parental reactions during feeding (9-12 months)**
The child seems to act deliberately "naughty" or mischievous during this stage, playing games with food just to see how his parents will react.

S.34 **Tests parental reactions at bedtime (9-12 months)**
The child tries out new and mischievous behavior just to see how his parents will react, testing their confidence as well as his independence.

S.35 **Engages in simple imitative play (9-12 months)**
The child can do simple imitations at this age. He may, for example, clap hands in imitation, grab at the spoon and try self-feeding, and brush his hair if he can acquire the hairbrush. These activities do not last very long, and they are not usually complete behavior sequences.

S.36 **Explores environment enthusiastically—safety precautions important (9-12 months)**
The child is more physically than socially oriented. Interest in people, language, and social games may decrease, although it definitely should not disappear. The child's interest focuses on his motor skills, his immediate environment, and those objects he can explore and discover independently. Do not dampen the child's excitement about his physical world and his increasing self-confidence by limiting or discouraging his active behavior.

S.37 **Likes to be in constant sight and hearing of adult (12-13 months)**

S.38 **Gives toy to familiar adult spontaneously and upon request (12-15 months)**
The child is already capable of voluntary and purposeful release. The child uses this interaction in a sociable way.

S.39 **Displays independent behavior; is difficult to discipline (the "No" stage) (12-15 months)**
The child seems to say "No" to almost every suggestion. This extremely important stage is critical to the child's growth as an independent, self-confident person. This stage should be encouraged, not discouraged; it is the ability to say "No" that counts. This does not mean that parents should allow the child to "rule the roost." They must still use positive guidance to control the child and must not allow the child to control them.

S.40 **Acts impulsively, unable to recognize rules (12-15 months)**
The child cannot really understand or attend to rules because he has such little control over his impulses. Rules are ignored not out of defiance, but because he cannot stop himself.

S.41 **Attempts self-direction; resists adult control (12-15 months)**
The child learns to assert and control himself. This is just another facet of the "No" stage and the child's urge for independence.

S.42 **Displays frequent tantrum behaviors (12-18 months)**
The child exhibits tantrum behaviors that disturb adults. Almost everyone has a different idea of just what constitutes a tantrum. Perhaps the best way to define tantrums is according to the reaction of the adults who are subjected to them. If the adult feels distressed enough about a

child's display of negative emotion to wish to "do something" about the behavior, then we will call it a tantrum. One adult may see any angry crying or frustrated yelling as a tantrum, even if the behavior lasts only a few seconds. Another form of tantrum may be a kicking, screaming, hysterical scene of 45 minutes' duration that is repeated many times a day. Whatever the definition, our suggestions within the text are applicable if the child's behavior is disturbing.

S.43   **Needs and expects rituals and routines (12-18 months)**
The child becomes ritualistic about familiar routines and demands a repetitive pattern for some daily activities.

S.44   **Begins to show a sense of humor—laughs at incongruities (12-18 months)**
The child learns what things are normal and abnormal in the environment. If the unusual or strange events are not frightening, the child may see them as "silly" and laugh. This early sense of humor is usually evidenced in the familiar home environment.

S.45   **Enjoys imitating adult behavior; responds well to the introduction of new tasks (12-18 months)**

S.46   **Plays ball cooperatively (12-15 months)**
The child cooperates happily in a give-and-take game. He can tolerate releasing the ball, knowing it will be rolled or tossed right back.

S.47   **Shows toy preferences (12-18 months)**
The child shows his developing ability and his unique personality when compared to other children in his preference for dolls versus books versus blocks versus trucks, active versus quiet play. Certain toys appeal to him, while others are ignored.

S.48   **Displays distractible behavior (12-15 months)**
A child at this age typically "flits" from one thing to another. He is quickly bored, easily distracted, and literally incapable of sitting still for extended periods of time. This is too normal to worry about as long as he plays or explores constructively at least some of the time.

S.49   **Tends to be quite messy (12-18 months)**
The child does not have a sense of neatness or order, and usually revels in making messes with just about everything.

S.50   **Enjoys being center of attention in family group (12-18 months)**
The child loves to be admired and watched in the family group, even if shy and self-conscious around others. He often repeats activities to attract attention and, in general, is very demanding of this attention.

S.51   **Hugs and kisses parents (14-15½ months)**

S.52   **Imitates doing housework (15-18 months)**
The child's imitation is very simple, incomplete, and of short duration. He is copying his parents because he loves to do so. This imitation is a good sign that the child is developing normally in identification with the parents.

S.53 Expresses affection (18-24 months)

S.54 Shows jealousy at attention given to others, especially other family members (18-24 months)
The child evidences jealousy not in words but in negative behavior. He may become aggressive, loud, noisy, destructive, babyish, or whiny, or act overly dependent or demand parental help unnecessarily. These actions prove a need for extra attention, even though he does not know what is wrong.

S.55 Shows a wide variety of emotions: fear, anger, sympathy, modesty, guilt, embarrassment, anxiety, joy (18-24 months)
The child pushes himself along toward being grown up and displays a wide range of emotions. This is a natural development. Negative emotions should be mild and occupy a minor portion of the child's day.

S.56 Desires control of others—orders, fights, resists (18-24 months)

S.57 Feels easily frustrated (18-24 months)
The child can stand very little challenge or thwarting, and is as easily frustrated by his own inability as by parents' limits or demands upon him.

S.58 Interacts with peers using gestures (18-24 months)
The child may push, pull, or grab at toys. He may also hit. Most of his interaction is still aggressive, although there are occasional pats, offering of toys, or waves of "bye-bye" to another child.

S.59 Engages in parallel play (18-24 months)
The child plays beside or around other children. He watches others intently. However, he does not really interact or play games with other children at this time.

S.60 Enjoys solitary play (coloring, building, looking at picture books for a few minutes) (18-24 months)
The child cannot play alone, even for a few minutes, at all times. Occasionally at first, and more frequently later, he can attend to toys and play alone for longer and longer periods of time. Do not interrupt him!

S.61 Enjoys rough-and-tumble play (18-24 months)

S.62 Experiences a strong sense of self-importance (18-24 months)
The child begins to feel he is the center of the universe and expects others to act accordingly. He is often described as "selfish," but he is actually learning to feel self-respect and to become an individual. It is a very important stage of development if the child is to grow up to be an independent and happy adult.

S.63 Attempts to comfort others in distress (22-24 months)

S.64 Defends possessions (23-24 months)
The child has developed a sense of possession and ownership and is also self-confident enough to defend his possessions from others.

S.65 **Distinguishes self as a separate person; contrasts self with others (24-36 months)**
The child really begins to understand now that he and his body are separate from his parents and the rest of the world. The dawning realization that he alone is responsible for himself and his body, this awareness of body integrity, is powerful and frightening. The child may become afraid of injury, fearful under some circumstances, worried about body differences, modest.

S.66 **Displays shyness with strangers and in outside situations (24-30 months)**
The child may place fingers in his mouth, refuse eye contact, hide his face or hide behind and cling to the parent when approached by strangers or other children. He may seem especially shy at school.

S.67 **Holds parent's hand outdoors (24-30 months)**

S.68 **Feels strongly possessive of loved ones (24-36 months)**
The child really knows to whom he "belongs" and is strongly and permanently attached to the primary caretakers. He wants the sole attention of these loved ones and is often jealous of attention paid to others or of affection between parents. The birth of a sibling at this time can create strong feelings of jealousy.

S.69 **Displays dependent behavior; clings and whines (24-30 months)**
The child strongly feels dependence on and need for the parents. The two-year-old child is at a peak age for whining, fussing, and clinging, especially at bedtime. At other times, he may feel independent and want to be left alone.

S.70 **Enjoys a wide range of relationships; meets more people (24-36 months)**

S.71 **Says "No," but submits anyway (24-30 months)**

S.72 **Tends to be physically aggressive (24-30 months)**
The child can be very aggressive, hitting, biting, and pinching. These aren't "bad habits" that are being picked up from peers or even from home; instead, most of this behavior is natural and disappears with adult encouragement.

S.73 **Enjoys experimenting with adult activities (24-30 months)**
The child continues to love play that imitates adult activities. As the play is continued, it becomes more varied and complex. The mother and her activities around the house are usually the most visible and therefore the most imitated. The child thinks of his behavior as "real work" to be proud of, not as imitative play.

S.74 **Frustration tantrums peak (24-30 months)**
The child displays frustration tantrums that are internally caused. These tantrums are not a sign that negative behavior has been reinforced by adults.

S.75 **Relates best to one familiar adult at a time (24-36 months)**

S.76 **Engages best in peer interaction with just one older child, not a sibling (24-36 months)**

S.77   Dramatizes using a doll (24-30 months)
The child's doll play is very helpful and important. The child learns to identify with adults by mimicking adult behavior with dolls.

S.78   Initiates own play, but requires supervision to carry out ideas (24-36 months)
The child thinks of things to do and then becomes frustrated because he cannot carry out his plans. He definitely needs tactful adult help.

S.79   Fatigues easily (24-30 months)
A child may be cranky, irritable, whiny, clingy, or aggressive, or may throw tantrums. Fatigue is often the first thing to consider. A child can usually handle only thirty minutes or so of an exciting activity before falling apart. This is especially true of peer play, group activities, or special events.

S.80   Dawdles and procrastinates (24-30 months)
The child may continue this very difficult and frustrating habit of dawdling and procrastinating for years if it is not tackled now or pre-vented before it starts. There are many reasons for beginning this behavior, but they all originate with adults. A child is *never* naturally lazy or dawdling.

S.81   Values own property; uses word "mine" (24-30 months)

S.82   Takes pride in clothing (24-30 months)
The child enjoys compliments he receives about his appearance. This behavior is most common when encouraged, as it often is in little girls' dressing up, but it is appropriate and important for both sexes.

S.83   Becoming aware of sex differences (24-30 months)
The child is aware of being a boy or a girl and knows the sex of others, but may sometimes make mistakes. The child also becomes aware of genital differences.

S.84   May develop sudden fears, especially of large animals (24-30 months)
The child may develop sudden fears that seem to arise out of the blue. Animals can be particularly frightening, but anything may be feared at this sensitive age.

S.85   Separates easily from mother in familiar surroundings (30-36 months)
The child can cope with separation fairly well by now. The shy, dependent child may still have difficulty. This is a personality difference that is not necessarily due to "bad" handling.

S.86   Shows independence; runs ahead of parent outdoors, refuses to have hand held (30-36 months)
The child feels proud and practices his independence by refusing "babyish" contact with the parent.

S.87   Demonstrates extreme emotional shifts and paradoxical responses (30-36 months)
The child has emotional ups and downs that are indicative of how hard this third year is on the child as well as the parents. This is the age when the child really does not "know his own mind." He contradicts himself and is frustrated with his own indecision. His reactions are almost always intense.

S.88 Begins to obey and respect simple rules (30 months and above)

S.89 Tends to be dictatorial and demanding (30-36 months)
The child constantly orders others around and exhibits generally irritating attitudes. He behaves like "royalty" and is furious if not obeyed. Despite its difficulty, this is an important time for the child. He is learning in this exaggerated way to be an assertive, competent, self-confident individual. It is hard on the child as well as the parents.

S.90 Talks with a loud, urgent voice (30-36 months)

S.91 Resists change; is extremely ritualistic (30-36 months)
The child is very sure of the way things are supposed to be; any disruption appears to be quite threatening to the newfound understanding of order and routine.

S.92 Experiences difficulty with transitions (30-36 months)
The child experiences emotional distress of varying severity when faced with transitions. A transition involves any movement from one activity to another. The child usually experiences transitional problems between sleeping and awakening, playing and being asked to sleep, playing and being stopped for lunch, indoor and outdoor play, and upon first arrival at school or play group.

S.93 Participates in circle games; plays interactive games (30 months and above)

S.94 Takes pride in own achievements; resists help (30-36 months)

Cognitive Skill Definitions

C.01 Quiets when picked up (0-1 month)
The child stops crying, momentarily, when picked up.

C.02 Shows pleasure when touched or handled (0-6 months)

C.03 Responds to sounds (0-1 month)
The child may show a sound has been heard in various ways: quieting after having been active; changing breathing pattern; becoming more active after having been quiet by kicking his feet, moving his arms, widening his eyes, or making a verbal sound.

C.04 Responds to voice (0-2½ months)
Initially, the child shows awareness of a sound by a response such as a blink of an eye or a startle response, depending on the intensity of the sound. The child quickly adjusts to the sound and the response diminishes. The child adjusts to almost any kind of environmental noise and sleeps in quiet or noise, whichever is typical of the child's environment. A change either way (to more noise or more quiet) is apt to result in a response of increased activity or alertness demonstrating awareness of the change.

C.05 Inspects surroundings (1-2 months)
The child begins to visually inspect the environment.

C.06 **Shows active interest in person or object for at least 1 minute (1-6 months)**
The child interacts with a person or object for 1 minute.

C.07 **Listens to voice for 30 seconds (1-3 months)**
The child soberly regards the face of the adult speaking to him and seems to listen intently as the adult continues to talk.

C.08 **Shows anticipatory excitement (1½-4 months)**
The child shows the ability to anticipate something that is about to happen: a change in the surrounding environment, such as Mom smiling and talking to the child; a change in the child's situation, such as getting picked up; a change in the child's condition, such as being fed.

The child shows anticipation in various ways: kicking, smiling, vocalizing, body tensing, quieting, or becoming more active from a quiet state.

C.09 **Reacts to disappearance of slowly moving object (2-3 months)**
The child watches a slowly moving object disappear and continues to search for it for a few seconds at the place at which it disappeared.

C.10 **Searches with eyes for sound (2-3½ months)**
In these activities, the adult must make sure the child is in a position to search for a sound by using his eyes (not by turning his head). The child searches for the sound, but need not find it and look toward it.

C.11 **Inspects own hands (2-3 months)**
The child looks at and really inspects his hands, moving them, watching what they do without a toy.

C.12 **Watches speaker's eyes and mouth (2-3 months)**

C.13 **Begins play with rattle (2½-4 months)**
The child plays with a rattle placed in his hand by regarding, shaking, mouthing, or waving it for very short periods of time. Choose rattles that do not break easily, expose sharp edges, or have small particles that fall out.

C.14 **Enjoys repeating newly learned activity (3-4 months)**
The child purposefully hits or moves a toy at least three or four times to keep it active in movement or sound (or both).

C.15 **Uses hands and mouth for sensory exploration of objects (3-6 months)**
The child explores objects by mouthing, patting, touching, rubbing, hitting them with his hands, or banging them against another object.

C.16 **Turns eyes and head to sound of hidden voice (3-7 months)**
The child turns to mother's voice when she is near and later localizes it even if she is hidden from view.

C.17 **Plays with own hands, feet, fingers, toes (3-5 months)**
The child touches, clasps his hands, and reaches for his feet and toes (not necessarily looking at what is being done). In general, the activities described for play with hands can be done with other body parts with little or no modification.

C.18   Awakens or quiets to mother's voice (3-6 months)
The primary reason for using the soothing voice in conjunction with awakening or quieting is to begin the development of a good feeling, a sense of security, with a melodic human voice.

C.19   Localizes sound with eyes (3½-5 months)
The child finds a sound that is close by, to the left, right, above, and below his eyes. The child must be in a position in which the child is physically capable of finding the sound by using his eyes.

C.20   Finds a partially hidden object (4-6 months)
The child successfully uncovers a partially covered, nonsymmetrical toy or object (such as a doll or car).

C.21   Continues a familiar activity by initiating movements involved (4-5 months)
The child must indicate a desire to continue a pleasant familiar activity by appropriately moving the specific body part involved.

C.22   Localizes tactile stimulation by touching the same spot or searching for object that touched body (4-6 months)
The child searches for the object that was felt or localizes the body part touched. Use normal firm pressure when touching and rubbing.

C.23   Plays with paper (4½-7 months)
The child enjoys crumpling, tearing, and pulling paper.

C.24   Touches toy or adult's hand to restart an activity (5-9 months)
The child begins to learn that objects can have independent actions. The child watches an action toy in operation until it stops, and then tries to start it again by touching the toy or the hand of the person who originally started the toy.

Later the child begins to explore for direct causes of the action observed and eventually tries to start it the way the child sees it started.

C.25   Reaches for second object purposefully (5-6½ months)
The child holds an object in one hand and reaches for a second object purposefully. The child reaches for the object with either hand, whether or not there is already a toy in that hand. The child need not be successful in obtaining the second object.

C.26   Works for desired out-of-reach object (5-9 months)
The child reaches repeatedly for a toy or object without necessarily obtaining it. Give the toy to the child after a few attempts if the child does not succeed. The child's persistence is rewarded only if there is repeated success in obtaining the object. Be careful not to tease the child.

C.27   Distinguishes between friendly and angry voices (5-6½ months)
The child responds in a different manner to pleasant and angry voices even when the child cannot see the facial expression.

C.28   Hand regard no longer present (5-6 months)
If the child has been progressing sequentially, the child has many things to do and has much to see and play with by this developmental age. The child should not be looking at the hands constantly or for any period of time. If hand regard occupies much of the child's day, seek professional help.

C.29   **Brings feet to mouth (5-6 months)**
After playing with his feet, the child begins to explore bringing them to his mouth.

C.30   **Shows interest in sounds of objects (5½-8 months)**
The child shows interest in the sounds objects make by actively hitting, banging, or shaking different toys. The child uses a single toy to make different sounds by doing different things with it, hitting it on or against different surfaces.

C.31   **Anticipates visually the trajectory of a slowly moving object (5½-7½ months)**
The child appropriately switches his glance from the point of disappearance of an object to the expected point of reappearance.

C.32   **Finds hidden object using 1 screen, 2 screens, then 3 screens (6-9 months)**
The child finds an object the child sees hidden under a screen. *Do not* move the screens around and make this a guessing game.

C.33   **Plays peek-a-boo (6-10 months)**
The child responds with delight when his eyes or face or a parent's face is uncovered suddenly.

C.34   **Smells different things (6-12 months)**
The child uses his sense of smell to explore the environment. Use specific activities to encourage the child to use this sense in learning about the environment and discriminating differences.

C.35   **Plays 2-3 minutes with single toy (6-9 months)**
The child is actively involved with a single toy for 2 to 3 minutes.

C.36   **Slides toy or object on surface (6-11 months)**
The child slides the toy or object as a way of exploring the object and the environment.

C.37   **Follows trajectory of fast-moving object (6-8 months)**
The child follows and finds a rapidly moving or falling object with his eyes after the object passes behind obstacles.

C.38   **Looks for family members or pets when named (6-8 months)**

C.39   **Responds to facial expressions (6-7 months)**
The child's facial or bodily movements change appropriately in response to adult emotions.

C.40   **Retains two of three objects offered (6½-7½ months)**
The child reaches for an object and retains it while reaching for a second object. When a third object is offered, the child retains both objects or drops one while reaching for the third object. The child retains the third object.

C.41   **Turns head and shoulders to find hidden sound (7-10 months)**
The child turns head and shoulders to locate hidden sounds at a distance.

C.42 **Imitates familiar, then new gesture (7-11 months)**
The child imitates gestures he can do spontaneously and then imitates new gestures.

C.43 **Responds to simple request with gesture (7-9 months)**
The child responds with an appropriate gesture to a simple verbal request. The verbal request is accompanied by a gesture.

C.44 **Looks at pictures 1 minute when named (8-9 months)**
The child enjoys looking at pictures for 1 minute with an adult who names and points to the pictures.

C.45 **Retains two objects and reaches for third (8-10 months)**
The child retains an object in each hand and reaches to secure a third object without dropping one. The child may try to obtain the third object by using his mouth or by purposefully putting one toy down to reach for the third object.

C.46 **Overcomes obstacle to obtain object (8-11 months)**
The child obtains a toy or object by reaching over or around an obstacle or by removing the barrier.

C.47 **Retrieves object using other material (8-10 months)**
The child pulls the material on which a toy or object rests to obtain the toy.

C.48 **Listens selectively to familiar words (8-12 months)**
The child shows signs of understanding familiar words. If you ask a child to "Get the ball," the child shows signs of looking, scanning, or appearing to know the word "ball," which are appropriate responses. The child does not actually "get" the ball, but it is important that the child show you understanding of the word "ball" or any other familiar word.

C.49 **Finds hidden object under three superimposed screens (9-10 months)**
The child finds an object the child sees hidden under three layers of screens placed one at a time on the object.

C.50 **Guides action on toy manually (9-12 months)**
The child tries to make a stopped action toy perform by manually putting it through its action.

C.51 **Throws objects (9-12 months)**
The child throws an object and observes where it goes and its effects.

Throwing objects may develop accidentally as the child, in learning voluntary release, shakes his hands to remove objects and finds they get flung a distance and bounce and roll. These kinds of observations and experiences are important to learning. Throwing objects should not be the primary or only interaction between child and object. It is a behavior that develops naturally and is part of children's play, in addition to other play behaviors. Provide lots of appropriate toys and experiences for throwing. Do not become overly concerned about the throwing of objects. All this will help the child move on to developing other schemata. Throwing things just to get attention, even if the attention is negative, is different from the play activity.

C.52 **Drops objects systematically (9-12 months)**
The child drops objects repeatedly and intentionally. This behavior appears as the child learns to let go of things, observing the path of moving objects and listening to the sounds objects make when they hit the floor.

C.53 **Uses locomotion to regain object and resumes play (9-12 months)**
The child plays with a toy that has at least two essential parts. When one part is moved, the child uses a form of locomotion to regain the part, then resumes play. A child may push, drag, or carry one part of the toy to resume play.

C.54 **Listens to speech without being distracted by other sources (9-11 months)**
Children may become so engrossed in their immediate activities and play that they are unaware of or appear undistracted by the external environment.

It is very important that the child attend only to the "important" sounds. Everyone should be able to screen out unimportant sounds, such as traffic noises and some conversations.

C.55 **Knows what "No-No" means and reacts (9-12 months)**
The child stops what he is doing briefly when an adult says "No."

C.56 **Responds to simple verbal requests (9-14 months)**
The child responds to verbal requests, such as "Come Here," "Up," or "Don't touch," without the gestures that usually accompany such requests. The child responds with gestures.

C.57 **Removes round piece from formboard (10-11 months)**
A formboard is a shape puzzle; the round shapes are easiest to remove.

C.58 **Takes ring stack apart (10-11 months)**
The child removes all the rings on the ring stack toy with some adult encouragement.

C.59 **Demonstrates drinking from a cup (10-15 months)**
Give the child a child-size cup or a play cup similar to one the child uses. The child should "drink" although there is nothing in the cup.

C.60 **Enjoys looking at pictures in books (10-14 months)**
The child enjoys looking at pictures in books with some adult participation.

C.61 **Unwraps a toy (10½-12 months)**
The child unwraps an object loosely wrapped with paper.

C.62 **Hidden displacement one screen (11-13 months)**
The child finds an object hidden by displacement. The child watches as an object is placed into a container. The container is hidden under a screen and the child cannot see the object being removed from the container and left under the screen. The child searches for the object by looking into the container and then by looking under the screen.

C.63 **Places cylinders in matching hole in container (11-12 months)**
The cylinder can be a spool, juice can, or peg.

C.64 **Stacks rings (11-12 months)**
The child stacks rings in any order using a ring stack with a center that is uniform in size.

C.65 **Moves to rhythms (11-14 months)**
The child spontaneously moves the whole body rhythmically in response to music, but not necessarily in time to the music.

C.66 **Imitates several new gestures (11-14 months)**
The child imitates several new gestures and combines two simple gestures in imitation.

C.67 **Hands toy back to adult (12-15 months)**
The child understands that you caused the action of a toy. The child tries to continue the action of the toy when it stops by giving the toy back to you and then waits for you to activate it again.

C.68 **Enjoys messy activities, such as finger painting (12-15 months)**

C.69 **Reacts to various sensations, such as extremes in temperature and taste (12-15 months)**
The child reacts with facial expressions or body movements.

C.70 **Shows understanding of color and size (12-18 months)**
The child shows a preference for a certain color (or colors). Awareness of size is seen in the exploratory use of formboards and nesting cans.

C.71 **Places round piece in formboard (12-15 months)**
A formboard is a shape puzzle; the round pieces are easiest to insert.

C.72 **Nests two, then three cans (12-19 months)**
The child fits together two round containers by putting the smaller one into the larger container. The child then fits together three containers. The child may put the middle container into the largest container and then add the smallest one, or may put the smallest one into the middle container and put both inside the largest one.

C.73 **Understands pointing (12-14 months)**
The child visually follows your pointing or uses his index finger to point at people and things.

C.74 **Pulls string horizontally to obtain toy (12-13 months)**
The child obtains an out-of-reach toy by pulling on a string attached to the toy. The stringed toy is placed on a table so that the child pulls horizontally.

C.75 **Makes detours to retrieve objects (12-18 months)**
The child goes around obstacles to obtain a desired object that can't be reached by direct crawling or creeping.

C.76 **Looks at place where ball rolls out of sight (12-13 months)**
The child watches a ball roll out of sight and continues to look for it at the point it disappeared.

C.77 **Recognizes several people in addition to immediate family (12-18 months)**
The child may indicate recognition by looking at or pointing to the person named. Recognition may also be indicated by a lack of stranger anxiety and by a willingness to interact freely.

C.78 **Hidden displacement two screens (13-14 months)**
The child finds an object hidden by displacement when two screens are used (see C.62). Be sure to leave the object under the same screen.

C.79 **Pulls string vertically to obtain toy (13-15 months)**
The child sees a desired object that is attached to string as it is lowered beneath a barrier. The child pulls the string upward to obtain the object.

C.80 **Hidden displacement three screens (14-15 months)**
The child finds an object hidden by displacement when three screens are used (see C.62). The object should be under the same screen.

C.81 **Hidden displacement two screens alternately (14-15 months)**
The child finds an object hidden by displacement when it is randomly hidden under one of two screens. The child finds the object by removing the correct screen. The child should not randomly search under all the screens, but should look only under one screen.

C.82 **Pats picture (14-15 months)**

C.83 **Helps turn pages (14-15 months)**
The child helps an adult turn pages of a book.

C.84 **Imitates "invisible" gesture (14-17 months)**
An "invisible" gesture is one the child does but cannot see himself perform (such as nodding the head).

C.85 **Matches objects (15-19 months)**
The child matches two objects that are exactly the same from a group of three objects.

C.86 **Places square piece in formboard (15-21 months)**
A formboard is a shape puzzle.

C.87 **Indicates two objects from a group of familiar objects (15-18 months)**
The child points to, touches, or picks up two different objects at the same time out of a group of three to five objects upon request.

C.88 **Brings objects from another room on request (15-18 months)**
The child must be able to bring something from the room he is in before he is able to bring an object from another room.

C.89 **Turns two or three pages at a time (15-18 months)**
The child turns pages by pushing many pages over at a time. The child learns to turn one page at a time at a later age.

C.90 **Identifies self in mirror (15-16 months)**
The child may point to his image in the mirror or indicate self-recognition in other ways. The child may at first find it easier to recognize family members in the mirror.

C.91   **Identifies one body part (15-19 months)**
The child identifies one body part by pointing, touching, or moving the part named.

C.92   **Recognizes and points to four animal pictures (16-21 months)**
The child points to or touches the appropriate picture out of a choice of four pictures when asked.

C.93   **Understands most noun objects (16-19 months)**
The child knows the names of most common objects in the child's environment and looks at or points to them on request.

C.94   **Series of hidden displacements: object under last screen (17-18 months)**
The child finds an object, when hidden by a series of displacements, under the last screen.

C.95   **Solves simple problems using tools (17-24 months)**
The child purposefully uses an unrelated object to obtain a desired result.

C.96   **Imitates several "invisible" gestures (17-20 months)**

C.97   **Points to distant objects outdoors (17½-18½ months)**

C.98   **Attempts and then succeeds in activating mechanical toy (18-22 months)**
The child searches for a way to reactivate a toy that has stopped. The child did not see the toy activated.

C.99   **Uses play dough and paints (18-24 months)**
The child explores and manipulates play dough and enjoys a variety of painting activities.

C.100   **Pastes on one side (18-24 months)**
The child applies paste on one side of a shape and turns it over to stick on paper.

C.101   **Paints within limits of paper (18-24 months)**
The child paints or colors inside the limits of a large piece of paper (about 18 by 22 inches).

C.102   **Points to several clothing items on request (18-20 months)**

C.103   **Explores cabinets and drawers (18-24 months)**

C.104   **Matches sounds to animals (18-22 months)**
The child shows understanding of the sounds that animals make. The child spontaneously vocalizes the sound of animals when the child sees them. The child points to the correct animal when another person vocalizes the animal sound. The child responds correctly when asked, "What does the [animal] say?"

C.105   **Rights familiar picture (18-24 months)**
The child spontaneously corrects a familiar picture that is presented upside-down or moves to the other side of the picture.

C.106   Enjoys nursery rhymes, nonsense rhymes, finger plays, poetry
(18-30 months)

C.107   Matches objects to pictures (19-27 months)
The child puts the object on or points to the matching picture out of a
choice of three to four pictures.

C.108   Sorts objects (19-24 months)
The child separates objects into three groups. Each group has three to
five identical objects.

C.109   Assembles four nesting blocks (19-24 months)
Nesting containers are square boxes of different sizes that fit together.

C.110   Recognizes self in photograph (19-24 months)
The child points to or picks up a picture of himself from a choice of two
photographs. Each photograph should have only one person in it. A
child may find it easier to recognize family members in photographs
before recognizing his own image.

C.111   Identifies three body parts (19-22 months)
See C.91.

C.112   Understands personal pronouns, some action verbs, and adjectives
(20-24 months)
The child shows understanding of a pronoun by carrying out a simple
direction given without gestures. The child performs a familiar action
upon request.

C.113   Series of hidden displacements: object under first screen
(21-22 months)
The child finds an object, when hidden by a series of displacements,
under the first screen. (See C.62 and C.94.)

C.114   Places triangular piece in formboard (21-24 months)
A formboard is a shape puzzle.

C.115   Remembers where objects belong (21-24 months)
The child, with adult assistance, can put some of the child's toys and
familiar objects away.

C.116   Turns pages one at a time (21-24 months)

C.117   Points to five to seven pictures of familiar objects and people
(21-30 months)
The child points to or touches the appropriate picture out of a choice of
four pictures when asked.

C.118   Matches sounds to pictures of animals (22-24 months)
The child demonstrates understanding of the sounds animals make
using pictures of the animals.

C.119   Identifies six body parts (22-24 months)
See C.91.

C.120   Plays with water and sand (24-36 months)
The child uses water and sand imaginatively and purposefully.

C.121 Pastes on appropriate side (24-30 months)
The child independently applies paste to the appropriate side of a shape and turns it over to stick onto a paper.

C.122 Demonstrates awareness of class routines (24-27 months)
The child anticipates the next classroom activity when given environmental or verbal cues. A routine helps the children feel more comfortable in the classroom. They know there is a certain order to the class day and can anticipate activities (such as snacks or painting time). A routine lets them be more independent and helps teach time concepts.

C.123 Understands concept of one (24-30 months)
A child points to a set of one out of a choice of two sets, such as a set of one apple and a set of two bananas. The child also answers, verbally or with gestures, the question, "How many do you have?"

C.124 Identifies rooms in own house (24-28 months)
The child, on request, goes to or points to different rooms in the house, such as the kitchen or bathroom.

C.125 Demonstrates use of objects (24-28 months)
The child responds correctly to questions involving the functions of objects, such as a comb, telephone, or shoes. For example, "What do you do with a shoe?" A gesture is acceptable.

C.126 Identifies clothing items for different occasions (24-28 months)
The child indicates appropriate clothing for several specific activities or occasions.

C.127 Enjoys tactile books (24-29 months)
Tactile books are ones that have pop-up pictures, textured pieces glued on the pages, or things for the child to do (such as pull a tab, smell, scratch, or turn a wheel between two pages). Most of these books need to be handled more gently than ordinary books and are usually more costly to buy or take more time to make.

C.128 Finds details in favorite picture book (24-27 months)
The child looks at and points at several fine details in favorite pictures in books both spontaneously or when named.

C.129 Recognizes familiar adult in photograph (24-28 months)

C.130 Engages in simple make-believe activities (24-30 months)
The child begins to initiate make-believe activities at this age. The child begins to separate reality and fantasy, but the two are still often mixed. The activities the child engages in are short, discrete pieces of drama and are active imitations of actions previously seen or experienced. If an adult participates, the child usually is unable to reverse the adult's role (in other words, the child cannot respond as if the adult is the child, even if pretending to be Mommy or Daddy).

C.131 Knows more body parts (24-28 months)
The child can identify more body parts, now including smaller parts of the body, such as the wrist, elbow, and knee.

C.132 Selects pictures involving action words (24-30 months)
The child points to several pictures depicting familiar actions on request.

C.133 Obeys two-part commands (24-29 months)
The child obeys a simple command related to two objects but requiring only one action, such as "Give me the shoe and the ball."

C.134 Understands complex and compound sentences (24-27 months)
The child remembers and understands more complex language structures as language experiences and skills increase.

C.135 Gives one out of many (25-30 months)
The child gives or takes one of something from a larger grouping. Be careful that unintentional cues are not given.

C.136 Matches shapes—circle, triangle, square (toys) (26-30 months)
The child matches two shapes that are exactly alike.

C.137 Matches colors (black, white) (26-29 months)
The child matches objects of the same color from a group of three objects.

C.138 Knows own sex or sex of others (26-33 months)
Children enjoy imitating the different people they know at this age. They make no discrimination of sex roles, although they are aware of sex differences. Girls' imitating traditional male roles or boys' playing with dolls or dressing up in Mom's clothes should be accepted as a natural part of play and growing up.

C.139 Matches identical simple pictures of objects (27-30 months)
The child identifies from a group of three pictures of objects the two that are the same.

C.140 Listens to stories (27-30 months)

C.141 Understands many action verbs (27-30 months)
The child shows understanding of action verbs by doing the actions on request or by pointing to pictures describing the actions.

C.142 Identifies objects with their use (28-34 months)
The child points to the correct object when the function of the object is described.

C.143 Identifies body parts with their function (28-34 months)
The child indicates with word or gesture the appropriate functions of body parts.

C.144 Matches primary colors (29-33 months)
See C.137.

C.145 Matches similar pictures of objects (30-36 months)
The child identifies different pictures of the same object.

C.146 Sorts shapes—circle, triangle, square (toys) (30-36 months)
The child groups objects by their shapes.

C.147 Completes three- or four-piece puzzle (30-36 months)
The child completes a puzzle of an object, person, or animal with three or four related pieces.

C.148 Stacks rings in correct order (30-36 months)
The child independently stacks rings in correct order on the ring stand. The child may make self-corrections while proceeding.

C.149 Points to larger or smaller of two spoons (30-36 months)

C.150 Understands concept of two (30-36 months)
The child, on request, gives you two objects from a group of objects.

C.151 Identifies familiar objects by touch (30-36 months)
The child selects on request a familiar object without looking at it.

C.152 Enjoys being read to and looks at books independently (30-36 months)

C.153 Plays house (30-36 months)

C.154 Points to six body parts on picture of a doll (30-36 months)

C.155 Understands more adjectives (30-33 months)
The child shows understanding of more adjectives by labeling or, more frequently, by picking out the object or feature described.

C.156 Sorts colors and points to several colors when named (33 months and above)
The child groups three to five objects of the same color, using objects that are identical except for color.

C.157 Identifies longer stick (33 months and above)
The child picks the longer (2 to 3 inches longer) of two sticks.

C.158 Begins to pick longer of two lines (33-36 months)

C.159 Understands all common verbs, most common adjectives (33-36 months)
The child understands almost all verbs and most common adjectives, and may ask when the word is not understood. This is a continuation of development in understanding verbs and adjectives.

Language Skill Definitions

L.01 Cry is monotonous, nasal, one breath long (0-1½ months)
The child's cry is a total response seen throughout the body as well as heard at birth and during the first month. At first the cry is undifferentiated and not modified by mouth opening and closing.

L.02 Cries when hungry or uncomfortable (0-1 month)
The child's cry is the first form of communication. It is imperative to attend to the child's cries to help develop a pattern of interaction. The child learns these sounds are useful and have meaning to others.

L.03 Makes comfort sounds—reflexive vocal (0-2½ months)
A child who is feeling good makes comfort sounds. These sounds are usually accidental, the result of changes in tension of the muscles used for speech. Some of the sounds are /k/, /d/, "aaah," or "nnn."

L.04 **Makes sucking sounds (½-3 months)**
A child who is feeling comfortable and relaxed may make these sounds. These sounds are usually reflexive, the result of changes in tension of the muscles used for sucking.

L.05 **Cry varies in pitch, length, and volume to indicate needs such as hunger, pain (1-5 months)**
The child's only way to obtain attention is by crying. Respond to the crying by meeting the child's needs. The child learns these sounds are useful and have meaning to others. The child should not be allowed to cry for long periods of time unattended. Try to find out why the child is unhappy. Many parents can recognize the child's problem by the way the child is crying.

L.06 **Laughs (1½-4 months)**
The child chuckles or laughs out loud in response to an environmental stimulus instead of cooing or smiling to show pleasure.

L.07 **Coos open vowels (aah), closed vowels (ee), diphthongs (oy as in boy) (2-7 months)**
The child's developmental pattern in the production of vowel sounds starts from the simple vowel sounds to the complex diphthongs. (Diphthongs are vowels that go from one sound to another.) The open vowel sounds are the first and easiest sounds, requiring the opening of the mouth with vocalization and no rounding of the lips. The closed vowel sounds follow and the mouth is not open as wide.

L.08 **Disassociates vocalizations from body movement (2-3 months)**
The child no longer vocalizes primarily in conjunction with body movements, and instead separates vocalization from body movement. The child begins to lie quietly and vocalize, cooing or laughing in response to stimulation.

L.09 **Cries more rhythmically with mouth opening and closing (2½-4½ months)**
The child modifies crying by rhythmically opening and closing the mouth at a very early age. This is a normal developmental stage that occurs with maturation. Listen for changes in the child's cry. These changes show an increase in coordination of the muscles involved in respiration and phonation.

L.10 **Squeals (2½-5½ months)**
The child produces loud, sudden bursts of vowel sounds when excited.

L.11 **Responds to sound stimulation or speech by vocalizing (3-6 months)**
The child vocalizes in response to sound and continues an interchange of sounds.

L.12 **Laughs when head is covered with a cloth (3½-4½ months)**
Not every child goes through this stage. The child who does enjoy this stage laughs with delight when the head is briefly covered with a cloth.

L.13 **Babbles consonant chains "babababa" (4-6½ months)**
The child discovers the voice and all the funny sounds it can produce as coordination of lips, tongue, and jaw improves. In fascination, the child produces and repeats sounds in long strings, such as "babababa," and later the couplet "baba." The child also uses sounds other than "baba." If the child fails to babble or decreases babbling, it is a warning sign suggesting possible hearing problems.

L.14 **Vocalizes attitudes other than crying (joy, displeasure) (5-6 months)**
The child indicates feelings with voice quality, tone, and inflection, and is not limited to crying or laughing.

L.15 **Reacts to music by cooing (5-6 months)**
Infants coo, a melodic, soft vowel sound, when happy or contented. All infants do not react to music by cooing.

L.16 **Looks and vocalizes to own name (5-7 months)**
The child looks for the speaker and often coos when hearing the child's name.

L.17 **Babbles double consonants "baba" (5-8 months)**
The child produces "couplets" of double syllables instead of long chains as coordination of lips, tongue, and jaw improves. Occasionally, parents interpret these couplets as meaningful words.

L.18 **Babbles to people (5½-6½ months)**
The child participates in conversation using babbling sounds. The child or the adult may start the interchange.

L.19 **Waves or responds to bye-bye (6-9 months)**
The child moves a hand for "bye-bye" in stages, first with help, then in imitation, and later on request or spontaneously.

L.20 **Says "dada" or "mama," nonspecifically (6½-11½ months)**
The child often says "dada" or "mama" as the first sounds produced. As parents respond to and encourage these sounds, they become useful and meaningful to the child.

L.21 **Shouts for attention (6½-8 months)**
The child shouts to attract attention after learning that adults will respond to sounds the child makes.

L.22 **Produces these sounds frequently in babbling: /b/, /m/, /p/, /d/, /t/, /n/, /g/, /k/, /w/, /h/, /f/, /v/, /th/, /s/, /z/, /l/, /r/ (7-15 months)**
The child generally makes all these sounds in vocal play. Letter sounds are listed in the sequence in which they usually appear.

The first consonant sounds are often bilabials (sounds produced by using both lips, such as /m/, /b/, /p/). These sounds may be heard in conjunction with feeding, the "lip-smacking" sounds. The /d/ and /t/ sounds may also be heard during feeding time. The rest of the sounds generally appear in the order given. The more difficult sounds, requiring more precise movements, will develop as oral musculature coordination improves.

You will probably hear at some time during the child's babbling all the sounds that appear in your expressive language. This does not mean these sounds are immediately used in talking, since precise coordination is required to change quickly from one sound to another to make a word. The same pattern of development of sounds produced in babbling, such as /b/ before /sh/, will be heard later in the development of consistent articulation of words, such as "boy" before "shoe."

L.23 **Vocalizes in interjectional manner (7½-9 months)**
The child produces noises that sound like exclamations.

L.24 **Babbles with inflection similar to adult speech (7½-12 months)**
The child is tuning in to the specific patterns, the intonations, and the melody of language. This is an extremely important stage of development. The child's babbling sometimes sounds like adult sentences (for example, the accent may be placed on final syllables, making a sentence sound like a question).

L.25 **Babbles single consonant "ba" (8-12 months)**
The child begins to break strings of consonant sounds to produce only single consonant sounds. Encourage this development.

L.26 **Shows understanding of words by appropriate behavior or gesture (9-14 months)**
The child's responses and simple gestures show understanding of common language experiences.

L.27 **Babbles in response to human voice (11-15 months)**
The child replies to vocal stimulation with a collection of babbling sounds, partial words, and intonation patterns. The child attempts to "communicate" with melody and intonation patterns sounding like sentences. The child's sound-making is directed to the person talking to the child.

L.28 **Babbles monologue when left alone (11-12 months)**
The child enjoys hearing and playing with sounds the child can make.

L.29 **Says "dada" or "mama" specifically (11-14 months)**
The child's babbling until this point is usually nondirected. The child begins to direct babbling sounds of "dada" and "mama" specifically to the parents around this time because the parents respond and reinforce these sounds.

L.30 **Repeats sounds or gestures if laughed at (11-12½ months)**
The child repeats an activity that brought attention from others. This is a specific repetition, not done by chance, and occasionally the child adds embellishments to amuse an audience.

L.31 **Speech may plateau as child learns to walk (11½-15 months)**
The child, when concentrating energies on mastering the task of walking, appears to plateau or even regress in expressive language skills. As the child gains confidence in walking, language skills are "regained."

L.32 **Unable to talk while walking (11½-15 months)**
The child must concentrate when learning a skill, and may not be successful if energies are put into two activities at once. As the child becomes more competent in walking and talking, the child begins to do both at the same time. (This is closely related to L.31.)

L.33 **Omits final and some initial consonants (12-17 months)**
The child is often inarticulate during initial months of experimentation with a newly acquired speech ability. The child often omits or distorts the initial and final consonant sounds in words and short phrases. Articulation, as a fine motor skill, requires maturation and practice.

L.34 **Babbles intricate inflection (12-18 months)**
The child babbles many sounds using inflection patterns heard in adult speech. The child makes statements, scolds, asks questions, and tells stories, all without words but with eloquent inflection, pitch, and rhythm.

L.35   **Experiments with communication; not frustrated when not understood (12-17½ months)**
The child experiments with new sounds, words, and short phrases. The child's "talking" is often nondirected and seems more like a game or an experiment.

The child carries on a monologue, "talking" to people, animals, and inanimate objects. The child seldom shows concern or frustration when there is a lack of feedback or a reply. However, adults should continue to reply in the most appropriate way possible.

L.36   **Uses single-word sentences (12-14 months)**
The child's first words are utterances that have articulation qualities like the adult's pronunciation of the word. The words are recognizable even to a stranger and are used meaningfully.

L.37   **Uses expressive vocabulary of one to three words (12-15 months)**
The child may expressively have about one to three words that are used correctly and may imitate many more words. In a linguistic sense, expressive maturity is not generally based on quantity, but on the quality of expression.

L.38   **Vocalizes or gestures spontaneously to indicate needs (12-19 months)**
The child vocalizes words or sounds to attract attention and uses gestures to help communicate to others. Some common gestures are a nod of the head for "Yes," a twist of the wrist for "All gone," and a wave of the hand for "Bye."

L.39   **Greets with verbal cues (12-15 months)**
The child is greeted verbally by an adult, without the use of gesture. The child responds with a wave and later with a verbal "Hi."

L.40   **Uses exclamatory expressions ("uh-oh," "no-no") (12½-14½ months)**
The child begins to use the expressions "oh," "uh-oh," and "no-no" appropriately.

L.41   **Says "No" meaningfully (13-15 months)**
The child says "No" appropriately, often accompanied by a head shake or by turning away.

L.42   **Names one or two familiar objects (13-18 months)**
The child names familiar objects spontaneously or on request.

L.43   **Attempts to sing sounds to music (13-16 months)**
The child does not sing sounds on key. The child's first effort to sing is actually "talking" (or yelling) to music.

L.44   **Uses voice in conjunction with pointing or gesturing (14-20 months)**
The child indicates needs and wants by vocalizing along with pointing or gesturing.

L.45   **Uses 10 to 15 words spontaneously (15-17½ months)**
The child uses 10 to 15 words spontaneously in self-expression.

L.46   **Vocalizes wishes and needs at the table; names desired items (15-17½ months)**
The child asks for milk or a cookie spontaneously. Word approximations, such as "mi" or "coo-ie" may be used.

L.47 **Makes sounds in babbling, but often substitutes those sounds in words (15½-21 months)**
The child makes sounds in babbling but does not use the sounds correctly yet in words. The child may say /sh/ in babbling but substitute /t/ for /sh/ in the word "shoe." It is easier for the child to produce strings of the same sounds than to make the rapid changes required for articulation in words.

L.48 **Jabbers tunefully at play (17-19 months)**
The child discovers the value of talking. The child begins to talk to get and maintain an adult's attention, to see if speech continues to be useful in controlling the environment, to practice this new skill, and to enjoy the sound of the voice.

L.49 **Echoes prominent word or last word spoken (17-19 months)**
The child usually imitates the last spoken word as a clue to help remember directions. Do not overreact because you do not want to encourage the echoing of all speech so that the child fails to use spontaneous speech. Usually the imitation of the last word spoken is done by a child as a clue for remembering directions.

L.50 **Uses expressive vocabulary of 15 to 20 words (17½-20½ months)**
The child uses 15 to 20 words spontaneously.

L.51 **Uses jargon with good inflection and rate (18-22 months)**
The child's use of jargon, the meaningless repetition of consonant sounds using speech inflection patterns, is a natural development. Jargon is most often heard when the child is in solitary play, practicing the sounds, inflections, and fluency of speech. The child may use a few understandable words within the jargon. Some children do not go through a prolonged jargon stage. Do not worry if the child progresses directly to speech. Also, do not imitate jargon. If we imitate or respond as if we understand, the child may begin to think the jargon has meaning to us.

L.52 **Uses own name to refer to self (18-24 months)**
The child gives the first name when asked or uses the first name spontaneously.

L.53 **Imitates environmental sounds (18-21 months)**
The child imitates environmental sounds in play. These may be animal, nature, or machine sounds.

L.54 **Imitates two-word phrases (18-21 months)**
The child says simple two-word phrases in imitation. This usually begins when the child has an expressive vocabulary of 20 to 30 words.

L.55 **Attempts to sing songs with words (18-23 months)**
The child attempts to sing with or without others, using a few words. The child may be off-key and use the same words over and over.

L.56 **Names two pictures (19-21½ months)**
The child labels two different pictures spontaneously or when asked, "What is this?"

L.57 **Uses two-word sentences (20½-24 months)**
The child begins to form short two-word phrases and sentences while expanding a vocabulary of single words to 20 or 30 words.

258

L.58 **Uses nouns, verbs, modifiers (20½-24 months)**
The child will use different parts of speech, such as nouns, verbs (especially action verbs) and modifiers (such as adjectives) as expressive vocabulary increases.

L.59 **Tells experiences using jargon and words (21-24 months)**
The child's jargon peaks and begins to decline; you will probably hear more words within the jargon. The child will try to tell experiences, filling in with jargon when lacking words.

L.60 **Uses intelligible words about 65 percent of the time (21½-24 months)**
The child speaks in words that can be understood although not articulated properly. Articulation skills and intelligibility improve as a child's fine motor skills develop. If the child is not intelligible 65 percent of the time at this stage and there is no physical disability involving the articulators (tongue, lips, jaw, soft palate) the causes may be:

a. General delayed development, including fine motor skills.

b. Hearing loss or previous hearing loss that was present while the child was beginning to talk. Even a mild temporary hearing loss associated with an ear infection can affect articulation development.

c. Lack of good speech models.

d. Idiopathic. This means no one really knows the cause.

L.61 **Names three pictures (21½-24 months)**
The child labels three different pictures spontaneously or when asked, "What is this?"

L.62 **Uses elaborate jargon (22-24 months)**
The child usually peaks at this developmental stage in the use of jargon. You will probably note a decrease in jargon as the child learns to use words and phrases.

L.63 **Imitates four-word phrases (22-24 months)**
The child repeats simple four-word sentences immediately after you say them, such as "Amber's cat and dog," "Boy running to Mom," "Don't do that, Kitty," "Give me more juice."

L.64 **Sings phrases of songs (23-27 months)**
The child sings phrases of songs. The child attempts to follow a tune, but may be off-key.

L.65 **Produces the following sounds clearly: /p/, /b/, /m/, /k/, /g/, /w/, /h/, /n/, /t/, /d/ (24-27½ months)**
The child produces these sounds in words, especially at the beginning of words. The child may not use these sounds all the time.

L.66 **Uses pronouns (24-30 months)**
The child uses pronouns spontaneously instead of the child's name. Usually the first pronouns are self-centered (me, mine) or used in commands ("You come!").

L.67 **Uses three-word sentences (24-30 months)**
The child develops three-word sentences first in imitation. The child begins to use longer sentences, as well as a larger repertoire of words, as ideas and thoughts the child wants to share are developed.

L.68 **Uses past tense (24-30 months)**
The child begins to use past tense in telling about experiences. The child may over-regulate the verbs by using "ed" incorrectly (for example, "runned"). This over-regulation shows the child is learning and using grammatical rules automatically.

L.69 **Uses expressive vocabulary of 50 or more words (24-30½ months)**
The child uses 50 or more words spontaneously to express ideas and thoughts. These words include nouns, verbs, pronouns, and adjectives.

L.70 **Names five pictures (24-29 months)**
The child labels five different pictures spontaneously or when asked "What is this?"

L.71 **Imitates spontaneously or requests new words (24-27 months)**
The child imitates words others have been heard to use or asks for new words by saying, "What's this?" or even, "How do you say it?"

L.72 **Experiments with communication; frustrated when not understood (24-28½ months)**
The child becomes frustrated and may even cry when unable to express wants and needs verbally. A little frustration provides the motivation to develop better language skills, but too much hinders development.

L.73 **Relates experiences using short sentences (24-34 months)**
The child uses short sentences to tell about experiences in the recent past. This may be completely spontaneous or may require a question, encouragement, or both to tell more.

L.74 **Answers questions (24-36 months)**
The child answers simple questions about experiences. The child may not answer a question if it seems redundant or if the listener does not need further information.

L.75 **Formulates negative reasoning (24-36 months)**
The child disagrees with an adult over something the child knows, indicating either with gesture or verbally an understanding of what "not" means.

L.76 **Uses size words (25-30 months)**
The child must understand the meaning of size words before being able to use them. The child is likely to ask for "the big one" (cookie, glass, paper) first when this understanding begins. Since size is relative, you may wish to present both big and little concepts simultaneously.

L.77 **Uses plurals (27-36 months)**
The child uses plurals, often over-regulating at first. The child says "books," "blocks," "shoes," but also "foots" and "mans."

L.78 **Refers to self using pronoun (27-40 months)**
The child uses "I" or "me" consistently instead of the child's own name. If the child becomes a little confused on the use of "me" and "you," be patient and provide models for the child to hear.

L.79 **Produces sounds correctly at beginning of words (27½-32 months)**
The child produces most consonant sounds correctly at the beginning of words. Some sounds, such as /s/, /z/, /sh/, /ch/, /r/, /l/, may still be distorted or another sound may be substituted for them. Correct sound

production requires a great deal of fine motor coordination of the lips, tongue, jaw, and soft palate. It is especially difficult to change rapidly from one consonant sound to another. This is one reason why initial sounds are produced first, and middle and final sounds are omitted.

L.80   Verbalizes one preposition (28-33 months)
The child must understand prepositions before using them verbally.

L.81   Frustrated if not understood; utterances have communicative intent (28½-36 months)
The child attempts to communicate ideas and thoughts rather than simple needs or wants. When not understood, the child may become very frustrated, cry, become very angry, or simply say "Never mind," or "Forget it," and give up.

L.82   Replaces jargon with sentences (29-31 months)
The child's use of jargon decreases and finally disappears as expressive vocabulary and linguistic competence increase.

L.83   Names eight or more pictures (29-36 months)
The child labels eight or more familiar pictures spontaneously or when asked, "What is this?"

L.84   Repeats words and sounds (29-36 months)
The child repeats words and sounds automatically when happy or excited. Do not ask the child to stop, repeat, or slow down. Sometimes this nonfluency is labelled "stuttering." Actually, it is part of a normal pattern as the child develops proficiency with more complicated grammatical structures and vocabulary. It is most often seen during emotional periods, including stress, but also when the child is tired or not feeling well. Do not require speech at these times; be a careful, patient listener. If you are worried about this, talk to a speech pathologist.

L.85   Talks intelligently to self (29½-36 months)
The child talks intelligently while developing vocabulary and ease in talking. The child talks to toys and describes play.

L.86   Uses most basic grammatical structures (30-36 months)
The child has learned the basic rules for grammar structure and can manipulate them to suit needs.

L.87   Over-regulates and systematizes plurals and verbs (foots, doed) (30-36 months)
The child's language is delightful at this stage. This is a natural development that gives us "half-shut moons" and excited shouts of "I doed it!" Enjoy it. The child learns the exceptions simply by listening to the surrounding speech models. You can help this learning by correctly repeating the child's utterances, providing a good model. Over-regulation shows the child is learning and applying automatically the grammatical structures of our language.

L.88   Vocalizes for all needs (30-31½ months)
The child has vocabulary and linguistic systems adequate to indicate needs verbally rather than through gesture.

L.89   Gives full name on request (30-33 months)

L.90 **Participates in storytelling (30-36 months)**
The child helps to tell a familiar story by adding words and comments and by anticipating events in the story. The child may correct the adult if the adult omits details.

L.91 **Recites a few nursery rhymes (30-36 months)**
The child recites a short nursery rhyme with a minimum of verbal or gesture prompting from an adult.

L.92 **Uses expressive vocabulary of 200 or more words (30½-35 months)**
The child's expressive vocabulary follows receptive vocabulary development. The child uses 200 or more different words expressively and understands even more.

L.93 **Verbalizes two prepositions (33-35½ months)**
The child uses two different prepositions spontaneously.

L.94 **Begins to respond to opposite analogies (33-36 months)**
The child gives the opposite of a word when the word is presented in a sentence or as a question (for example, The stove is hot and the refrigerator is _____; the refrigerator is not hot, it is _____).

L.95 **Repeats five-word sentences (33½-36 months)**
The child mimics a few five-word sentences and begins to use them spontaneously in conversations.

L.96 **Relates experiences more frequently using short sentences (34 months and above)**
The child uses short sentences to tell about past experiences as well as plans for the near future. This may be completely spontaneous or may require a question and prompting to tell more.

L.97 **Asks questions beginning with "what," "where," "when" (34½ months and above)**
The child asks questions using "what," "where," and "when" in addition to asking questions by intonation.

L.98 **Uses intelligible words about 80 percent of the time (35 months and above)**
The child speaks in words that can be understood, although they may not be articulated properly. Articulation skills and intelligibility improve as the child's fine motor skills develop.

If the child is not intelligible 80 percent of the time by this age and there is no physical disability involving the articulators (tongue, lips, jaw, soft palate) the causes may be:

a. General delayed development, including fine motor skills.

b. Hearing loss or previous hearing loss which was present while the child was beginning to talk. Even a mild, temporary hearing loss associated with an ear infection can affect articulation development.

c. Lack of good speech models.

d. Idiopathic. This means no one really knows the cause.

L.99 **Uses expressive vocabulary of 300-1,000 words (35 months and above)**
The child's linguistic maturity by now should be developed to the point of decreasing percentages of nouns and increasing percentages of adjectives, adverbs, verbs, and other words that indicate linguistic growth.

The variability of expressive vocabulary length at age three is great, depending upon the amount of exposure to verbal input, the environmental factors of family, amount, and type of interaction with peers, amount of materials and exploration, and physical and mental development.

The receptive vocabulary is normally many times the expressive vocabulary; the child should understand much more than the child expressively displays. Emphasis should be placed on using the receptive abilities of the child to develop the expressive talents. Considerable dysfluencies still exist with the tremendous growth of vocabulary and "rules" and experimentation; be patient and model correct responses without formal correction. Keep the learning experience a happy one. Keep speech and language learning positive!

L.100 **Verbalizes three prepositions (35½ months and above)**
The child uses three different prepositions spontaneously.

Gross Motor Skill Definitions

GM.01 **Neck-righting reactions (0-2 months)**
This reaction occurs in order to keep the head in proper alignment with the trunk. When the head is turned to one side, the body follows by rolling over. This reaction eventually helps the child learn to roll and assume the hand-knee position.

GM.02 **Turns head to both sides in supine (0-2 months)**
The child tends to keep the head on the side rather than in midline at this stage. It is important that the child turn to both sides to avoid muscle tightness or flattening of the head on one side.

GM.03 **Lifts head in prone (0-2 months)**
The child should briefly raise the head off the support when lying on the stomach. The head must be in midline, not turned to the side.

GM.04 **Holds head up 45° in prone (0-2½ months)**
The child's head should come up high enough to form about a 45° angle to the child's base of support when placed in prone position. The child's face should be forward in midline.

GM.05 **Holds head to one side in prone (0-2 months)**
The child's head should naturally turn to either side when placed face down on the stomach. If the head stays in midline, there is a danger of suffocation.

GM.06 **Lifts head when held at shoulder (0-1 month)**
The child will momentarily lift the head when held upright at an adult's shoulder.

GM.07 **Holds head up 90° in prone (1-3 months)**
The child's head should come up high enough to form a 90° angle to the child's base of support when placed in prone position.

GM.08 **Holds head in same plane as body when held in ventral suspension (1½-2½ months)**
The child's head should be held at the same level as the body (the legs will hang down) when the child is held horizontally in midair.

GM.09 **Extends both legs (1½-2½ months)**
The child is now moving out of a totally flexed posture into one of more extension. Check to see if the child's legs stay almost flat on the table when lying in supine and prone.

GM.10 **Rolls side to supine (1½-2 months)**
The child can turn to lie on the back when placed in a side-lying position.

GM.11 **Kicks reciprocally (1½-2½ months)**
The child, when excited, will kick the legs up and down in an alternating fashion while lying in supine.

GM.12 **Extensor thrust inhibited (2-4 months)**
This reflex is normally present during the first two months of life, but begins to diminish by now and becomes integrated into other more functional activities. With the child lying in supine and the legs held loosely flexed to the chest, scratch the sole of one foot. If the leg extends strongly, the extensor thrust is present. If the leg stays flexed, the response is inhibited.

GM.13 **Flexor withdrawal inhibited (2-4 months)**
This reflex is normally present during the first two months of life, but begins to diminish by now and becomes integrated into other more functional activities. With the child lying in supine position, scratch the bottom of one foot with a fingernail. If the leg forcefully pulls into flexion, the flexor withdrawal reflex is present. If there is a mild removal of the foot, but not the entire leg, the reflex is inhibited.

GM.14 **Assumes withdrawal position (2-3½ months)**
When the child is lying in supine, observe to see if a position of total flexion of arms and legs is sometimes assumed.

GM.15 **Holds chest up in prone—weight on forearms (2-4 months)**
Place the child on his stomach. See if the head and chest are lifted with some weight on the forearms. This is sometimes referred to as the "puppy position."

GM.16 **Rotates and extends head (2-3 months)**
Place the child in prone position. Observe to see if the child can lift his head into extension and then turn it to both sides.

GM.17 **Rolls prone to supine (2-5 months)**
Rolling usually starts by moving the head. Then the rest of the body moves as one piece. The child should demonstrate the roll two or three times to be sure the roll was purposeful rather than accidental.

GM.18   **Holds head beyond plane of body when held in ventral suspension (2½-3½ months)**
The head should be higher than the level of the body when the child is held horizontally in midair. The hips may come up into some extension.

GM.19   **Asymmetrical tonic neck reflex inhibited (3-5 months)**
This reflex is normally present during the first three months of life, but it begins to diminish now and becomes integrated into other more functional activities. The asymmetrical tonic neck reflex (ATNR) is also called the "fencer position." When the head is turned to the right, the right arm extends and the left arm flexes. The legs are sometimes also affected; the right leg flexes and the left leg extends. When the head is turned to the left, the extremities move in the opposite direction.

GM.20   **Holds head in line with body when pulled to sitting (3-6½ months)**
Raise the child from supine to sitting by slowly pulling the child's hands. The child should lift the head and hold it steady as soon as the head leaves the floor.

GM.21   **Holds head steady in supported sitting (3-5 months)**
The head should maintain a steady position without bobbing forward or to the side when the child is held in an upright position.

GM.22   **Sits with slight support (3-5 months)**
The child should maintain a sitting position with a small amount of support at the lower back.

GM.23   **Bears some weight on legs (3-5 months)**
The child should take some weight on the legs, as opposed to letting the knees collapse into flexion when held in a standing position. Be sure the feet are flat, the legs slightly apart, and the knees slightly bent when working on activities.

GM.24   **Moro reflex inhibited (4-5 months)**
This reflex is normally present during the first four months of life, but begins to diminish by now and becomes integrated into other more functional activities. It is elicited by a sudden loud noise or a sudden change of head position. The arms extend rapidly and then circle back into flexion as if to cling. If this reflex remains strong after four months, it seriously impairs continued motor development, throwing the child off balance in upright positions.

GM.25   **Protective extension of arms and legs downward (4-6 months)**
The child is held in the air by the trunk face down. Rapid movement toward the floor should elicit arm and leg extension as the child readies protection against a fall.

GM.26   **Bears weight on hands in prone (4-6 months)**
A child placed in the prone position should lift head and chest and support weight on the hands, with elbows extended. This is sometimes called the "extended puppy position."

GM.27   **Extends head, back, and hips when held in ventral suspension (4-6 months)**
The child's head should be raised above the level of the body, the back should be held straight, and the hips should be extended at the same level as the back when the child is held in midair around the trunk.

GM.28   **Rolls supine to side (4-5½ months)**
Rolling should be accomplished by moving the head to the side. The shoulders and the hips will follow. The child should demonstrate the roll two or three times to be sure the roll was purposeful rather than accidental.

GM.29   **Sits momentarily leaning on hands (4½-5½ months)**
Place the child in a sitting position. The child's trunk naturally flexes forward. Place the child's hands on the floor or on the child's knees and let go cautiously. The child should hold this position 1 to 2 seconds.

GM.30   **Demonstrates balance reactions in prone (5-6 months)**
Place the child on a surface that can be tilted. The child's head, trunk, and extremities act to prevent a fall by moving in a direction opposite to the tilt.

GM.31   **Circular pivoting in prone (5-6 months)**
The child moves in circles on his stomach although unable to crawl forward or back.

GM.32   **Moves head actively in supported sitting (5-6 months)**
The child should be able to turn his head in all directions, maintaining good control when sitting with good trunk support.

GM.33   **Holds head erect when leaning forward (5-6 months)**
The child is placed in a sitting position and given trunk support. The child's head should be fully erect.

GM.34   **Sits independently indefinitely but may use hands (5-8 months)**
Place the child in a sitting position. Withdraw your support when the child is well balanced with or without using the hands. The child should maintain this position for at least 5 minutes.

GM.35   **Raises hips pushing with feet in supine (5-6½ months)**
Place the child in supine with hips and knees flexed and feet held flat on the floor. Encourage the child to lift his hips by patting the child's bottom.

GM.36   **Bears almost all weight on legs (5-6 months)**
Place the child in standing position. Cautiously remove your support. The child should be able to hold most of his own weight, requiring help mainly for balance.

GM.37   **Lifts head and assists when pulled to sitting (5½-7½ months)**
Place the child in the supine position. Hold the child's hands and pull him slowly up to sitting. The child should bring up his head and pull actively with his hands against your grip.

GM.38   **Rolls supine to prone (5½-7½ months)**
Rolling should be accomplished by moving the head to the side. The shoulders and hips will follow. The child should demonstrate the roll two or three times to be certain the roll was purposeful rather than accidental.

GM.39   **Body righting on body reaction (6-8 months)**
Turn the child's head to one side while in supine. The child should roll over segmentally with the shoulders turning first, followed by the pelvis, then the legs. The child should not roll stiffly as one piece.

GM.40   Demonstrates balance reactions in supine (6-7 months)
Place the child on a surface that can be tilted. The child's head, trunk, and extremities act to prevent a fall by moving in a direction opposite to the tilt.

GM.41   Protective extension of arms to side and front (6-8 months)
Place the child in a sitting position. Push the child off balance suddenly toward the front or side. The child should protect from a fall to the side by extending one arm and catching his weight. For protection from a fall to the front, the child should extend both arms and catch his weight.

GM.42   Lifts head in supine (6-8 months)
Observe the child in the supine position to see if head flexion occurs. Place a toy on the child's chest to encourage head lifting.

GM.43   Holds weight on one hand in prone (6-7½ months)
Place the child in the prone position and offer a toy. The child should be able to hold weight on one hand and take the toy with the other hand.

GM.44   Gets to sitting without assistance (6-10 months)
Observe to see if the child can sit up independently from either a prone or a supine position, using any method.

GM.45   Bears large fraction of weight on legs and bounces (6-7 months)
Place the child in supported standing and observe any bouncing movements of the legs.

GM.46   Stands, holding on (6-10½ months)
Place the child in standing position at a railing he can hold. Let go cautiously; the child should be able to hold the position. When the child is active in this position, the feet should be flat on the floor and the knees apart and slightly bent.

GM.47   Pulls to standing at furniture (6-10 months)
The child holds onto furniture and pulls up to a standing position without assistance from an adult. The child pulls to standing primarily by using the arms. The legs may straighten at the same time or one at a time.

GM.48   Brings one knee forward beside trunk in prone (6-8 months)
Lift the child's hip slightly on one side and watch for natural hip and knee flexion of the same side. The abdomen should remain flat on the floor. Observe the child in play to see if this occurs naturally.

GM.49   Crawls backwards (7-8 months)
Observe to see if the child moves backwards on the abdomen by pushing with the arms. The child may do this spontaneously while experimenting with movement. Teaching should be confined to the more functional forward movements.

GM.50   Demonstrates balance reactions on hands and knees (8-9 months)
Place the child on hands and knees on a surface that can be tilted. The child's head, trunk, and extremities act to prevent a fall by moving in a direction opposite to the tilt.

GM.51   Sits without hand support for 10 minutes (8-9 months)
Place the child in the sitting position. Give the child activities that will occupy the hands so they will not be used for support.

GM.52   **Crawls forward (8-9½ months)**
Place the child in the prone position. The child should be able to move forward on his abdomen by pulling with the arms and pushing alternately with the legs. The child may go backwards by pushing with the arms during the first attempts to crawl. Continue to present toys in front of the child. Show the child how to use the legs to crawl forward.

GM.53   **Makes stepping movements (8-10 months)**
The child spontaneously makes walking-type movements when held in standing.

GM.54   **Assumes hand-knee position (8-9 months)**
Observe to see if the child can independently assume the hand-knee position with his abdomen off the floor.

GM.55   **Demonstrates balance reactions in sitting (9-10 months)**
Place the child in sitting position on a surface that can be tilted. The child's head, trunk, and extremities act to prevent a fall by moving in a direction opposite to the tilt.

GM.56   **Protective extension of arms to back (9-11 months)**
Place the child in sitting position. Push the child suddenly backwards. The child should protect from a fall by catching his weight on one arm.

GM.57   **Goes from sitting to prone (9-10 months)**
Place the child in sitting position. Observe to see if the child can independently lower onto the floor into prone.

GM.58   **Lowers to sitting from furniture (9-10 months)**
Place the child in standing position by a piece of furniture. Remove your support and see if the child can independently lower safely into a sitting position. Compared to a fall, this is a slower and more controlled movement.

GM.59   **Creeps on hands and knees (9-11 months)**
The child moves forward on hands and knees with his abdomen off the ground. The child uses a reciprocal pattern moving opposite hands and knees: right hand, left knee, left hand, right knee.

GM.60   **Stands momentarily (9½-11 months)**
Place the child in a standing position. Hold the child from behind and gradually decrease your support until the child briefly stands alone.

GM.61   **Walks holding on to furniture (9½-13 months)**
The child is unsupported by an adult and takes a few steps, holding the furniture for support.

GM.62   **Extends head, back, hips, and legs in ventral suspension (10-11 months)**
The child's head, back, hips, and legs are held extended when the child is held in midair around the trunk.

GM.63   **Pivots in sitting—twists to pick up objects (10-11 months)**
The child can move in a circle in a sitting position.

GM.64   **Creeps on hands and feet (10-12 months)**
The child has both feet and both hands on the floor with arms and legs extended. The child "walks" forward in this position. This is also known as "plantigrade creeping" or "bear walking."

GM.65 **Walks with both hands held (10-12 months)**
The child can walk forward three or four steps when an adult holds both of the child's hands.

GM.66 **Stoops and recovers (10½-14 months)**
The child bends down from a standing position and regains standing without need for support.

GM.67 **Stands by lifting one foot (11-12 months)**
The child rises to a standing position by pulling to kneeling, lifting one foot, and finally standing up. The child will be holding onto something for support.

GM.68 **Stands a few seconds (11-13 months)**
Place the child in a standing position. Remove your support. The child should remain standing 2 to 3 seconds.

GM.69 **Assumes and maintains kneeling (11-13 months)**
In kneeling, full body weight is supported on the knees. (The child should not sit on the feet; the hips should be extended.) Observe to see if the child can move from a sitting to a kneeling position without using any support.

GM.70 **Walks with one hand held (11-13 months)**
The child walks five to six steps while an adult holds one hand.

GM.71 **Stands alone well (11½-14 months)**
Place the child in a standing position and remove support. The child should remain standing at least 10 seconds.

GM.72 **Walks alone two to three steps (11½-13½ months)**
The child walks independently without support, using two to three unsteady steps.

GM.73 **Demonstrates balance reactions in kneeling (12-15 months)**
Place the child in kneeling position on a surface that can be tilted. (The child should not sit on the feet; the hips should be extended.) The child's head, trunk, and extremities act to keep the body upright by moving in a direction opposite to the tilt.

GM.74 **Falls by sitting (12-14 months)**
Place the child in a standing position. The child moves to the floor by letting go of support and sitting down.

GM.75 **Stands from supine by turning on all fours (12½-15 months)**
The child should be able to assume a hands-feet position, then rise to a standing position without support.

GM.76 **Walks backwards (12½-21 months)**
The child independently walks in a backward direction for 6 feet without support.

GM.77 **Throws ball underhand in sitting (13-16 months)**
The child throws the ball forward by positioning the arm down at the side with the palm of the hand up.

GM.78   **Creeps or hitches upstairs (13½-15 months)**
Creeping means moving on hands and knees (some children may use hands and feet). Hitching means moving while in a sitting position.

GM.79   **Walks without support (13-15 months)**
The child walks most of the time for long distances and seldom falls down. No support is necessary. (Some children quite normally start to walk as early as 9 months or as late as 18 months.)

GM.80   **Walks sideways (14-15 months)**
The child moves sideways without support; the feet are not expected to cross over.

GM.81   **Runs—hurried walk (14-18 months)**
The child is technically walking rapidly, one foot on the ground at all times. The body is held stiffly upright and the eyes are fixed on the ground.

GM.82   **Bends over and looks through legs (14½-15½ months)**
The child's knees are slightly bent while looking backwards between the legs.

GM.83   **Demonstrates balance reactions in standing (15-18 months)**
Place the child in a standing position on a surface that can be tilted. The child's head, trunk, and extremities act to prevent a fall by moving in a direction opposite to the tilt.

GM.84   **Walks into large ball while trying to kick it (15-18 months)**
The child kicks a ball by walking toward the ball and moving it forward by bumping a leg or the body into it.

GM.85   **Throws ball forward (15-18 months)**
The child is in standing position and throws the ball in any manner, overhand or underhand.

GM.86   **Walks with assistance on 8-inch board (15-17 months)**
The child walks at least 3 feet on an 8-inch-wide plank raised 1 to 2 inches from the floor with someone holding the child's hand.

GM.87   **Pulls toy behind while walking (15-18 months)**
The child walks independently and holds the string of a pull toy. (Children learn to push before they learn to pull.)

GM.88   **Throws ball overhand landing within 3 feet of target (16-22 months)**
The child is in standing position and throws by bringing the hand up beside the head. The ball should travel 3 feet and land within 3 feet of the target.

GM.89   **Stands on one foot with help (16-17 months)**
The child can lift one foot and balance on the other when supported.

GM.90   **Walks upstairs with one hand held (17-19 months)**
The child walks upstairs by placing one foot up and then moving the other foot onto the same step.

GM.91   **Carries large toy while walking (17-18½ months)**
The child carries a large object with one or both hands without assistance.

GM.92 **Pushes and pulls large toys or boxes around the floor (17-18½ months)**
The child performs this activity without assistance.

GM.93 **Walks independently on 8-inch board (17½-19½ months)**
The board is 8 inches wide, 6 feet long, and 1 to 2 inches off the floor.
The child walks the entire length without assistance.

GM.94 **Tries to stand on 2-inch balance beam (17½-18½ months)**
The board is 2 inches wide, 6 to 8 feet long, well supported on each end,
and 3 to 4 inches off the ground. Demonstrate standing on the balance
beam. Ask the child to try. The child should step up on it with only one
foot, without holding onto any support.

GM.95 **Backs into small chair or slides sideways (17½-19 months)**
Use a child-size chair. The child approaches the chair from the front
or the side and sits on it without assistance.

GM.96 **Kicks ball forward (18-24½ months)**
The child in standing position kicks a ball with one foot without
assistance.

GM.97 **Throws ball into a box (18-20 months)**
The child in standing position throws a ball into a box placed one
foot away.

GM.98 **Moves on ride-on toys without pedals (18-24 months)**
The child can propel a wheeled vehicle forward without assistance.

GM.99 **Runs fairly well (18-24 months)**
"Running" means neither foot is touching the ground during one
phase of the movement. The child is well balanced and arms and legs
alternate smoothly.

GM.100 **Climbs forward on adult chair, turns around, and sits (18-21 months)**
The child does this without assistance.

GM.101 **Walks downstairs with one hand held (19-21 months)**
The child walks downstairs by placing one foot down and then
moving the other foot on the same step. (Alternating feet is a more
advanced skill.)

GM.102 **Picks up toy from floor without falling (19-24 months)**
The child can squat down or bend over and pick up a toy and maintain
sufficient balance to stand up again.

GM.103 **Squats in play (20-21 months)**
The child has sufficient balance to play on the floor for several minutes
in a squatting position.

GM.104 **Stands from supine by rolling to side (20-22 months)**
From a supine position, the child rolls to the side and sits up, using the
hands for support. The child then stands up without assistance or
holding onto a support.

GM.105 **Walks a few steps with one foot on 2-inch balance beam
(20½-21½ months)**
The child walks with one foot on the balance beam. The other foot is on
the floor. The child receives no assistance.

GM.106 Walks upstairs holding rail, both feet on step (22-24 months)
The child's foot movements do not yet alternate. The child receives no adult assistance.

GM.107 Jumps in place both feet (22-30 months)
The child jumps up with both feet lifting off the ground at the same time.

GM.108 Goes up and down slide (23-26 months)
The child climbs a ladder and goes down the slide independently.

GM.109 Stands on tiptoes (23-25½ months)
The child comes up on the toes either spontaneously or on request.

GM.110 Walks with legs closer together (23-25 months)
The child previously walked with legs apart (abducted). The child can now balance better and bring the legs closer together (adducted) for a smoother gait.

GM.111 Catches a large ball (24-26 months)
The child in standing position catches a ball at least 12 inches in diameter.

GM.112 Rides tricycle (24-30 months)
The child moves forward on a tricycle, sometimes using the pedals, sometimes with feet on the ground. The child pushes the tricycle with feet on the ground to turn corners.

GM.113 Imitates simple bilateral movements of limbs, head, and trunk (24-36 months)
The child should be able to imitate movements he sees another make: up and down, front to back, and sideways. The arms should be able to cross in front of the body.

GM.114 Walks upstairs alone—both feet on step (24-25½ months)
The child walks upstairs without assistance from an adult or a railing. The foot movements do not alternate.

GM.115 Walks downstairs holding rail—both feet on step (24-26 months)
The child's foot movements do not alternate. The child receives no adult assistance.

GM.116 Jumps a distance of 8 to 14 inches (24-30 months)
The child jumps forward with both feet lifting off the floor at the same time and landing at the same time.

GM.117 Jumps from bottom step (24-26½ months)
The child jumps without adult assistance from a 7-inch step using both feet at the same time.

GM.118 Runs; stops without holding and avoids obstacles (24-30 months)
The child performs this activity independently and without falling.

GM.119 Walks on line in general direction (24-26 months)
Draw a 10-foot line on the floor. Demonstrate by walking on it. Ask the child to imitate you. The child should walk in the same direction as the line, but need not keep the feet on the line.

GM.120 **Walks between parallel lines 8 inches apart (24-30 months)**
Place two 10-foot lines on the floor 8 inches apart. Demonstrate by walking between the lines. Ask the child to imitate you. The child should walk the entire distance.

GM.121 **Stands on 2-inch balance beam with both feet (24½-26 months)**
Demonstrate by standing on the balance beam. Ask the child to imitate you. The child should stand on the beam with both feet for 2 or 3 seconds.

GM.122 **Imitates one foot standing (24-30 months)**
The adult demonstrates the one-foot-standing position. The child should imitate without assistance.

GM.123 **Walks downstairs alone—both feet on step (25½-27 months)**
The child walks downstairs without assistance from an adult or a railing. The foot movements, however, do not alternate.

GM.124 **Walks on tiptoes a few steps (25½-30 months)**
The child stands on tiptoes without assistance and takes two to three steps forward. (The child's knees and hips should be straight.)

GM.125 **Jumps backwards (27-29 months)**
The child jumps backwards with both feet lifting off the floor at the same time and landing at the same time.

GM.126 **Attempts step on 2-inch balance beam (27½-28½ months)**
Demonstrate by walking on the balance beam. Ask the child to imitate you. The child should have both feet on the beam and should attempt to walk forward.

GM.127 **Walks backward 10 feet (28-29½ months)**
The child does this without assistance.

GM.128 **Jumps sidewards (29-32 months)**
The child jumps sidewards with both feet lifting off the floor at the same time and landing at the same time.

GM.129 **Jumps on trampoline with adult holding hands (29-31 months)**
The child's feet should lift off the trampoline surface at the same time.

GM.130 **Alternates steps part way on 2-inch balance beam (30-32 months)**
The child should take at least two alternating steps on the balance beam.

GM.131 **Walks upstairs alternating feet (30-34 months)**
The child walks up regular-size stairs without using a railing or the assistance of an adult. One foot is placed on each step alternating with the other foot.

GM.132 **Jumps over string 2 to 8 inches high (30-36 months)**
The child jumps with both feet together. The child should be able to jump 2 inches high by the age of 30 months and about 8 inches high by the age of 36 months.

GM.133 **Hops on one foot (30-36 months)**
The child hops on one foot and hops forward.

GM.134   **Jumps a distance of 14 to 24 inches (30-34½ months)**
See GM.116.

GM.135   **Stands from supine using a sit-up (30-33 months)**
From a supine position, the child sits up by curling the body forward and using the hands for support. The child stands up without assistance or holding onto a support.

GM.136   **Stands on one foot 1 to 5 seconds (30-36 months)**
A child holds this position for 1 to 3 seconds without help. The time is increased to 5 seconds by the age of 36 months.

GM.137   **Walks on tiptoes 10 feet (30-36 months)**
The child does this without assistance. Hips and knees should be straight.

GM.138   **Keeps feet on line for 10 feet (30-32 months)**
The child walks on a 10-foot-long line without stepping off at all.

GM.139   **Uses pedals on tricycle alternately (32-36 months)**
The child propels and steers a tricycle without assistance.

GM.140   **Walks downstairs alternating feet (34 months and above)**
The child walks down regular-size stairs without using a railing or the assistance of an adult. One foot is placed on each step alternating with the other foot.

GM.141   **Climbs jungle gyms and ladders (34½-36 months)**
Playing on jungle gyms encourages total body coordination, development of an understanding of body positions in space, muscle strengthening, and the understanding of spatial relationships.

GM.142   **Catches an 8-inch ball (35 months and above)**
The child in standing position catches a ball of at least 8 inches in diameter.

GM.143   **Jumps a distance of 24 to 34 inches (34½-36 months)**
See GM.116.

GM.144   **Avoids obstacles in path (34½-36 months)**
The child does not fall or bump into obstacles that are in the child's way.

GM.145   **Runs on toes (34½-36 months)**
The child runs on toes without assistance in a smooth, easy manner.

GM.146   **Makes sharp turns around corners when running (34½-36 months)**
The child turns easily when running without losing balance or falling down.

Fine Motor Skill Definitions

FM.01 **Regards colorful object momentarily (0-1 months)**
The child regards, glances, or looks at a colorful object for one second.

FM.02 **Moves arms symmetrically (0-2 months)**
The child moves the arms together with random movements to the sides. The whole body may respond to a stimulus.

FM.03 **Regards colorful object for few seconds (½-2½ months)**
The child looks at a colorful object for 4 to 5 seconds.

FM.04 **Follows with eyes moving person while in supine (½-1½ months)**
The child follows a moving person with the eyes while lying on his back. The child may stop doing this after three to four months of age.

FM.05 **Stares and gazes (1-2 months)**
The child looks at an object or person for a prolonged period of time.

FM.06 **Follows with eyes to midline (1-3 months)**
The child visually tracks an object from the side he is facing to the midline.

FM.07 **Brings hands to midline in supine (1-3½ months)**
The child brings the hands to the middle of his body while lying on his back.

FM.08 **Activates arms on sight of toy (1-3 months)**
The child moves his arms about when seeing a toy.

FM.09 **Blinks at sudden visual stimulus (2-3 months)**
The child blinks when an object is suddenly brought close to his eyes.

FM.10 **Follows with eyes past midline (2-3 months)**
The child visually tracks an object past the midline.

FM.11 **Follows with eyes downward (2-3 months)**
The child visually tracks an object downward, but often inconsistently.

FM.12 **Indwelling thumb no longer present (2-3 months)**
The child's thumb is no longer held flexed in his hand.

FM.13 **Grasps toy actively (2-4 months)**
The child maintains grasp of an object placed near or in his hand.

FM.14 **Looks from one object to another (2½-3½ months)**
The child looks briefly at one object then at another object when both are held within his visual field.

FM.15 **Keeps hands open 50% of the time (2½-3½ months)**
The child's hands are open and not fisted about half the time.

FM.16 **Reaches toward toy without grasping (2½-4½ months)**
This is a beginning reach in which the arms move generally toward a visual stimulus.

FM.17 **Follows with eyes 180° (3-5 months)**
The child visually tracks an object 180°.

FM.18 **Follows with eyes, moving object in supported sitting (3-4½ months)**
The child visually tracks a moving object while held in a sitting position or placed in a seat.

FM.19 **Follows with eyes upward (3-4 months)**
The child visually tracks an object upward.

FM.20 **Grasp reflex inhibited (3-4 months)**
The child's grasp reflex is a response that occurs when pressure or stimulation is applied to the palm; the fingers close into a tight grasp. This reflex begins to diminish from about three months of age.

FM.21 **Clasps hands (3½-5 months)**
The child brings hands to midline and grasps them.

FM.22 **Uses ulnar palmar grasp (3½-4½ months)**
The child grasps an object placed in his hand. The child uses an ulnar palmar grasp (grasps the object with the ring finger and little finger against his palm).

FM.23 **Looks with head in midline (4-5 months)**
The child prefers to look at an object in supine with his head usually held at midline. The limbs are symmetrical in posture and the asymmetrical tonic neck reflex is inhibited.

FM.24 **Follows with eyes without head movement (4-6 months)**
The child visually tracks an object within his visual field without turning his head.

FM.25 **Keeps hands open most of the time (4-8 months)**
The child's hands are relaxed and remain open most of the time.

FM.26 **Reaches for object bilaterally (4-5 months)**
The child uses both hands to reach for an object.

FM.27 **Reaches for toy followed by momentary grasp (4-5 months)**
The child reaches and maintains grasp of an object momentarily.

FM.28 **Uses palmar grasp (4-5 months)**
The child grasps an object against the palm without use of his thumb.

FM.29 **Reaches and grasps object (4½-5½ months)**
The child reaches and maintains grasp of an object.

FM.30 **Uses radial palmar grasp (4½-6 months)**
The child uses a radial palmar grasp (grasps an object with thumb, index, and middle fingers against his palm).

FM.31 **Regards tiny object (4½-5½ months)**
The child looks at an object about the size of a pellet or raisin.

FM.32 **Looks at distant objects (5-6 months)**
The child shows visual interest in objects at a distance.

FM.33 **Drops object (5-6 months)**
The child drops an object rather than purposefully releasing it.

FM.34 **Recovers object (5-6 months)**
The child picks up an object after dropping it if the object is within easy reach.

FM.35 **Retains small object in each hand (5-6 months)**
The child holds a small object in each hand simultaneously for a short period of time.

FM.36 **Watches adult scribble (5½-7 months)**
The child watches while an adult scribbles on paper.

FM.37 **Reaches for object unilaterally (5½-7 months)**
The child reaches for an object with one arm. Unilateral reaching may occur with either arm at this age.

FM.38 **Transfers object (5½-7 months)**
The child grasps an object with one hand, then transfers the object to the other hand.

FM.39 **Bangs object on table (5½-7 months)**
The child bangs an object on the table or any hard surface during play.

FM.40 **Attempts to secure tiny object (5½-7 months)**
The child makes attempts to grasp a pellet-sized object; the attempts are not necessarily successful.

FM.41 **Manipulates toy actively with wrist movements (6-8 months)**
The child grasps, explores, and manipulates a toy with active rotary wrist movements.

FM.42 **Reaches and grasps object with extended elbow (7-8½ months)**
The child reaches directly with extended elbow and grasps an object.

FM.43 **Uses radial digital grasp (7-9 months)**
The child grasps an object with the thumb, index, and middle fingers without use of his palm.

FM.44 **Rakes tiny object (7-8 months)**
The child grasps at a pellet-sized object (such as a raisin) with a raking motion. The child flexes the fingers toward the palm without using his thumb.

FM.45 **Uses inferior pincer grasp (7½-10 months)**
The child grasps a small object with his index finger and thumb. The thumb is positioned at the lateral or lower part of the index finger.

FM.46 **Bangs two cubes held in hands (8½-10 months)**
The child grasps a 1-inch cube in each hand and hits them together.

FM.47 **Removes pegs from peg board (8½-10 months)**
The child removes previously placed pegs from the peg board.

FM.48 **Takes objects out of container (9-11 months)**
The child empties or removes objects from a container by dumping it over or by taking out the objects one by one.

FM.49 **Extends wrist (9-10 months)**
The child extends the wrist during play or during the manipulation of objects.

FM.50 **Releases object voluntarily (9-11 months)**
The child releases an object in a controlled, purposeful, and intentional manner.

FM.51 **Pokes with index finger (9-12 months)**
The child uses his index finger to poke or feel objects.

FM.52 **Uses neat pincer grasp (10-12 months)**
The child grasps a tiny object the size of a raisin with precise thumb and index finger opposition.

FM.53 **Tries to imitate scribble (10½-12 months)**
The child holds the crayon and makes contact with the paper in imitation but does not necessarily make marks on the paper.

FM.54 **Uses both hands freely; may show preference for one (11-13 months)**
The child uses either or both hands during play. The child may show a preference for one hand; do not insist upon one hand over the other. Do not worry if there is no preference sometimes.

FM.55 **Grasps crayon adaptively (11-12 months)**
The child grasps the crayon and positions one end of the crayon toward the paper.

FM.56 **Puts objects into container (11-12 months)**
The child puts objects or toys into a large container.

FM.57 **Supinates forearm (11-12 months)**
The child actively supinates the forearm (turns the forearm over so the palm is facing up). The child reaches and grasps for an object with forearm in midsupination (the forearm is positioned with the thumb side of the hand up).

FM.58 **Places one block on top of another without balancing (11-12 months)**
The child puts one block on top of another without releasing the second block, or without accurately balancing the second block on the first (as in a tower). (A block is about 1½-inches square, while a cube is 1-inch square.)

FM.59 **Marks paper with crayon (12-13 months)**
The child makes contact with the crayon on the paper and makes visible marks on the paper.

FM.60 **Puts three or more objects into container (12-13 months)**
The child consecutively puts three or more objects or cubes into a container the size of a cup or bowl. The child may need some encouragement to complete the task.

FM.61 **Builds tower using two cubes (12-16 months)**
The child places one 1-inch cube on top of another and releases the top cube. The cube is balanced on top of the other cube to build a tower of two cubes.

FM.62 **Places one round peg in pegboard (12-15 months)**
The child puts at least one round peg (¾-inch in diameter) in the peg board.

FM.63 **Points with index finger (12-16 months)**

FM.64 **Inverts small container to obtain tiny object after demonstration (12½-18 months)**
Give the child a small container with a tiny object in it to see if the child will spontaneously invert the container to obtain the object. The opening of the container should be about ⅝ to ¾-inch so the child cannot put a hand into it.

FM.65 **Scribbles spontaneously (13-18 months)**
The child grasps a crayon and scribbles spontaneously without assistance.

FM.66 **Inverts small container spontaneously to obtain tiny object (13½-19 months)**
The child turns the container over spontaneously to obtain the tiny object without a demonstration. The opening of the container should be about ⅝-inch to ¾-inch in diameter so the child cannot put a hand into it.

FM.67 **Puts many objects into container without removing any (14-15 months)**
The child puts at least eight objects into a container without removing any in the process.

FM.68 **Uses both hands in midline; one holds, other manipulates (16-18 months)**
The child holds the object or toy at midline. One hand holds the toy while the other manipulates, explores, or feels the toy.

FM.69 **Builds tower using three cubes (16-18 months)**
The child balances three 1-inch cubes, one on top of the other.

FM.70 **Places six round pegs in peg board (16-19 months)**
The child places at least six round pegs (¾-inch in diameter) in the peg board without removing any in the process. Urge the child to keep going and "put them all in."

FM.71 **Imitates vertical stroke (18-24 months)**
The child watches while you draw a vertical stroke and imitates it with your vertical stroke in view. The child's stroke is acceptable if the line is drawn within 30°.

FM.72 **Builds tower using four cubes (18-22 months)**
See FM.61.

FM.73 **Imitates circular scribble (20-24 months)**
The child observes while you scribble continuous circles and then imitates with your scribble in view.

FM.74 **Strings one 1-inch bead (20-23 months)**
The child strings at least one 1-inch bead with a heavy corded string.

FM.75   **Imitates horizontal stroke (21-24 months)**
The child observes while you make a horizontal stroke and then imitates with your horizontal stroke in view.

FM.76   **Folds paper imitatively, not precisely (21-24 months)**
The child folds paper over once in imitation; the fold is not exact or precise.

FM.77   **Builds tower using six cubes (22-24 months)**
See FM.61.

FM.78   **Holds crayon with thumb and fingers (23-25 months)**
The child holds a crayon with thumb and fingers rather than in a fisted hand.

FM.79   **Imitates three-block train using cubes (23-26 months)**
The child watches you make a train using three cubes (1-inch square) and successfully aligns them horizontally with your model in view.

FM.80   **Strings three 1-inch beads (23-25 months)**
See FM.74.

FM.81   **Snips with scissors (23-25 months)**
The child cuts with scissors, taking one snip at a time rather than doing continuous cutting.

FM.82   **Imitates a cross (24-36 months)**
The child watches you draw a cross and imitates it with your cross in view.

FM.83   **Makes first designs or spontaneous forms (24-35 months)**
The child begins to make definite and controlled strokes that appear to be spontaneous designs or forms. The child is beginning to manipulate the crayon with the thumb and fingers and therefore make smaller, more controlled forms or marks.

FM.84   **Puts tiny objects into small container (24-30 months)**
The child puts a tiny object such as a pellet or raisin into a small bottle with a ⅝- to ¾-inch opening.

FM.85   **Folds paper in half (24-30 months)**
The child folds a piece of paper in half and creases it without crumpling the paper.

FM.86   **Copies a circle (25-36 months)**
The child copies or reproduces a circle from a model without observing a demonstration.

FM.87   **Builds a tower using eight cubes (28-31 months)**
The child successfully builds a tower of at least eight cubes.

FM.88   **Snips on line using scissors (28-35 months)**
The child cuts with one snipping movement at a time on a drawn line.

FM.89   **Holds pencil with thumb and finger; adult-like grasp (29-31 months)**
The child holds a pencil with thumb and fingers in an adult-like grasp.

FM.90   **Places six square pegs in peg board (29-31 months)**
The child places at least six square pegs (about ⅝-inch) in the peg board.

FM.91   **Imitates three-block bridge using cubes (31 months and above)**
Using three cubes (1-inch square), the child builds a three-block bridge after a demonstration and with the model in view.

FM.92   **Builds tower using nine cubes (32-36 months)**
The child builds a tower using nine cubes (1-inch square).

FM.93   **Strings ½-inch beads (33½ months and above)**
See FM.80.

Self-Help Skill Definitions

SH.01   **Opens and closes mouth in response to food stimulus (0-1 month)**
The child opens and closes the mouth in response to the food stimulus when the cheek or the area around the mouth is touched with the nipple.

SH.02   **Coordinates sucking, swallowing, and breathing (1-5 months)**
The child sucks a number of times in succession, rests, sucks a number of times again, and rests, developing a regular pattern of sucking, swallowing, and breathing while feeding at the breast or bottle.

SH.03   **Sleeps nights for 4- to 10-hour intervals (1-3 months)**
The child's sleep needs vary widely during the first year, but each child will take as much sleep as needed if the environment provides the opportunity. Sleep patterns may change from day to day. Nothing needs to be done about this.

SH.04   **Stays awake for longer periods without crying, usually in p.m. (1-3 months)**

SH.05   **Naps frequently (1-3 months)**
The child will take as much sleep as needed. Sleep patterns can vary widely.

SH.06   **Suck-and-swallow reflex inhibited (2-5 months)**
The child automatically closes lips around the nipple and sucks several times before swallowing. This is the suck-and-swallow reflex seen from birth to about 2 months. From about 2 months on, the child develops a more voluntary sucking-and-swallowing pattern.

SH.07   **Brings hand to mouth (2-4 months)**
The child brings hand to mouth for oral stimulation and exploration.

SH.08   **Swallows strained or pureed foods (3-6 months)**
The child swallows strained foods fed with a spoon.

SH.09   **Brings hand to mouth with toy or object (3-5 months)**

SH.10   **Recognizes bottle visually (3½-4½ months)**
The child shows visual recognition of the bottle or breast by facial or body expression, by an open mouth, or by sucking motions.

SH.11   **Uses tongue to move food in mouth (4-8½ months)**
The child uses the tongue to move food before swallowing.

SH.12   **Rooting reflex inhibited (4-6 months)**
The rooting reflex is seen for about the first four months, and may continue for up to eight months of age before it completely diminishes. This reflex is exhibited when the child's cheek or area around the mouth is touched and he turns his head toward the stimulus with open mouth, as if in search of food.

SH.13   **Pats bottle (4-5 months)**
The child periodically pats the bottle while it is held for him during feeding.

SH.14   **Sleeps nights 10 to 12 hours with night awakening (4-8 months)**
The child sleeps 10 to 12 hours at night and awakens at least once. The child who has been sleeping through the night may begin to awaken to play or perhaps to fuss a little. This at times may be related to teething, or it may be just a desire to have fun.

SH.15   **Naps two or three times each day, 1 to 4 hours (4-8 months)**
The child takes two to three naps during the day of one to four hours duration, varying according to his needs.

SH.16   **Places both hands on bottle (4½-5½ months)**
The child places both hands on the bottle while the bottle is held for him during feeding.

SH.17   **Mouths and gums solid foods (5-8 months)**
The child mouths and gums solid foods, such as a teething biscuit or graham cracker.

SH.18   **Holds own bottle (5½-9 months)**

SH.19   **Bites food voluntarily (6-8 months)**
The child begins to develop voluntary biting, a controlled bite with vertical jaw movement. The bite reflex, the strong closure of the jaw when the gum or teeth is stimulated, is diminished.

SH.20   **Drinks from cup held by another (6-12 months)**

SH.21   **Feeds self a cracker (6½-8½ months)**
The child holds and self-feeds a cracker, hard toast, or cookie.

SH.22   **Bites and chews toys (7-8 months)**
The child mouths, bites, and chews toys for sensory exploration.

SH.23   **Drools less except when teething (7-12 months)**
The child drools less except when teething or when concentrating on or attempting a particular gross or fine motor task.

SH.24   **Chews food with munching pattern (8-13½ months)**
The child begins to chew; jaw movements are on the vertical plane (up and down) with biting or munching movements.

SH.25 **Finger feeds self (9-12 months)**
The child self-feeds, using hands or fingers.

SH.26 **Holds spoon (9-12 months)**
The child holds or grasps a spoon in fisted hand.

SH.27 **Sleeps nights 12 to 14 hours (9-12 months)**
The child's sleep pattern is usually fairly regular by now. The child sleeps through the night for about 12 to 14 hours. Allow opportunity for the child to get as much sleep as needed.

SH.28 **Naps once or twice each day 1 to 4 hours; may refuse morning nap (9-12 months)**
The child begins to give up the morning nap but gets desperately tired. It may help to move lunch time to as early as 11 a.m., then put the child down for an early afternoon nap. The nap may be from one to four hours in duration.

SH.29 **Cooperates with dressing by extending arm or leg (10½-12 months)**
The child voluntarily moves arms or legs while being dressed. This item does not refer to negative behavior that may cause the child to refuse to cooperate with dressing.

SH.30 **May refuse foods; appetite decreases (12-18 months)**
The child begins to refuse food. Refusing food is a behavior that may continue throughout the toddler stage. The behavior may be inconsistent. At some time the child may eat meals then resume again the behavior of refusing foods. This is normal behavior for the toddler. This is a growth stage in which one good meal or the equivalent of one good meal from the three meals of the day is adequate. Food dislikes and inconsistency of appetite may continue throughout toddlerhood.

SH.31 **Brings spoon to mouth; turns spoon over (12-15 months)**
The child usually grasps the spoon with a fisted hand, brings the spoon to mouth, and licks it, but has difficulty preventing the spoon from turning over.

SH.32 **Holds and drinks from cup with some spilling (12-18 months)**
The child holds and drinks from a child's cup with some spilling, especially when drinking or putting the cup down on the table.

SH.33 **Holds cup handle (12-15½ months)**
The child develops better control of his hands and can hold the handle or handles of a cup with his fingers.

SH.34 **Shows bladder and bowel control pattern (12-18 months)**
The child's frequency of urination will decrease and he will begin to show some regularity by being dry for about one- to two-hour intervals. Bowel movements may occur after a meal. A pattern of regularity and control is forming. At this point the child's pattern of elimination is still automatic and not yet voluntary.

SH.35 **Indicates discomfort over soiled pants verbally or by gesture (12-18 months)**
Awareness of soiling and wetting is shown when the child indicates discomfort over soiled pants. Watch for signs such as the child hiding his face, showing you his wet pants, or trying to take them off. He may

be indicating also by stopping during an activity, grimacing, straining, touching his genitals, or squatting. The child may touch his wet diaper, may hear the sound of urination, or look down while making a puddle. The child may say, "shi-shi," "wee-wee," or "do-do."

SH.36 Sleeps nights 10 to 12 hours (13-18 months)
The child sleeps through the night for about 10 to 12 hours.

SH.37 Naps once in afternoon 1 to 3 hours (13-18 months)
The child takes one nap a day, usually in the afternoon, for about one to three hours.

SH.38 Scoops food, feeds self with spoon with some spilling (15-24 months)

SH.39 Removes socks (15-18 months)
The child pulls his socks off.

SH.40 Removes hat (15-16½ months)
The child takes his hat off.

SH.41 Places hat on head (16½-18½ months)

SH.42 Gives empty dish to adult (18-19 months)
The child hands the empty dish to the adult after finishing eating or to request more food. He will usually first give the empty dish to a familiar person or whoever feeds him. If the adult is not available, the child might drop the dish on the floor.

SH.43 Distinguishes between edible and inedible objects (18-23 months)
The child knows what can be eaten. It is normal for a child at this age to want to taste objects. It is important to keep hazardous and poisonous objects away from the child.

SH.44 Chews completely with rotary jaw movements (18-24 months)
The child chews food well with rotary jaw movements. The tongue moves the food in the mouth from side to side and front to back. The child can chew meat and other tough foods.

SH.45 Gives up bottle (18-24 months)
The child gives up drinking from the bottle. He may want or ask for the bottle until age three or four. Very gradual weaning to perhaps one bottle a day may be necessary. Breast feeding should continue as long as mother and child are able to or want to continue.

SH.46 Removes shoes when laces undone (18-24 months)
The child takes shoes off alone. Shoes should be very easy to remove with laces loosened or removed, ready to slip off.

SH.47 Unzips, zips large zipper (18-21 months)

SH.48 Sits on potty chair or on adaptive seat on toilet with assistance (18-24 months)
The child sits on the potty chair or adaptive seat on a regular toilet when placed or assisted by an adult. The child may or may not be successful each time on the potty.

SH.49   May be toilet-regulated by adult (18-24 months)
The child can be considered toilet-regulated even if he does not yet indicate his need to use the toilet, but can be "caught" in time by an adult.

SH.50   Plays with food (19-23 months)
A child normally plays with food. If food play becomes a problem (such as throwing or dumping), teach the child that he cannot play with the food in such a way. If food play continues, casually end the meal. Be consistent with your routine.

SH.51   Washes and dries hands partially (19-24 months)
The child washes and dries hands partially, requiring assistance to complete the job.

SH.52   Anticipates need to eliminate; uses same word for both functions (19-24 months)
The child shows awareness of wanting to urinate or have a bowel movement, and may use the same word for both urination and bowel movement.

SH.53   Delays sleeping by demanding things (19-31 months)
The child refuses to sleep and fusses or demands things to delay bedtime.

SH.54   Holds small cup in one hand (20-30 months)
The child holds a small cup with or without a handle in one hand and drinks from it with minimal spilling.

SH.55   Opens door by turning knob (21-23 months)

SH.56   Helps with simple household tasks (21-23 months)
The child has fun helping you and doing something "adult." Do not expect a perfect job or insist that the child do or complete the tasks. It may sometimes take you longer to finish your tasks or perhaps it will double your duties, but do not ignore or discourage the child's efforts. Much learning takes place for the child. Praise all attempts.

SH.57   Puts shoes on with assistance (21-30 months)
The child needs assistance in putting shoes on. The amount of assistance the child may need will depend on the type of shoes worn. Shoes with fastenings (buckles, laces) or special shoes with high tops or shoes with braces may require more assistance. The child will need help in putting shoes on the correct feet.

SH.58   May have definite food preferences (23-25 months)
The child may have definite food preferences at this age. The child may crave one food (such as bananas) and eat it to the exclusion of everything else. This is normal, although not all children do this. Some children under two-and-a-half years old have been found to have some fruit or vegetable as a preferred food. After that age, meats gradually become favorites.

SH.59   Unwraps food (23-25 months)
The child removes the wrapper from the food and eats the food.

SH.60 Understands and stays away from common dangers (stairs, glass, strange animals) (24-30 months)

SH.61 Handles fragile items carefully (24-26 months)
The child can handle fragile items carefully and does not throw or break them.

SH.62 Helps put things away (24-29½ months)

SH.63 Holds spoon in fingers, palm up (24-30 months)
The child holds the spoon in the fingers or between thumb and index and middle fingers with forearm supination (palm up) in adult-like fashion. The child should have voluntary supination in order to hold the spoon in this manner. The child may still occasionally grasp the spoon in a fisted hand with forearm pronation (palm down).

SH.64 Pulls down pants with assistance (24-26 months)
The child pulls down pants over the hips with assistance.

SH.65 Unbuttons large buttons (24-25 months)
The child unbuttons large flat round buttons at least 1 inch in diameter.

SH.66 Washes hands (24-30 months)
The child washes hands alone, but may need a little help to do a thorough job.

SH.67 Brushes teeth with assistance (24 months and above)
The child begins to brush teeth but requires assistance to brush thoroughly.

SH.68 Anticipates need to eliminate in time (24-36 months)
The child may indicate need to eliminate by gesture, or signal, or verbally, in time to use the toilet.

SH.69 Uses toilet with assistance; has daytime control (24-36 months)
The child uses the toilet during the day. The child may still have occasional accidents, and may need reminding and assistance with clothing and wiping.

SH.70 Undresses with assistance (26-32 months)
The child undresses with physical and verbal help, and also needs help undoing fastenings.

SH.71 Pulls up pants with assistance (26-28 months)
The child pulls up pants over the hips with assistance.

SH.72 Dresses self with assistance (28-32 months)

SH.73 Wipes nose with assistance (29-31 months)
The child wipes the nose with some help, but may not be able to blow the nose yet.

SH.74 May reject many foods (29½-31½ months)
The child may want only certain kinds of foods or will eat only one kind of food for several days in succession. The child's appetite may decrease according to the level of activity or motor development. The child may eat only one good meal a day. This is all right as long as the child is not

ill. Part of the reason for these demands is increased cognitive awareness and memory. The child can remember a food he likes and asks for it, requesting foods eaten before but not directly visible. The child is learning where things belong, so may want to have dishes arranged the same or "correct" way. The child may also notice any change in seating arrangements or in the child's place at the table.

SH.75 **Insists on doing things independently (30 months and above)**

SH.76 **Knows proper place for own things (30-36 months)**
The child demonstrates this knowledge by fetching an object on request.

SH.77 **Pours liquid from small container (30-36 months)**

SH.78 **Uses fork (30-36 months)**
The child uses a child-size fork or a salad fork to pierce or scoop food.

SH.79 **Uses napkin (30-36 months)**
The child uses a napkin to wipe mouth and hands.

SH.80 **Hangs clothing on hook (30 months and above)**

SH.81 **Buttons large buttons (30-36 months)**
The child buttons large round buttons at least 1 inch in diameter.

SH.82 **Dries hands (30-36 months)**
The child dries hands with a towel after washing them, but may need a little help to do a thorough job.

SH.83 **Helps with bathing self (30 months and above)**

SH.84 **Distinguishes between urination and bowel movements (30-36 months)**
The child can verbally or by gesture distinguish between bladder and bowel movements, and may tell you before or after eliminating.

SH.85 **Serves self at table with little spilling (31 months and above)**
The child self-serves finger foods or small portions of some foods under supervision.

SH.86 **Shows interest in setting table (31 months and above)**
The child enjoys feeling "grown up" and helping with grown-up activities, such as setting the table.

SH.87 **Verbalizes need to use toilet; has occasional accidents (31 months and above)**
The child tells you of a need to use the toilet but still has occasional accidents.

SH.88 **Takes responsibility for toileting; requires assistance in wiping (31 months and above)**
The child goes to the bathroom and lowers underpants to use the toilet. The child may need assistance getting on and off the toilet, and may also need help wiping. Teach the child to flush the toilet, if flushing is not a frightening experience, and to wash and dry his hands.

SH.89 **Sleeps 10 to 15 hours daily (31 months and above)**
The child is sleeping enough if not terribly fussy or cranky. The amount of sleep the child needs will vary according to the child. Schedule changes made upon the child, such as school, or other new situations or demands, should be taken into consideration. There are times when the child may need more rest.

SH.90 **May awaken crying from dreams (31 months and above)**
The child's crying from dreaming is usually distinguishable from other crying. It sounds very distressed and fearful.

SH.91 **May eliminate naps (31 months and above)**
The child may take only occasional naps and then gradually take no naps at all. The child may need only to lie down and rest or engage in a quiet activity, such as listening to a story or a record. The child may nap only when especially tired.

This might be the time when a short nap may be too much nap and the child will stay awake and active until very late in the evening. Or, if the child does not take a nap during the day, the child may go to sleep very early in the evening and awaken after a couple of hours. This becomes the nap, and the child is awake and alert until much later in the evening. This period will pass shortly. Try to tolerate and handle this period by continuously adjusting the child's schedule.

SH.92 **Dresses with supervision, requires assistance with fastenings (32 months and above)**
The child undresses and dresses with minimal assistance, but still needs supervision and some verbal assistance, and will need help with the fastenings.

SH.93 **Blows nose with assistance (32-34 months)**
The child may need a demonstration or reminder to blow the nose, and may need help with wiping after blowing.

Involve the family in your early intervention plans . . .

PLANNING FAMILY GOALS
A Systems Approach to the IFSP
by Jennifer Olson, Ph.D., and Kathy Kwiatkowski, M.S.

This theory-driven model of IFSP development gives information on best practices in transition, family involvement, and collaboration with agencies. You'll learn valuable strategies to help you improve the quality of special education services to children from birth to 3 years and their families. Three different models—family systems theory, family stress theory, and ecological—show you how to plan and provide early intervention services.
Catalog No. 7802-Y   **$35**

POSITIONING FOR PLAY
Home Activities for Parents of Young Children
by Rachel B. Diamant, M.S., OTR

Teach parents therapeutic play activities to stimulate and develop motor skills in their children. Use this collection of 100 reproducible activity sheets with parents of children birth to 3 years who have developmental delays or are at risk. Choose activities from 10 developmental skill positions. Clear introductions for each section help increase parents' understanding of the developmental skill.   **Catalog No. 4231-Y**   **$39**

NORMAL DEVELOPMENT COPYBOOK
by Marsha Dunn Klein, M.Ed., OTR, Nancy Harris Ossman, B.S., OTR, and Barbara Tracy, B.S., PT

Completely reproducible, you'll find all your favorite pictures from the *Normal Development Poster Set.* Each page features a developmental age, skill illustration, and space for you to suggest "Helpful Hints." Individualize pages by writing at-home activities for reaching goals. As a special plus, 24 "Developmental Sequence" pages illustrate skill acquisition in a glance. On one convenient page you'll have pictures and steps showing a task through completion—a great overview for parents!
Catalog No. 4732-Y   **$39**

CHARLOTTE CIRCLE INTERVENTION GUIDE FOR PARENT-CHILD INTERACTIONS
by Mary Lynne Calhoun, Ph.D., Terry L. Rose, Ph.D., and Donna E. Prendergast, M.Ed.

This supplemental curriculum guide facilitates behaviors that support social interaction skills in children from birth to two years. Use the meaningful activities in six curriculum areas to promote responsive interactions between caregiver and child. Each unit contains background information, reproducible parent handouts, sample IFSP goals, lesson plans, and data collection strategies.   **Catalog No. 7721-Y**   **$39**

FAMILY-CENTERED INTERVENTION PLANNING
A Routines-Based Approach
by R. A. McWilliam, Ph.D.

Use this structured manual to work collaboratively with families creating early intervention programs. Based on the tested Family-Centered Intervention Plan (FCIP), this multicultural resource easily adapts to your clients and their parents. Present alternative routine-based treatments and let parents decide the best approach for their child.
Catalog No. 7819-Y   **$33**

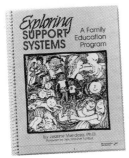

EXPLORING SUPPORT SYSTEMS
A Family Education Program
by Jeanne Mendoza, Ph.D.

Help families of high-risk, handicapped, recently diagnosed, or at-risk infants, toddlers, and preschoolers build support systems with this comprehensive manual. Lead families through a series of six sessions and follow up with a seventh home visit. Sessions address the types of stress that family members may face and explore available support systems. You'll have instructor and parent materials in one convenient, completely reproducible manual.

Catalog No. 7768-Y   **$39**

PARENT ARTICLES FOR EARLY INTERVENTION
Edited by Marsha Dunn Klein, M.Ed., OTR

These articles give parents practical information on therapeutic ways to interact with their child who has special needs. Written in clear, everyday language for parents of children ages birth through three who have physical and communication disorders. Articles include normal development, therapeutic handling, and daily living activities.

Catalog No. 7549-Y   **$45**

FACILITATING FAMILY-CENTERED TRAINING IN EARLY INTERVENTION
by Tess Bennett, Ph.D., Donna E. Nelson, M.S., and
Barbara V. Lingerfelt, M.A.

Use these five modules in workshops to train professionals working with families of young children with special needs. Participants learn how to implement state-of-the-art early intervention for children and their families. Topics include building a trusting relationship with the family, using effective strategies for intervention in the classroom, planning smooth transitions, and more! You'll have reproducible training materials in a handy three-ring binder.

Catalog No. 7737-Y   **$49**

ORDER FORM

Ship to:

INSTITUTION: _____

NAME: _____

ADDRESS: _____

CITY:_____ STATE:_____ ZIP:_____

☐ Please check here if this is a permanent address change.

Telephone No._____ ☐ work ☐ home

Payment Options:

☐ My check is included.

☐ Purchase order enclosed. P.O.# _____
(Net 30 days)

☐ Charge to my credit card. ☐ VISA ☐ MasterCard ☐ Discover

Card No. ☐☐☐☐☐☐☐☐☐☐☐☐☐☐☐☐

Expiration Date: Month_____ Year _____

Signature_____

QTY.	CAT. #	TITLE	AMOUNT

Please add 10% for shipping and handling. 8% for orders over $500.
Arizona residents add sales tax.
Canada: Add 22% to subtotal for shipping, handling, and G.S.T.

Payment in U.S. funds only.   **TOTAL**

MONEY-BACK GUARANTEE
You'll have up to 90 days of risk-free evaluation of the products you ordered. If you're not completely satisfied with any product, we'll pick it up within the 90 days and refund the full purchase price! *No Questions Asked!*

FOR PHONE ORDERS
Call (602) 323-7500. Please have your credit card and/or institutional purchase order information ready.
Monday–Friday 9 AM–6 PM Central Time
Voice or TDD / FAX (602) 325-0306

We occasionally backorder items temporarily out of stock. If you do not accept backorders, please advise on your purchase order or on this form.

Send your order to:

Communication Skill Builders
3830 E. Bellevue / P.O. Box 42050-Y / Tucson, AZ 85733